Developing a Successful Subsidiary Strategy

Most books on business strategy approach the subject from a corporate perspective, covering topics such as the vision for the business, the marketplace, competition and differentiation. However, the reality is that most managers work in sub-units or subsidiaries of the business and they are not involved in corporate strategy formulation. Their strategic concerns are with the positioning and future trajectory of their own units within the complex internal ecosystem in which they exist. If these units are to survive and grow, the middle managers responsible for them must plan their future, maximise their value-add and compete for resources within the internal market of their corporations. Such internal markets are becoming increasingly volatile due to general economic conditions but also given the questioning of globalisation and increasing corporate concerns about the frailties of international supply chains as brought into sharp focus by the COVID-19 crisis and the war in Ukraine.

This book provides practical perspectives for these business unit managers and a step-by-step toolkit that can be used by management teams to develop a successful subsidiary strategy that acknowledges these challenges while maximising their contribution to corporate objectives. It is based on the author's 30 years of experience as an executive in a complex multinational (IBM) organisation, supplemented by academic study at Master's and PhD levels. The material covered has been verified through workshops over a 3-year period with the senior leadership teams of over 30 multinational subsidiaries operating from Ireland.

Developing a Successful Subsidiary Strategy

A Step-by-Step Toolkit for Managers

Paul Lyons

Routledge
Taylor & Francis Group

A PRODUCTIVITY PRESS BOOK

First published 2024
by Routledge
605 Third Avenue, New York, NY 10158

and by Routledge
4 Park Square, Milton Park, Abingdon, Oxon, OX14 4RN

Routledge is an imprint of the Taylor & Francis Group, an informa business

ISBN: 9781032545738 (hbk)
ISBN: 9781032544038 (pbk)
ISBN: 9781003425502 (ebk)

DOI: 10.4324/9781003425502

Typeset in Garamond
by Deanta Global Publishing Services, Chennai, India

To Ethna, Aoife and Donal

Contents

List of Figures

Preface

In the early 1990s, I was a young manager in a small software development centre that IBM Europe, Middle East and Africa (EMEA) set up a few years previously in Dublin, Ireland. This centre had been established after the case was made by the IBM Ireland sales and marketing unit to EMEA headquarters (HQ) that it had become increasingly challenging to promote the company's products to the government and other large clients without showing that IBM was also making a positive investment contribution to this growing economy. The availability of a ready supply of IT graduates at cost rates that were still low by European standards convinced HQ to invest in this new international software development centre. After a successful start-up, the new subsidiary quickly grew to over 250 employees, which was a significant number compared to the local IBM Ireland sales and marketing organisation of around 450 people.

The subsidiary was initially established as part of the company's pan-European IT organisation and was tasked with developing internal IT applications in areas such as HR and sales administration for IBM country operating units across EMEA. After the first few years of successful operation, concerns arose among the management team that its positioning as an IT centre – which was a cost burden to IBM EMEA – could limit the potential for the subsidiary, given the increasing internal pressures on cost at a time when IBM's dominance of the IT industry was waning significantly. Without endorsement by their corporate sponsors, the ambition was formed to migrate away from internal IT work and towards licensed software development, which would be revenue-earning. This would be of greater value to the corporation than IT applications for internal use and would therefore offer a safer harbour for the fledgling subsidiary as IBM's operating costs came under increasing pressure. The strategy was firstly to offer sub-contracted services to incumbent software product laboratories around the world, but particularly in the USA where Irish-American executives had an emotional affinity with Dublin. Effectively, this was a Trojan Horse strategy, aimed at securing entry and then normalisation within the software product division. The strategy proved successful, and the Dublin centre was named as a software product development laboratory in 1994.

As a young manager, it was an education to observe my more savvy colleagues as we worked together to navigate the politics inherent in this strategy: carefully briefing incumbent sponsors overseeing the EMEA IT organisation to avoid them feeling threatened by these moves, building relationships within the global software product development organisation to earn initial low-level responsibilities as a satellite of their labs, managing the coexistence of workload from both sources while prioritising where to assign the strongest skills, while all of the time remaining focused on strong delivery, the promotion of successes and the playing-down of failures.

For a number of my more senior management colleagues who had developed the early part of their careers in the relatively small IBM Ireland sales and marketing office, this was the fulfilment of a career ambition to be globally recognised within the corporation and to be involved in the design of some of the company's most exciting new software products. While I shared this sense of achievement, coupled with a sense of nationalistic pride, I was only at the start of my career journey and was more concerned with where we would go from here. My manager at the time agreed that we needed to find the impetus for the next phase of the strategy and with his support I undertook an executive Masters in Management with an action-learning emphasis on strategy formulation. I learned a lot about the strategy development process but was surprised by the dearth of insight in the literature into the business development issues facing subsidiaries operating within complex corporate internal markets. Literature on organisational strategy was generally focused on an overall company level, with little recognition that business units within multinational structures also require strategies to optimise their contribution to corporate objectives while navigating the complications of the internal market within which they operate.

This interest in strategy formulation from the subsidiary perspective remained as my career continued to develop and as I led a series of large international shared services units – each one seeking to solidify and develop its role in the face of internal and external competition. As the company increased its presence in the outsourced services market I managed large client contracts, where customers outsourced services to IBM that were previously delivered internally. I oversaw teams of up to 3,000 staff across a network of global delivery centres in Europe and Asia delivering these services. This provided a new dimension to my interest in internal business unit strategy, as I observed clients' executives making decisions about outsourcing versus insourcing and the interplay between internally and externally provided services. The strategic agendas of client executive management as they balanced between their internal shared services subsidiaries and outsourced providers were particularly interesting to observe.

I left IBM in 2013 to pursue the long-held ambition to undertake a PhD aimed at exploring the phenomena that I had experienced as a practising subsidiary manager. My research focused on the formation and evolution of relationships between service providers and service sponsors, with particular attention to services outsourcing. The literature reviews that I completed as part of the research process found relatively little progress on internal business unit strategy within corporations in the intervening period since I had investigated this as part of my Master's studies in the 1990s.

After I completed my PhD, I was pleased to be contacted by David Cornick – a former IBM colleague. In the late 1990s, David and I had been fortunate to work as part of an Ireland executive team led by William Burgess, who was a particularly ambitious and charismatic IBM Ireland CEO. Under William's leadership, this team successfully encouraged a series of IBM international divisions to sponsor Foreign Direct Investment (FDI) projects which grew the company's presence in the country to over 5,000 employees, mostly located at a new Technology Campus on the outskirts of Dublin. This workload also went through a series of transitions to reflect the changing nature of the Irish labour market and also significant changes in IBM's business as the corporation's strategy moved from an orientation around manufacturing to one that was more software and services based.

As we reminisced about the successes, setbacks and sheer hard work that this had involved, David briefed me on a request that had been made of him by the Irish Management Institute to develop a programme of workshops for the senior management teams of FDI subsidiaries, to help them to develop growth strategies within their parent corporations. The initiative was sponsored by the IDA Ireland – the government agency tasked with encouraging inward FDI in Ireland and developing its potential. This was a recognition that FDI success for a country like Ireland does not end with the announcement of a new investment and a smooth start-up. Decades of experience have shown that the most successful and sustained investments – such as those by Boston Scientific, Dell, Intel and Pfizer – have evolved over time. They have been shaped and reshaped by strong leadership and changes in direction, driven by market events, corporate changes and a continued focus on opportunity development. Fundamentally, this shows that subsidiaries require a clear strategy and strong leadership to survive and thrive.

In 2019, we began the development of the resulting programme, titled *Leading with Strategic Intent*. To date, the senior management teams of over 30 subsidiaries have attended the programme which is delivered through a series of workshops over a nine-month period. This book provides an extended version of the strategy recommendations that provide a foundation for the programme. After this, the teams go on to develop their detailed thinking on value proposition development, talent management and stakeholder engagement as it applies to their particular environments. For the sake of brevity and because they are so individual to each organisation, these latter topics are only given brief treatment in this text.

Many of the ideas that are contained in the book are those that resonated from my extra-curricular studies and which provided the most practical insight when I was operating as a subsidiary leader. These ways of viewing things helped me when navigating the terrain within the complex and highly political environment that is typical of large organisations. These ideas have been further refined through the development of the Leading with Strategic Intent programme, not least by recognising those that proved to be of most practical benefit to the participating senior management teams as they tried to make sense of their own disparate and intricate environments.

Ultimately, the motivation for a subsidiary leader should be to ensure that the organisation maximises its potential to contribute to corporate success. Dysfunctional moves – that may deliver short-term benefits to the local organisation at the expense of the wider corporate agenda – will ultimately come back to haunt the subsidiary through reputational damage or some other form of revenge. At the most fundamental level, no growth strategy pursued by a subsidiary will achieve the support it requires unless the organisation is seen to be delivering its basic mandates successfully. The strategic desire to contribute more may be admirable, but a qualifier for having these ambitions is the continuing effective delivery of current responsibilities.

Equally, a mature headquarters organisation should have the confidence to tolerate and even encourage subsidiary ambitions that extend beyond the boundaries of their current mandates. Just as a good manager should not limit the development of an ambitious employee, nor should a headquarters constrain the potential for a subsidiary. Without such ambition, a subsidiary may struggle to retain the most energetic managers, and without such boundary challenges, a headquarters risks underutilising resources that may nudge the wider organisation to the next level. Of course that is as long as existing responsibilities are fulfilled at a superior level.

This book is founded on the premise that organisations should always have a strategy. This includes business units and subsidiaries operating within larger organisational networks. Business conditions will always be challenging, whether that be the result of external events or internal pressure to improve. While the ideas, process and tools described in this book are not designed as a response to any specific environmental conditions, there is no doubt that subsidiaries today face particular pressures in the wake of the COVID-19 crisis, the economic impacts of the war in Ukraine and speculation that there will be some retrenchment from the march of globalisation that has shaped business and economies in the past 30 years.

All of these factors emphasise the need for subsidiary leaders, now more than ever, to be proactive in strategising for the success of their organisations. The ideas presented in this book provide a vocabulary, a process and a toolkit to shape this planning. Not every idea and construct presented here will resonate with every subsidiary. However, it is hoped that they will nonetheless trigger your thinking and set you on the road to planning how the potential of your subsidiary can be unlocked to deliver maximum benefit to your parent organisation.

Acknowledgements

I would like to thank my family – Ethna, Aoife and Donal – for their constant support and encouragement throughout my career and while I was writing this book. Aoife deserves special thanks for proofreading some of the early chapter drafts – although I think she enjoyed the opportunity to exact revenge for my pernickety feedback on her essay drafts while she was studying.

The finished work would not have been possible without the input of colleagues who also built much of their careers in subsidiary management. Many of my own formative management experiences were shared with my friend and colleague David Cornick, who deserves special recognition for his directorship of the IMI/IDA Leading with Strategic Intent[1] programme for subsidiary managers. David always acted as a challenging, but constructive sounding board for materials created for this audience. He also provided much encouragement and excellent feedback when he reviewed the first draft of this book.

I am also indebted to the executive mentors and instructors on this programme for their openness when sharing experiences from their own careers. I am particularly grateful to Jeff Caselden, Brian Hayes, Elizabeth Reynolds and Margit Takacs for reviewing drafts and for providing such helpful improvement suggestions. I am especially thankful to Paddy Barr for the insights that he gave me based on his own experience in book publishing.

Cyrilla Costello and the teams at IMI and IDA Ireland also deserve thanks for their foresight in recognising the need to fill this gap in management education offerings. The leadership teams of the over 30 companies that have attended the programme to date also played a major role in the development of this material, by articulating where it was successful (or not) in shaping their strategic thinking.

Ed Delany's work on subsidiary maturity phases is referenced in the early chapters of the book. I would like to thank Ed for this, but particularly for the spotlight that he put on subsidiary management and for working with me as I grappled with the subject when I studied for my executive Masters in the early 1990s. I was also very grateful to Ed for reviewing the first draft of this text and for his helpful input.

I am also very appreciative of the management colleagues with whom I worked throughout my own career as a subsidiary manager. Later, when I could take the time for fulltime academic research into the subject, I was fortunate to have the support of the excellent faculty at Trinity Business School, who helped my transition from a practising manager to a more dispassionate observer. I would particularly like to thank Professor Louis Brennan who acted as my PhD supervisor and writing mentor, and who also provided much encouragement and practical advice when I was seeking a publisher for this manuscript.

Note

1. IMI, "Leading with Strategic Intent (Fdi)," https://www.imi.ie/leading-with-strategic-intent/.

About the Author

Paul Lyons has practical experience in business unit and subsidiary management from his 30 years with IBM. During this time, he managed large international shared services centres and was consistently successful in growing these by adding more value to the corporation. He also worked at a headquarters level and oversaw international business units operating from Bulgaria, India, Ireland, the Philippines, Poland and the United Kingdom. He supported clients at a CxO level in planning and executing their organisational strategies. Throughout this time Paul maintained a deep interest in strategy formation at a business unit level – with an emphasis on how units can optimise their contributions and positioning within the internal networks of their parent organisations. He studied this topic at Master's and PhD levels at Trinity Business School, Dublin. In recent years, he has supported a large number of multinational subsidiaries in the formation of their strategies and developed a range of tools that have proved highly effective for these management teams.

Chapter 1

Introduction

Ambitious managers want to gain more influence over their future and to plot a course which will enable their business to succeed and grow. This explains the popularity of books, academic articles, podcasts and other online contributions providing direction on how to develop the various dimensions of a business strategy. Typically, the strategy process involves analysing the operating environment and marketplace, establishing a vision of what the organisation can achieve in the future, making choices on focus areas and assigning short- and long-term actions to affect change and to work towards the strategic vision.

Yet, in all but the smallest companies, few managers will ever have the opportunity to contribute substantively to the development of an overall strategy for the business, as this activity typically remains under the control of the most senior corporate executives and their headquarters (HQ) staffs. This is not to suggest that managers throughout the organisation do not have a role in the strategy process. But in most cases, this role is limited to following corporate direction.

It is short-sighted to expect that in complex modern organisations, strategy-making should be solely in the realm of HQ, with all other constituents of the organisation required only to understand and follow. This overlooks the dynamism that should be a feature of vibrant and flexible companies. Such a linear and one-directional perspective on strategy assumes that a command and control hierarchy exists, although such rigid structures have limited effectiveness in complex networked organisations. It risks stifling the value-add contributions that can be made by business units outside HQ, based on their closer positioning to the marketplace. It can also thwart the

DOI: 10.4324/9781003425502-1

ambitions of line managers who want to develop their business units and boost their potential to contribute to corporate goals. This can ultimately lead to sub-optimisation of business units, frustration and attrition at all levels in the unit and even clandestine actions by managers who feel constrained by the boundaries to their strategic participation that are set by HQ.

This is not to suggest that business units should have the freedom to question corporate strategic direction or to follow a contrary path. However, managers in these units should still be empowered to interpret how their units can develop their organisations to support the strategy to best effect. They should be expected to deeply consider their own environment and their potential to increase their contribution to corporate goals. In doing so, they should also be encouraged to push the boundaries of their current responsibilities and to find ways of earning more responsibility. This will enable them to maximise the investments made in them by their parents and to develop energetic staff who are bought into corporate strategies and determined to exploit local capabilities to make the maximum possible contribution to the achievement of these strategies.

While most writings on business strategy approach the topic from the corporate perspective, this book is aimed at business unit managers seeking to create local strategies to develop their organisations within the corporate environments in which they operate. The strategic concerns of these managers are with the positioning and future trajectory of their own units within complex internal ecosystems. If their units are to survive and grow, the managers responsible for them must plan their future, maximise their value-add and compete for resources within the internal market of their corporation. This book outlines a process for doing this and provides a set of tools to enable this process.

The management audience for this book is therefore quite wide. Particularly in an international business context, most corporations structure their business units by establishing legal subsidiaries across multiple countries and continents. Recent estimates are that there are now over 60,000 multinational enterprises (MNEs) operating across the world, controlling more than 500,000 subsidiaries.[1] These subsidiaries represent a substantial proportion of company activities. For example, 33% of employees of US MNEs are now based in other countries.[2] This shows the scale and breadth of business activity that is executed by globally distributed business units.

For simplicity, from here on we will generally use the term *subsidiary* when referring to all business unit entities that can benefit from strategy-making. This reflects the reality that, particularly when firms are expanding internationally, they will normally establish entities in which they have direct ownership as separate legal subsidiaries in each new country where a presence is required. Historically, the geographic remoteness of these subsidiaries from HQ made it more challenging to integrate them into strategy development and caused managers in these regions to feel that HQ was not taking full advantage of the unique capabilities available in their region – even though these were often the very capabilities that attracted the corporation to invest in their region in the first place. In the little academic research that specifically investigates strategy development at the subsidiary level, a significant proportion of the data comes from countries such as Canada, Scotland and Ireland. These countries historically attracted high levels of foreign direct investment (FDI) from their larger neighbours (i.e., the UK and USA)[3] and the developing nature of these economies encouraged managers in these subsidiaries to be more ambitious in their strategic thinking. As a result, many of the early insights into subsidiary strategy and how this can be most effectively pursued within complex organisations emanated from business units operating from these countries.

So the strategy development process that is detailed throughout this book will, for convenience, refer to subsidiaries as the entities that are the focus of the strategy. However, these ideas can be applied more generally to any business unit that has a cohesive identity and seeks to maximise its contribution to the parent's success. This could include selected parts of a legal subsidiary that have meaningful linkages to each other through common reporting lines, co-location or other forms of shared infrastructure. However, it may exclude other parts of the subsidiary where no such operational synergies exist. It could include groupings of business units that happen to be incorporated across multiple legal subsidiaries – even across different countries. The subsidiaries in question do not have to be wholly owned to benefit from this process and they could include partnerships and joint ventures. The material covered here is also relevant to business units that operate within the same country as their HQ and therefore have not required the establishment of a separate legal subsidiary. In this way, the terms subsidiary and subsidiary strategy as used here can be applied as broadly as makes sense for the business unit in question.

The Right Time for Strategy

Strategy-making needs to start somewhere, but it should not be viewed as a finite process with fixed outputs and set timeframes. Of course, it is useful to set a strategic horizon and clear objectives, as we will discuss later. However, the world in which subsidiaries operate is often volatile, with change amplified by reorganisations within the corporation, movements in the market, developing conditions in the region and geopolitical events that shape the world in general. Therefore, it is important to remain flexible and to constantly monitor progress and external events to determine where adjustments are needed as the strategy progresses. As will be emphasised regularly throughout this book, in the subsidiary context it is also critical to ensure that existing responsibilities are executed satisfactorily before seeking to push beyond these into new areas of value-add.

Subsidiaries – like their parents – should always have a strategy if they are to take responsibility for their own future. The process that is outlined in this book describes how one can be established, but it can also be used to re-invigorate an existing strategy. The process is founded on a number of analytical tools that can be re-assessed regularly to confirm that the assumptions upon which the strategy was based still hold.

But, having emphasised that strategy formation and execution is a continuing process, it must be acknowledged that market conditions at the time of writing in 2023 bring increased urgency to the need for subsidiaries to assess their current positioning within their corporations, the risks that they face and the opportunities that can be exploited. Brexit and the America-First instincts of large sections of the US electorate have dented the free trade culture that has shaped the development of the world economy over the past 30 years, encouraging many to hypothesise about the demise (or not) of globalisation[4] and even the need to reshape the capitalist system that has largely underpinned the global trading environment as we know it.[5] The frailties of international supply chains, as highlighted by the COVID-19 crisis and the war in Ukraine, have caused some companies to reconsider their international investments. The resulting global economic pressures are requiring all companies to assess their cost bases. This has added to the environmental, social and geopolitical concerns that were already emerging about globalisation. Experience with offshoring and outsourcing has been mixed, leading some firms to consider reshoring[6] and raising further questions about the outlook for FDI in the coming years.[7] Although the OECD reported in April 2022 that FDI flows had bounced back to exceed pre-pandemic levels, they conclude that the outlook remains uncertain given the current geopolitical context.[8]

The COVID-19 pandemic highlighted another feature that will likely have significant enduring impacts. That is the enthusiasm with which employees embraced remote working as an alternative to commuting to an office. This is more applicable for services roles than for manufacturing workers, although it should be acknowledged that most manufacturing units also have services components for planning, logistics management and value-added customer support. Our experience with the benefits and downsides of remote working during the pandemic highlights how the co-location that forms a structural bond between subsidiary employees may not be as influential in the future. Even call centres which were the epitome of large labour-based services subsidiaries were successful in distributing their workload seamlessly across multiple individual employee homes.

The ability to share workload across multiple locations is not new. Indeed follow-the-sun shared services centres have managed cross-border workload for decades. However, each such centre typically had its own management structure and identity. The proliferation of remote working calls into question our very conception of a subsidiary as a cohesive and co-located business unit. The innovations in working practices that were forced on us by the pandemic proved what many in large organisations already knew – that particularly for services-oriented workload, effective teams can be formed across multiple countries and cultures. This brings into sharper focus how the subsidiary as an operating unit is no longer the only organisational form that can be used by a headquarters to take advantage of remote capabilities. It raises new questions for subsidiary general managers on how to justify their existence while taking advantage of practices that dilute the importance of co-location, as work can now be completed virtually and seamlessly across multiple sites. When a subsidiary's identity is no longer centred on a single physical location, and when its deliverables are no longer dependent on the co-location of its people, this places an even greater onus on managers to reassess and reshape the unit's value proposition. Having a well-formulated strategy to do so is therefore more important now than it ever was.

Against this backdrop, some soul-searching is required on whether you and your management colleagues have sufficient motivation at this time to try to influence what the future may hold. As you have taken the time to start reading this book, it is fair to assume that you have some level of personal interest in the topic. Your personal motivation may be fuelled by the expectation that the ideas that are presented here will provide you with perspectives to help make more sense of your subsidiary environment. The strategy development process that is described, and the templates that populate the process, will help you to define the way forward and to re-enforce your position as a leader with vision, with an appetite for change and with the energy to do something about it. Investing your personal intellectual capital in the process by familiarising yourself with the ideas explored in the following chapters will better position you to personally influence how the future evolves.

Developing and executing a strategy will require colleagues to share your motivation for the journey. In later chapters, we will explore the general sources of organisational motivation that might be developed across the subsidiary to power the additional effort required in addition to existing responsibilities and pressures. Some colleagues may begin from the perspective that your business unit should simply continue to focus exclusively on current responsibilities, and when these are performed to a superior level await whatever additional roles the parent organisation may wish to assign. The alternative of becoming more proactive in assessing options and pushing the boundaries requires more appetite for change throughout the organisation. The process that is outlined in the chapters that follow begins with actions to deeply assess the current roles and competencies of your organisation, including risks, weaknesses and future potential. This will develop a wider realisation of the need for change and where strategic initiatives should be focused. The toolkit of templates provides a roadmap for the journey. This will help to develop broader organisational motivation by giving clarity to colleagues on how the process will develop – allowing them to envisage how this potential can be exploited.

Current conditions certainly present particular challenges and opportunities for subsidiary managers. While these should not be underestimated, history indicates that the impacts of these events will pass. When they do, businesses as always will place new pressures on themselves to excel and combat competition. Current environmental challenges and opportunities will then be replaced, requiring further strategic responses. Therefore, the time is always right for strategic thinking, and the process presented in this book can be followed whatever the conditions, to develop a robust and living strategy.

Objectives and Origins

This book is written for managers and management teams seeking guidance on how to secure and grow their subsidiary organisations. It provides a practical perspective and a step-by-step toolkit that can be used to develop strategies that incorporate a realistic understanding of challenges, and importantly to plan how to address these by taking strategic actions that will maximise the potential of the subsidiary to add more value to the corporation. The concepts and tools presented in the following chapters draw on my personal experience over 30 years as a line manager and executive in a complex multinational, in both subsidiary and HQ functions. This also embeds observations from working with client MNEs on their organisational and sourcing strategies.

The insights that I developed into the relationships between subsidiaries and their HQ throughout my management career were complemented by my research into this subject at Masters and PhD level. This allowed me to assess academic contributions to our understanding of this field. I am very conscious that, to practising managers, academic literature can appear removed from reality and impenetrable. In common business parlance, the very word "academic" is often used to describe something that is hypothetical and not practical. I have certainly spent many hours wading through academic articles that did not resonate with me as a manager. I have also been fortunate to work with a number of very insightful and practice-oriented academics, but it is true to say that the majority of the academic community has not had the opportunity to practice as managers themselves. As a result, much of the formal academic research tends to look from the outside-in, motivated by a desire to observe and explain how phenomena manifest themselves. Practical guidance for managers on how to affect change tends to be presented in the literature almost as an afterthought, or as something that is left to practising managers to interpret and apply.

Despite this, I have also found that the literature contains many very useful contributions on the subject and many perspectives and theories that provide new insights into the complexities of the world in which subsidiaries operate. Part of my role here is to act as a filter to the range of ideas emanating from academic contributions and to offer interpretations of how they apply in practice. The footnotes that accompany each chapter are included to give credit to authors who have provided useful sources of ideas. The full references for these footnotes are included in the bibliography, should you wish to explore these sources more fully. In the limited number of instances where I elaborate on management theory or conceptual frameworks, I do so with the intention that the reader should use these as a lens to view their own environment and see whether this provides a new perspective or improves clarity. Even the best lenses may still leave some blurriness, but at least they help us to see things in a new way or bring some of the issues into focus.

The core material presented here has been verified through a series of workshops over a four-year period with the senior leadership teams of over 30 multinational subsidiaries participating in iterations of the IMI/IDA Leading with Strategic Intent programme.[9] The design of this programme required the full senior team from each subsidiary to attend these workshops. Between six and eight companies participated in each iteration of the programme, and this encouraged the sharing of experiences between companies – subject of course to any commercial sensitivities. The participating management teams came from a wide variety of manufacturing and services subsidiaries operating across multiple business sectors. Some were part of very large multinationals and operated within complex organisational networks. Others were from companies with much smaller numbers of international subsidiaries. Some of the participating subsidiaries were the result of acquisitions of smaller companies that had previously operated independently. Others had grown organically following initial FDI commitments by their parents. The parent corporations for these units originated in many different countries, adding to the rich blend of corporate cultures that contributed to the programme.

During each iteration of the programme, encouraging feedback was received from participating managers on the concepts and tools that were presented to stimulate their thinking and steer their strategy development process. Improvements were also made as the programme progressed, taking account of the ideas that resonated most with participants. A critical element of the programme was the assignment of a seasoned subsidiary executive as a mentor to each participating subsidiary. These mentors all had impressive track records in leading subsidiary organisations, so they were well-positioned to provide further input on programme materials and to assist management teams in applying these to their environments. Additionally, other experienced subsidiary leaders were invited as guest speakers to share their stories *in camera* and to encourage more discussion on the particular strategic challenges faced by subsidiaries.

This book benefits greatly from all of these practical insights – including participant feedback on the concepts and tools that proved most useful, suggestions from mentors on how these can be applied and particularly from the stories shared by participants, mentors and guest speakers of their own experiences in navigating the terrain within their respective companies.

Despite the range of contributing sources, it should also be emphasised at the outset that no single text can cover all of the complexity and nuances that exist in every subsidiary or other form of business unit. Indeed, a common initial reaction of subsidiary management teams to generalised frameworks is to stress that the environment in which they work is different. They are correct, but the differences are not always as significant as they think. Even if your situation does not exactly fit with a conceptual model that is presented in the chapters that follow, it is useful to consider HOW it is different.

Contents and Structure

Throughout the book, a toolkit of templates is presented to assist subsidiary managers in analysing their environments and making decisions on where to focus. It is intended that these templates should be used during team meetings of those involved in the strategy development process to pro-voke discussion and to provide vehicles for capturing consensus or areas of dispute for later resolution. A number of the templates and underlying con-cepts that are chosen for this purpose will already be widely understood by readers (e.g., SWOT analysis). Frameworks such as these that are already part of general management vocabulary are popular because they are intuitive and effective. Where possible, such commonly understood frameworks are preferred here as they have the added advantage of being familiar to those participating in the strategy development process.

The templates all have deliberately simple designs so that they can be easily replicated in a drawing tool such as MS PowerPoint, or even on a virtual or physical whiteboard. They are also provided on a larger scale in an appendix for ease of reproduction. Strategy development teams will get most benefit where they devote sufficient time to populating each template, while ensuring that all views are heard – especially those that do not reflect the popular consensus or preconceptions. As the book progresses, a case study is also developed to illustrate how the templates apply to a fictitious subsidiary.

That all being said, you should still feel free to be selective in deciding what is most appropriate to your particular circumstances. The concepts and templates that are described should still contribute to your general under-standing of subsidiary strategy and provide you with a vocabulary for debat-ing issues with colleagues. However, if after some reflection you conclude that a particular method does not map well to your environment or does not resonate with your organisation's culture, then you can move on, or even consider modifying it for your needs. As with all business strategies, there is no one-size-fits-all.

The body of the book is structured in three parts, to first introduce some of the fundamental ideas underpinning strategy and how this applies in a subsidiary context, to then show how your own subsidiary environment and potential can be analysed in detail and finally to guide the reader through the process of making choices, identifying required actions and managing change.

Part I is comprised of two chapters that provide foundations for the process of subsidiary strategy formulation that follows. In Chapter 2 (The View from the Top), the reader is encouraged to begin by considering the issues associated with subsidiary management from the corporate HQ perspective. Fundamentally, this requires a balance between giving direction and maintaining control, while also enabling all subsidiaries to deliver on their full potential for value-add. Chapter 3 (Subsidiary Evolution) considers how subsidiaries typically develop within corporate organisational structures. The phases that subsidiaries usually progress through as they mature are identified and the actions that can be taken to accelerate this evolution are explored.

Part II is made up of three chapters designed to encourage managers to deeply analyse their own subsidiary and the environment within which it operates. This reflects the need to challenge any preconceptions and to fully diagnose the current positioning of the subsidiary, prior to considering where to go from here and how to get there. This begins in Chapter 4 (What We Do: Analysing Our Charters) where tools are provided to enable an analysis of existing subsidiary responsibilities and areas that could be of future strategic value to the parent. Chapter 5 (How We Do It: Analysing Our Capabilities) then walks the reader through a process designed to highlight those areas where the subsidiary has strong competencies, as well as areas requiring development. Chapter 6 (Where We Do It: Analysing Our Environment) focuses on the environment in which the subsidiary operates and proposes how the internal and external forces that shape the climate surrounding the subsidiary can be analysed to consider their potential impact on the strategic direction.

The four chapters in Part III explore how strategic decisions can be made and appropriate actions can be enabled, taking account of the self-diagnosis discussed in the previous chapters. Chapter 7 (Making Strategic Choices) focuses on the process of making the choices that will form the backbone of a strategy. Chapter 8 (Exerting Influence) draws attention to the challenge of soliciting support across the parent organisation for any investment decisions needed to support the strategy. Chapter 9 (Managing the Change Within) draws attention to the leadership, change management and governance imperatives needed to orchestrate change within the subsidiary in support of the strategy's execution. Chapter 10 (Parental Responsibilities) discusses the responsibilities that fall on the parent organisation to facilitate subsidiaries in fulfilling their potential, while ensuring the smooth running of the network within which they operate.

Chapter 11 provides an overall Conclusion to the book.

Notes

1. Espace Mondial, "Multinational Corporations: World Atlas of Global Issues," https://espace-mondial-atlas.sciencespo.fr/en/topic-strategies-of-transnational -actors/article-3A11-EN-multinational-corporations.html#:~:text=At%20the %20present%20time%2C%20there,controlling%20more%20than%20500%2C000 %20subsidiaries.
2. Mark Goddard, "Activities of U.S. Multinational Enterprises, 2020" (USA Bureau of Economic Analysis, 2022).
3. Ed Delany, "Strategic Development of the Multinational Subsidiary through Subsidiary Initiative-Taking," *Long Range Planning* 33 (2000).
4. Martin Sandbu, "The Death of Globalisation Has Been Greatly Exagerated," *Financial Times*, 26 May 2022.
5. Rebecca Henderson, *Reimagining Capitalism: How Business Can Save the World* (Penguin Random House, 2020).
6. Jon Hay, "Esg, Trump and Covid Hasten Gathering Trend to Re-Shore," *Global Capital*, 9 July 2020.
7. Daniel Thomas, "Uk Manufactuers Reshore Supply Chains after Pandemic and Brexit," *Financial Times*, 16 May 2022.
8. OECD, "Fdi in Figures: April 2022" (OECD, 2022).
9. IMI, "Leading with Strategic Intent (Fdi)."

CORPORATIONS AND THEIR SUBSIDIARIES

This first part provides some background in Chapter 2 on how large corporations develop and how this influences their decision-making in relation to the establishment and subsequent management of subsidiaries. The intent of Chapter 2 is to put readers in the shoes of headquarters managers and to encourage greater reflection on their objectives and concerns. Chapter 3 then focuses on subsidiaries by discussing the ways in which they typically develop their roles within·the company over time. This chapter lays out some frameworks to help us understand the evolutionary pathways of subsidiaries as they mature and grow. The moves that trigger their evolution from one stage to the next are also discussed.

These chapters provide a general context for understanding the world of corporations and subsidiaries. This sets the foundation for the discussion on subsidiary strategy formulation that begins in Part II.

DOI: 10.4324/9781003425502-2

Chapter 2

The View from the Top

At its most fundamental level, the relationship between a subsidiary and its parent can be thought of as one between a supplier and a customer. The subsidiary seeks to develop its business by providing resources that maximise the value delivered to its sole customer. The parent wants the subsidiary to perform to its greatest potential as a supplier. However, it retains the right to seek alternative suppliers, while remaining subject to the constraints to any binding commitments that underpin the relationship (e.g., contractual agreements, sunk capital cost and exit costs). Best business practice suggests that everything should start with an understanding of the customer, so it is therefore worthwhile to begin by reflecting on what brings a parent to a point in their development where it requires subsidiaries, and what forces may influence future requirements and decision-making in relation to its subsidiaries.

Like customers, all parents are different, so it is not feasible to be overly prescriptive in this chapter on the influences that will be most relevant in your case. It is well established that the national culture characteristics from the parent's home country will have a significant influence on attitudes to subsidiary management.[1] For example, the headquarters (HQ) of a US multinational enterprise (MNE) is likely to adopt a very different subsidiary management style to that of a Chinese company that is expanding to international markets. Industry requirements will also cause differences, as can be considered when one contrasts how technology companies (e.g., Apple and Samsung) and professional services companies (e.g., KPMG and Accenture) interact with their respective satellite subsidiaries. Even within companies, cultures will differ based on occupational traits. For example,

DOI: 10.4324/9781003425502-3

units that are oriented around sales will be managed differently to those that are concerned with finance and business controls. When these factors are blended, and when any unique corporate culture traits of the company are added to the mix, multiple possible combinations exist. It is therefore not feasible to describe a set of influences that will apply equally, for example, to a sales subsidiary in a Chinese technology company and a finance unit in a US professional services company.[2]

Rather, the approach taken here is to explore the general factors that shape the development of organisations, and the issues that arise when the structure that emerges encompasses subsidiaries. Deeper understanding often comes from comparison, so while all of the elements that are explored here may not be applicable in your case, this discussion provides a reference point which you can contrast against your own parent's evolution and priorities. By using these general characteristics to reflect on the specifics of your own situation, you can begin to build a foundation of insights into your parent as a customer and how this may shape decision-making in relation to your subsidiary strategy as this emerges.

Subsidiaries within Global Supply Chains

International companies, by definition, use global supply chains either to give them access to new foreign markets or to take advantage of cost structures and other capabilities that are not readily available to them in their home country. Establishing subsidiaries is just one organisational approach to achieving this extended reach, and it is usually not the first step in developing a global supply chain.

Companies typically develop their production and sales processes in their home country before making some low-risk moves into exporting. Exporting usually starts with countries in close geographical proximity (e.g., firms in the Nordic countries usually start by exporting to other countries in that region) and/or to countries with a shared language or cultural affinity (e.g., between UK, USA, Ireland, Canada and Australia).[3] Having established an export market, companies typically increase their investments in those markets through formal engagements with local agents, often followed by the establishment of local sales offices.

This is a classic *multidomestic* expansion strategy, where presence in new remote markets is steadily developed until a local management structure is put in place. Each region is treated as an individual instance of the company that mirrors the structure adopted in the home market. In the early days of internationalisation, it was recommended that MNEs should set their strategic priorities by categorising target markets according to a combination of the market size and the local subsidiary's level of expertise in serving that market.[4] That is, the highest corporate strategic focus should be on the largest markets where the local subsidiary has demonstrated the highest level of competence. This basically viewed the world as a palette of regional markets, each of which could be developed at a different pace to others.

At the other end of the spectrum from the multidomestic organisational model is a *global* strategy that regards the world as one market, suitable for standardised products and common marketing methods. The corporate strategic emphasis in this case is on centralisation of competencies, consistency of practice and efficiency of operation globally.

The multidomestic versus global alternatives reflect a strategic choice between (a) the pressure for company products and services to take account of differences in regional preferences and (b) the pressure to achieve efficiencies by aggregating activity and maintaining consistency at a cross-regional level.[5] These options represent extremes, each with its advantages and disadvantages. Most firms will try to find the best of both worlds, although typically one of these strategic themes tends to dominate. Norms vary across industries. Consider for example the global nature of the IT industry compared to the regional structures that predominate in the food and beverage sector. Even within a given industry, different companies can have different emphases to their investments as they seek differentiation and competitive advantage. In the entertainment streaming sector, Disney relies largely on the global attraction of its content, whereas Netflix grew its global presence into targeted markets such as India by also investing in titles that would appeal to specific cultures.[6]

The nature of the cross-border investments that an MNE makes as part of its internationalisation strategy will vary depending on whether it is adopting a multidomestic strategy, a global strategy or a hybrid of these. Fundamentally, investment decisions boil down to the question of whether the MNE is motivated by the need to gain access to a new market, or whether it is seeking access to a capability that is not available as efficiently in the home country or in an existing international location where the company has a presence.

Market access investments usually entail the establishment of a sales or distribution network to service customers in a new region. Before online shopping and highly efficient global logistics networks, selling in a new region required prior investment in local sales outlets and distribution systems. These days, sophisticated web portals and digital marketing can satisfy much of the market access need, particularly for consumer products companies. This does not always negate the need to have a local presence for unlocking access to certain markets, such as the EU, or to overcome differences in regulations or standards. For example, after Brexit, to circumvent new customs clearance requirements, Amazon realised the need to establish a local distribution centre in Ireland, which was previously serviced from the company's UK hubs. However, even in cases such as this, the scale of the local presence can be limited and supplemented by shared international infrastructure.

Capability access investments aim to take advantage of resources that are not available to the same extent elsewhere. These can include natural resources, raw materials, supplier networks, supply chain infrastructure, employee skills, employment costs, government grants, preferential regulatory environments and tax regimes. In some cases, foreign direct investment (FDI) that may appear to be motivated by capability access can also have market access benefits. For example, making an inward investment in a country can also win flexibility from governments on how the company may trade in that market.

It should be noted that establishing a wholly owned subsidiary is not the only investment option open to an MNE looking for access to a new market or a new capability. A range of alternatives exist, depending on the scale of the investment that is affordable and the level of risk that the company is prepared to take.[7] Ultimately, this is a question of balancing the level of investment required against the need for operational control.[8] If the HQ requires strong control over the operation and is prepared to pay the price for this, then a wholly owned subsidiary may indeed be the best option. If limited control can be tolerated in a new market, in return for a low investment outlay, then a simple export or import agreement with a third party may be most appropriate. Between these extremes, a spectrum of foreign-entry forms can be considered for either market access or capability access, such as exporting/importing through a third party, franchising, licensing, joint ventures or acquisitions. Strategic outsourcing has also become a mainstay of corporate strategy-making, where *make-or-buy* decisions are made on sub-processes that are identified as core competencies which should be retained within the firm, versus those which are little more than a distraction for management and can therefore be outsourced to specialist providers.[9] Since the early 2000s, offshoring has emerged as a particular feature of outsourcing, whereby MNEs relocate workload to low-cost countries either by establishing new subsidiaries there (which are referred to as *captives*) or by using an established outsourcing provider to unlock access to new sources of capability while realising cost savings.

The most sophisticated MNEs adopt thoughtful sourcing strategies that find the optimal blend of wholly owned, collaborative and contractual relationships. Consider Microsoft for example. Although it operates a largely global strategy, it uses a mature network of wholly owned subsidiaries to serve regional markets and to provide shared services. It made 100% acquisitions of companies such as Skype and LinkedIn to complement its service offerings and market reach. Microsoft invested in the Caradigm joint venture with GE on health systems and also uses collaborative outsourcing partnerships such as that with Arvato Bertelsmann for cloud services. Outsourcing contracts are also in place for less strategic services such as facilities management and security. Relationships with certified partners and resellers are maintained in all markets to supplement Microsoft's sales coverage.

The incessant march of globalisation in recent decades created opportunities for countries with smaller market shares to lobby for subsidiary investment based on lower unit costs, government grants or preferential corporate tax regimes. Government agencies in countries like Ireland and Singapore aggressively competed for inward FDI and were hugely successful in doing so. For example, at the time of writing, 12.4% of the total working population in Ireland is directly employed by FDI companies, with a further 10% of national employment dedicated to servicing these companies.[10] Similarly, China, India, the Philippines and a host of Eastern European countries all presented attractive low-cost options that companies found it hard to ignore. China quickly established itself as a factory to the world, as India became a hub for call centres and IT services. Within a few short years, traditional hubs such as Ireland, Scotland, India and China faced new competition from previously under industrialised countries such as Slovakia, Bulgaria, Vietnam and Cambodia.

One feature of globalisation that we have seen in the last couple of decades has been the *fine-slicing* of organisational functions into more parts, carried out by increased numbers of specialised units.[11] The opening of cheaper labour markets, coupled with the abilities that global communications infrastructure and the Internet provided to monitor and direct remote sites, enabled companies to segment their processes into discrete elements and to assign these to in-house or outsourced providers with more granular mandates.[12] Spreading work across a larger number of internal and third-party units, each with more specialised responsibilities, should in theory improve each unit's efficiency and reduce confusion about who is responsible for what. However, it places a greater onus on HQ managers to ensure that all of the elements of the network operate seamlessly together across the global factory.

An MNE organisational model that fine-slices workload across larger numbers of specialised providers puts an increased emphasis on the efficiency of the global network that connects these providers. This network not only serves as a carrier for goods and services, and a channel for communication and relationship development between global supply chain entities. It also acts as the vehicle through which management direction is given. Yet, the more complex the network, the more challenging it becomes to rely on traditional management structures to apply control and give direction. Viewing the connections between internal and external providers as an organisational hierarchy becomes less meaningful as the lines of control proliferate and blur.

A more insightful perspective can be achieved by considering the MNE as an internal market system, arising from the need for modern organisations to balance flexibility, resource access and intense organisational learning.[13] Nodes in the network compete and collaborate to satisfy internal market needs. This is not to imply that this will ever have all of the characteristics of a typical free market system. It is unlikely, for example, that there will be open competition, full customer freedom to choose and a profit motive for product/service providers (at least, not for subsidiaries acting as cost-centres). However, this characterisation of the network within which subsidiaries operate as a market is often more satisfactory than implying that the system can be controlled through a management hierarchy. It recognises that competition exists and it implies that at least some level of independence is required by market participants.

However, markets require some level of regulation, so this raises questions about the rules of the game that HQ should set for the internal market. Should wholly owned subsidiaries be allowed the same freedom to invest that independent suppliers may enjoy? Should service users be allowed to choose an alternative if they take exception to what is being provided internally? How can the market be guided so that it caters for both long-term and short-term needs? If managing within a hierarchy was challenging for HQ and subsidiary managers, governing an internal market system does not make it much easier.

In Chapter 10 ("parental responsibilities"), we will discuss how the MNE can address the challenges discussed above. We will also consider the forces that may shape how MNE structures will continue to develop. However, even at this early stage, we should reflect on the concerns that HQ managers may have specifically in relation to subsidiaries. This will need to be borne in mind if your subsidiary is to flex its strategic muscles and push the boundaries of its current mandates.

Subsidiary Management Dilemmas for HQ

When navigating the organisational complexity that is discussed in the previous section, head office managers face a central dilemma in relation to how they should manage subsidiaries. These subsidiaries were established to give the company access to markets or resources that are not available through any other mechanism. In theory, the diversity of cultures, skills, costs and ideas that the subsidiary brings should contribute innovations that add to the richness of the organisation as a whole. On the other hand, corporate culture and identity should also be embedded in the subsidiary and it should build on the heritage of organisational learning that has brought the company to this point.

So, HQ expects difference, innovation and new sources of value-add from the subsidiary, but it also expects conformance and compliance. This is a conflict of objectives that can cause predicaments within the subsidiary.[14] How can it fully take advantage of its unique capabilities if it is constrained by corporate rules, norms and culture?

As the primary audience here is subsidiary leaders, it might be popular to recommend that head office managers should simply loosen the reins and let the subsidiary fulfil its potential to innovate within the internal market of the MNE. However, we have to accept that, if HQ took a totally hands-off stance, this would be a derogation of its duty to ensure that all parts of a corporation are integrated and share certain values, culture and objectives. Allowing free rein to a subsidiary also brings risks that could endanger the operations and reputation of the organisation as a whole. History is littered with examples of how the failure to control a subsidiary had contagious effects for the rest of the corporation.

BT Italia is a case in point. In 2019, Italian prosecutors alleged that top executives and a network of employees in this subsidiary had carried out frauds in bookkeeping that exaggerated revenues, fabricated contracts and falsified transactions to hide the unit's true financial position relative to bonus targets.[15] The scandal forced BT to write-off $685m and resulted in the resignation of BT's European CEO. It ultimately led to the breaking up of the Italian subsidiary, through the sale of parts of it to Telecom Italia.[16]

Shortfalls in subsidiary performance have seldom had a higher media profile than were seen at the height of the COVID-19 crisis. With govern-ments desperate for a path out of lockdowns, huge deals were done with pharmaceutical companies who committed to developing and supplying vaccines. AstraZeneca experienced significant political and legal pressure when it was accused of prioritising vaccine supplies to the UK, allegedly at the expense of its contractual commitments to the EU.[17] Under pressure to defend against accusations that it was missing commitments it made on vaccine delivery to the EU, the company revealed that its Belgian subsidiary had experienced operational problems which directly impacted its ability to meet manufacturing targets. Although legal actions were settled out of court, it will take longer to heal the wider relationship issues that these localised operational issues caused between AstraZeneca and the EU.

It is rare that we get insights into subsidiary underperformance like in the example of AstraZeneca's Belgium factory. Usually firms do not "wash their dirty linen in public" and problems within supply chains are hidden to avoid reputational damage. This does not mean that HQ generally gets what it needs from its subsidiaries. In 2007, a Forrester research report highlighted parent concerns that 60% of directly managed captive shared services cen-tres in India were struggling with attrition and costs.[18] The finding was quickly latched onto by outsource providers making the argument that an outsourced, rather than a captive subsidiary solution, would take this pain away. Irrespective of whether a captive or outsourced approach is taken to remote delivery, the research shows that maintaining strong performance in remote operations remains a challenge, even with significant investment of management time from head office.

Equally, real problems can arise when the head office is overly controlling and prescriptive about how a remote subsidiary should operate. Research has found that the '"headquarters knows best" syndrome' significantly inhibits the efforts of corporations to turn global presence into competitive advantage.[19] Too much emphasis by HQ managers on the largest markets causes them to overly focus on established regions without fully utilising untapped resources in smaller new markets. This syndrome limits the ability of distant subsidiar-ies to get access to the resources they need to exploit opportunities. An over-confidence and assertiveness by HQ staff discourages sharing of experience between subsidiaries so that organisational learning can improve. Importantly, the '"headquarters knows best" syndrome' has the effect of distancing HQ from regional customers, partners and other stakeholders, ultimately risking business in the very markets that remote subsidiaries were established to serve.

Sometimes expanding internationally by diligently replicating an operating model that has proved successful in a home market can be very successful (e.g., IKEA, Facebook). However, there are also many examples showing the dangers of imposing practices that are familiar to HQ managers, without taking account of the market nuances that local managers can highlight.

■ Home Depot's expansion into China failed because the company did not appreciate that DIY is not as popular a phenomenon there as it is in the US market. An abundance of cheap labour encourages Chinese people to feel that doing-it-themselves shows a lack of affluence and is even a source of embarrassment.

■ The foray by Target – the US retail giant – into the Canadian market only lasted from 2013 to 2015. Target sought economies of scale by replicating its US model and expanding quickly to 133 stores across Canada.[20] This did not allow time to adjust the immature supply chain to accommodate localised challenges, leading to empty shelves. A lack of attention to local market knowledge also caused the company to ignore Canadian customer sensitivities on price and product choice.

■ Walmart's entry to the German market similarly failed for a combination or reasons related to the inability to adjust their operating model to the local environment. Customers reacted against aspects of the standardised Walmart shopping experience, such as having greeters who smile and welcome people to the store. This was perceived to be insincere and grated on many Germans. Importantly, Walmart also underestimated the impact of German law which requires employers to recognise trades unions. From their US operations, they had no experience of working through unions and they struggled to get agreement to many of the work practices on which their model was founded.

■ As documented in the Academy Award winning documentary that was first shown on Netflix in 2019, the Chinese company Fuyao underestimated the challenges in imposing its management practices in the USA after it acquired the Moraine Assembly windshield manufacturing factory from General Motors.[21] Although the Ohio workforce were initially extremely pleased with the lifeline that this gave to the factory, they did not respond well to the regimented practices that their new managers attempted to replicate from their Chinese operations. This fly-on-the-wall documentary is an absorbing story of the collision of work cultures that are founded in contrasting values in relation to work safety, labour rights and worker autonomy.

■ Marketing sensitivities and language can also be underestimated by managers who are viewing a market remotely. Product names which have a different meaning in a local language can be a particular pitfall. Vauxhall, for example, ran into difficulties with its Nova range of cars in Spain, when it was discovered that "no va" in Spanish means "won't go." Orange, the UK telecommunications company, had to deal with extreme political sensitivities when planning its expansion into Northern Ireland. The local Loyalist community associates strongly with William of Orange and rally-around orange imagery. The company realised that their marketing tag-line of "The future is bright, the future is orange" would be particularly provocative for the Irish nationalist community in the Northern Ireland market.[22]

Overlooking local management intelligence is not the only danger that arises when HQ is too prescriptive in imposing its norms in other countries. There is also the risk that ideas developed by managers who are closer to the market will be ignored and this will lead to missed opportunities in new markets, or overlooked chances for production innovation.

In his seminal article on subsidiary evolution, which we will return to in some detail in the next chapter, Ed Delany recounts the story of the development of Bailey's Irish Cream by Gibney's of Ireland, a subsidiary of International Distillers & Vintners (IDV; now Diageo).[23] Gibney's had historically developed a small number of local products for sale in the Irish market alongside the popular international IDV brands. IDV did not pay much attention to this, as the Irish market was small and exports out of Ireland were insignificant. The Ireland management team recognised that if they hoped to increase their contribution to the parent they would have to develop a product that had growth potential outside the local market. Head office was not particularly enthusiastic about this prospect, but also did not object. Given Ireland's agricultural infrastructure and experience in overcoming problems associated with dairy product production, the unit worked with a local dairy co-operative to eventually develop Bailey's Irish Cream. Although initial expectations – both by the local subsidiary and HQ – were modest, the product has become one of the major Diageo global brands. Global IDV customers may never have had the opportunity to enjoy Bailey's if the

Gibney's team had not formed this ambition and if their HQ had not acqui-esced. A more controlling attitude in HQ would have stifled this innovation and caused the parent to miss out on a major new market.

Finding the right mix of direct management control and subsidiary empowerment is clearly a difficult balancing act for the HQ managers who will be held responsible for any performance or reputational issues that occur on their watch. It is also the case that HQ staff who are given responsibil-ity for interfacing with subsidiaries are often not best positioned to find this balance. In the early stages of a subsidiary's existence, operations experts in HQ can provide valuable assistance. However, as the subsidiary develops, it should get to a point where it has increased expertise, while in parallel the operational experience available from HQ becomes diluted through a lack of practice. Relationships can be particularly difficult if the HQ manager was previously operationally responsible for a function performed centrally before it was delegated to a subsidiary. In this case, rose-tinted perspectives on how things were done in the past can cause the HQ manager to forget that the subsidiary was established precisely because everything was not perfect in the old world. It can be hard for the HQ-subsidiary relationship to over-come the emotions felt by managers who may have had reservations about a decentralisation strategy in the first place. This can also make it difficult for more senior HQ executives to judicate when performance issues arise between subsidiaries and their HQ contact point.

It can also happen that as the subsidiary becomes more established, less senior people are assigned within HQ to act as the interface to the parent organisation. These people are in a difficult position. Their responsibility is to enable the subsidiary to maintain strong performance, but they are in the immediate firing line when HQ executives are dissatisfied. Sadly, staffers in these positions often feel that they are not demonstrating their worth unless they are drawing attention to issues. Their value proposition is that problems would be hidden if their role did not exist.

Even when a productive relationship is developed between the subsidiary and their upward-reporting lines, managers representing HQ interests can face a further dilemma. That is, they should remain open to the possibil-ity that alternative sourcing options exist for the functions assigned to the subsidiary. An HQ liaison who has been constructive and proactive in sup-porting the subsidiary in its development can understandably feel a sense of parental ownership for the unit. This may be good for the subsidiary, but can cause them to be blind to the flaws in the operation or to be too under-standing of the reasons for underperformance. To fulfil their obligations to the parent, HQ managers should retain a level of independence that allows them to consider whether an alternative delivery method – for example through sub-contracting, outsourcing or assignment to a different subsidiary – would improve efficiency or effectiveness.

The relationship between subsidiaries and their parent organisations has been characterised by some academic researchers as a constant "Us versus Them" tension between subsidiaries that push for autonomy and HQ organisations that push for control.[24] The reality in most cases is a bit more nuanced and incorporates a number of dilemmas as discussed above:

- How to realise the subsidiary's potential while maintaining control.
- How to promote global consistency while taking account of local market needs.
- How to balance corporate and local cultural influences.
- How to avoid the limitations of the "headquarters knows best" syndrome.
- How to define formal governance processes that should apply to the subsidiary.
- How to support the subsidiary while remaining open to other sourcing options.

HQ managers acting in loco parentis for the MNE have a difficult role to play in navigating this terrain. For their part, subsidiary managers can feel constrained, particularly when they are limited by the seniority of their reporting line into those functions in HQ that make strategy and resource-allocation decisions. It is important for subsidiary leaders to have a realistic appreciation of these dilemmas and to build relationships with HQ counterparts at all levels.

HQ and subsidiary managers share the common objective to achieve the best possible outcomes for the parent. While their perspectives and priorities may differ, they should both agree that navigating these dilemmas to unleash the potential of the subsidiary to contribute to these outcomes is a common cause.

Summary

This chapter was intended to provoke reflection on the expectations that your parent organisation may have of its subsidiaries and how they operate within its overall global supply chain. We also considered the challenges that HQ faces in finding the balance between empowering the subsidiary to maximise its potential, while maintaining control and avoiding negative impacts to other parts of the business. Although all of the features discussed above may not be visible in every organisation, this presents a backdrop against which you can compare and contrast your own MNE and develop more insight into the drivers that shape the environment within which your subsidiary operates. Deeply understanding this context will prove important later as you develop strategic options and plot a course through decision-making processes in your company.

In this chapter, we also introduced the concept of the MNE as an internal market, as distinct from a hierarchical organisational structure. However, we should not assume that HQ will always view their relationships with subsidiaries in the same way that they view third-party contractual relationships within this market. These relationships will differ in terms of their pricing structures, planning cycles, durations of relationships and recourse in the event of failure. Even if an internal relationship is governed by a memorandum of understanding, this is typically not legally enforceable and it is ultimately underwritten by the parent. At a more fundamental level, there are strategic reasons why the company chose an ownership relationship for the subsidiary and these reasons should be fulfilled. However, doing so raises dilemmas for HQ in relation to the posture it should adopt when managing the subsidiary, while remaining sensitive to the amount of control that it should cede to the internal market.

Investing in wholly owned subsidiaries is just one foreign-entry mode option that is available to corporations seeking to gain access to new markets or take advantage of new capabilities. Subsidiary managers who are motivated by the desire to gain autonomy from head office should recognise that one of the reasons why an MNE established a subsidiary instead of one of the other entry modes was to retain a degree of control commensurate with the investment risk and flexibility characteristics that ownership entails. Diluting the strength of this management line may feel liberating, but unless this is done thoughtfully it may lead to doubts on whether a wholly owned structure is still required. The close attention of a parent can be uncomfortable, but it is better than being neglected or, worse, replaced.

To provide additional foresight into where this strategic development may lead, it is useful to look at general profiles on how subsidiaries evolve and grow. This is the subject of our next chapter.

Notes

1. Howard Perlmutter, "The Tortuous Evolution of Multinational Enterprises," *Columbia Journal of World Business* 1 (1969).
2. Ed Schein, "Ed Schein – Let's Focus on (National, Organizational, and Occupational) Culture," (Youtube 2015).
3. Sjoerd Beugelsdijk et al., "Cultural Distance and Firm Internationalization: A Meta-Analytical Review and Theoretical Implications," *Journal of Management* 44, no. 1 (2018).
4. Christopher A. Bartlett and Sumantra Ghoshal, "Tap Your Subsidiaries for Global Reach," *Harvard Business Review* 64, no. 6 (1986).
5. J.D. Daniels, L.H. Radebaugh, and D.P. Sullivan, "Chapter 12: Country Evaluation and Selection," in *International Business: Environment and Operations* (Essex: Pearson Education Ltd, 2015).
6. L. Brennan, "How Netflix Expanded to 190 Countries in 7 Years," *Harvard Business Review Online* (2018).
7. Y. Pan and D.K. Tse, "The Hierarchical Model of Market Entry Modes," *Journal of International Business Studies*, no. 4 (2000).
8. J.J. Wild, K.L. Wild, and K.C.Y. Han, "Chapter 13: Selecting and Managing Entry Modes," in *International Business: An Integrated Approach* (Upper Saddle River, NJ: Prentice Hall, 2000), p. 470.
9. James Brian Quinn and Frederick G. Hilmer, "Strategic Outsourcing," *Sloan Management Review* 35, no. 4 (1994).
10. IDA Ireland, "Annual Report and Accounts 2020," (IDA Ireland, 2020).
11. Peter J. Buckley, "International Integration and Coordination in the Global Factory," *Management International Review* 51 (2011).
12. Thomas H. Davenport, "The Coming Commoditization of Processes," *Harvard Business Review* 83, no. 6 (2005).
13. Daniele Cerrato, "The Multinational Enterprise as an Internal Market System," *International Business Review* 15, no. 3 (2006).
14. G. Morgan and P.H. Kristensen, "The Contested Space of Multinationals: Varieties of Institutionalism, Varieties of Capitalism," *Human Relations* 59, no. 11 (2006).
15. Rob Davies, "Ex-Bt Bosses Named in Investigation into Alleged Fraud in Italy Unit," *The Guardian International Edition*, February 13 2019.
16. Nic Fildes, "Bt Breaks up Italian Business with Sale to Telecom Italia," *Financial Times*, December 10 2020.
17. Daniel Boffey, "Eu Starts Legal Action against Astrazeneca over Vaccine Shortfalls," *The Guardian International Edition*, April 26 2021.
18. Forrester, "Shattering the Offshore Captive Center Myth," (2007).
19. C. Bouquet, J. Birkinshaw, and J.-L. Barsouz, "Fighting the 'Headquarters Knows Best' Syndrome," *MIT Sloan Management Review* 2016, no. Winter (2016).

20. Hollie Shaw, "Target Corp's Spectacular Canada Flop: A Gold Standard Case Study for What Retailers Shouldn't Do," https://financialpost.com/news/retail-marketing/target-corps-spectacular-canada-flop-a-gold-standard-case-study-for-what-retailers-shouldnt-do.
21. Julia Reichert and Steven Bognar, "American Factory," (Netflix, 2019).
22. Patrick Tooher, "The Future's Not So Bright as Orange Gets the Red Light in Ulster," *Independent*, July 12 1996.
23. Delany, "Strategic Development of the Multinational Subsidiary through Subsidiary Initiative-Taking."
24. S.L. Patterson and D.B. Brock, "The Development of Subsidiary Management Research: Review and Theoretical Analysis," *International Business Review* 11 (2002).

Chapter 3

Subsidiary Evolution

The Oxford dictionary explains that the word *subsidiary* is derived from the Latin *subsidiarius*, which in turn is derived from *subsidium* meaning 'support or assistance'. The word is generally taken to mean something that is connected to a superior entity. A subsidiary company is defined as one that is owned or controlled by another company and therefore operates in a subservient manner.

This common interpretation of the word also reflects how subsidiaries were viewed by managers and academics alike in the early days of corporate expansion. At that time, the literature saw everything from the HQ perspective and positioned subsidiaries as entities that were established by the head office on an as-needed basis and directed through a hierarchical command and control structure. As global industries matured, the literature began to recognise that relationships between HQ organisations and subsidiaries are not always so rigid and that they also change over time. It became apparent to companies that giving more freedom and responsibility to subsidiaries could make global supply chains more innovative and flexible, to a level where this could become as important a competitive differentiator as the products or services that these supply chains carried.

This recognition of the potential additional value-add from differentiated supply chains encouraged subsidiaries to find new ways of adding value.[1] The most successful of these units adopted a more dynamic perspective on their role and actively pursued strategies to enhance this contribution.[2] Responsibility for developing the multiple dimensions of global supply chains also became more fragmented within headquarters organisations, resulting in multiple sponsors who could be lobbied for additional subsidiary investment. Regional subsidiaries often became homes for portfolios of multiple investments of varying sizes linking into different parts of the MNE.

This chapter explores the factors that drive these changes to subsidiary roles and the phases of subsidiary evolution that typically manifest themselves as the subsidiary develops. We will also investigate how this evolution can be accelerated.

However, before we delve into the patterns of subsidiary evolution, it is worth considering the motivating factors that are required to sustain this evolutionary journey. Understanding the sources of motivation (or the absence of these) is an important first step in verifying that these exist in sufficient strength to fuel the management effort needed to drive a subsidiary's evolution.

Why Bother?

If you are a subsidiary manager who has found the time to invest in reading this book, then you already have some degree of motivation in relation to the development of your organisation. It is nonetheless important to understand what the root of that motivation is. Is it likely to be lasting or is it driven by some recent, but passing frustration? Importantly, is it shared by management colleagues and their teams, at the levels needed to invest energy in new ventures while still managing existing responsibilities? It is unlikely that you and your team will be motivated by any single factor. However, it is worth reflecting on which of the following typical motivators are most applicable in your case.

Thrive and Survive

If any organisation, however, big or small, stands still, it runs the risk of stagnating and withering. In a dynamic business environment, where requirements change and internal and external competition are always a threat, unless the organisation is moving forward it is likely to slip backwards relative to its internal market network. Even if there are no direct internal or external competitors on the horizon, new technologies or processes may emerge that make current responsibilities less valuable to the parent.

The desire to constantly move forward and improve should therefore be a motivator for any strategy. The alternative is to fade into insignificance while others progress. In the worst case, this can result in the demise of the subsidiary.

Some subsidiaries may have the security of bricks-and-mortar investments, binding grant agreements with government agencies, or other structural bonds which will make it more difficult for their parent to reduce investment or to exit. However, nothing is forever. Many managers will look back with pride on the speed at which their subsidiary organisation was established and developed during its first phase of growth. Such quick start-ups are common as corporations seek to get an immediate return from their capital investments. However, this should also serve as a lesson that other sites can also be quick in stepping-up when they see an opportunity to supplement or replace an incumbent.

The 'fear of standing still' should always be a driver, as a subsidiary that does not thrive, may not survive.

Create Career Opportunities

A subsidiary with responsibility for more strategic functions will have greater power when negotiating for higher allocations of senior positions and rewards budgets. If the parent has rules in relation to the number of employees that must be overseen by managers at different levels of seniority, then the absolute number of workers that the subsidiary employs may also be an important driver when lobbying for promotions.

The subsidiary leadership team may therefore be motivated by the prospect that a strategy which earns more responsibility for the organisation will lead to more seniority and rewards for themselves. From the perspective of the general employee population, a larger subsidiary organisation also presents more opportunity for them to grow their careers into a greater variety of roles. For these reasons, the career opportunities that subsidiary development will provide for managers and employees will be an important response to the question 'What's in it for me?'.

Team Development

Good managers will aspire to leave an organisation in a better state than it was when they took over. Of course this can be demonstrated by improved operational performance, but managers should also recognise their responsibility to develop broader organisational capabilities, manifested through the skills and culture of the teams under their tutelage. If we believe the rhetoric that people are the most important asset and that they represent the future of the organisation, subsidiary leaders should accept responsibility for developing a culture of ambition and innovation in their teams.

The responsibility that falls on subsidiary leaders to lead by example, create a vibrant culture and act as a role-model for future leaders, should contribute to the motivation that drives subsidiary strategy and the evolution that results from this.

Align with Corporate Objectives

In complex and fragmented corporations, it can be difficult to appreciate the linkages between the activities of the subsidiary and the wider strategies of the parent. Which activities contribute most to corporate objectives and which ones can be deprioritised so that scarce resources are devoted to the most important areas? Developing a clear subsidiary strategy can solve this issue by forcing the local organisation to analyse whether all its activities are really in support of the corporate direction.

Subsidiaries that question how their role can be honed to add more value to the parent will be seen as more proactive and solution oriented. This should be appreciated by stakeholders who control how resources are allocated

Maintain Employee Loyalty

In healthy corporate cultures, subsidiary managers and their employees will have a strong pride in their corporations, based on what the parent organisation offers to the marketplace, how it operates and what it contributes to society. It is important for employees at all levels to feel this sense of belonging to the parent and a pride in how the subsidiary contributes to corporate successes. Having a clear ambition and development path for the subsidiary helps everyone to understand their contribution to team goals and instils a sense of purpose and accomplishment.

Subsidiaries that are only a few years in operation are likely to have been driven to date by the energy that gives momentum to the early stages of a start-up, such as the hiring phase, the bedding-in of facilities and the learning of new operational processes. However, teams can become weary of the constant pressure that this entails, and energy levels can fade. Communicating a new vision of what the future can hold for the subsidiary and how this will contribute to what their corporation aims to achieve gives people a new sense of commitment and renewed motivation to last the course.

Fulfil Subsidiary Potential

Strong subsidiaries have a local identity, with personal bonds formed across the organisation and with local partners. There will be a sense of pride in what is achieved as a team and a desire to build on successes to date. Subsidiaries will also have an identity within the communities in which they are located and they are likely to be valued contributors to the local economy. The community will expect that everything possible will be done to secure the subsidiary's position and to take advantage of everything it has to offer as a hosting location.

Subsidiary leaders should be motivated by their responsibility to tap into this potential and to develop their organisation so that it maximises its opportunity to serve customers, beat competition, increase shareholder returns and contribute to the community in which it operates.

Earn Increased Autonomy

Last but by no means least, the desire to increase the subsidiary's self-determination is often a fundamental motivator for managers. None of the other motivators above can be reliably achieved if the management of the organisation is totally at the behest of outside parties. Ambitious managers want to have the flexibility to lead their organisations without claustrophobic attention from above. As the subsidiary matures, it can earn increased autonomy for its operations and decision-making.

It is unlikely that a subsidiary can ever become fully autonomous, and indeed that level of autonomy would indicate a separation from the parent organisation that may ultimately prove self-defeating. However, it is reasonable for the subsidiary to pursue strategies that seek to improve its position of influence within the corporate structure so that it can earn more control over its operations and its future trajectory.

Evolution Phases

As will be clear from the previous chapter, international subsidiaries can operate concurrently in three markets:

1. The *local* market, where they may promote the company's products but where they also compete for talent and other resources to support their operations,
2. The *global* market, where they may support the company's activities internationally, and
3. The *internal* market within their corporations, where they compete for resources and mandates.

If productivity depends on the scale of an operation, then an initial significant investment will be required to establish the subsidiary's infrastructure, facilities, technology, staffing, etc. In cases like this, the responsibilities assumed by the new subsidiary will often be transferred from another site. In other instances, a smaller-scale initial investment may be possible, and the subsidiary can grow organically in line with the parent company's development. As discussed in the previous chapter, an alternative option for the parent is to grow its subsidiary network through the acquisition of an established entity.

Whether the subsidiary was established through a large initial investment, through organic growth, or through an acquisition, its strategic positioning within the parent can change over time. The theory that subsidiaries follow an evolutionary path within their markets has been explored from various perspectives.

In 1990, Sargeant proposed how subsidiaries that are established as *local market* representatives of a corporation typically evolve.[3] He identified phases of childhood, adolescence and adulthood as the subsidiary grows more effective in representing the parent's brand and is capable of customising this as required to cater to local market preferences.

Later, Julian Birkinshaw proposed stages of evolution for sales subsidiaries operating in *global* markets. He described phases of increasing responsibility as the subsidiary extended its scope from being only focused on the local market, to eventually having global responsibilities (i.e., local sales subsidiary, local sales with manufacturing, regional hub, world product mandate).[4]

In 2000, Long Range Planning published Ed Delany's seminal article providing a comprehensive model of the evolution stages of subsidiaries within their *internal* markets, as their prowess in local and global markets also increased.[5] This article drew attention to the initiatives that subsidiaries of decentralised organisations take to defend their existing mandates, to consolidate their position within the wider organisation and to proactively develop their activities to create new platforms for growth.

Delany's perspective challenged the traditional portrayal of the relationships between HQ and subsidiaries as a hierarchy directed from the top. Rather, it should be understood as a dynamic non-hierarchical structure where multiple centres of control within the parent interact with multiple subsidiaries, each with different degrees of responsibility and autonomy. Shifts in power happen between players and no one unit dominates the rest. A corollary of this perspective is that successful subsidiaries evolve over time by shifting their power-position within their company and by out-manoeuvring competitors. Of course, this is consistent with our previous characterisation of the corporation as a networked internal market, and it is therefore more in-tune with the climate within which most subsidiaries currently operate.

Delany's eight-stage model of subsidiary evolution emerged from his research work with managers from 28 Irish subsidiaries and was validated by 12 consultants who had extensive experience in working with subsidiary management teams. It is founded on the finding that, at the point where they are established, subsidiaries can initially be positioned at any stage in the evolution path. Their progress after that is driven by deliberate strategic actions to steadily improve their position within a lifecycle of development. It should be noted that progress through the evolutionary stages is not inevitable. Just as it is possible to quickly move through the stages, it is also very possible for a subsidiary to slip downwards, before settling and potentially progressing again. Evolution should therefore be considered like a game of snakes and ladders, rather than an inevitable progression.

The evolutionary stages identified by Delany are shown in Figure 3.1, including a summary of the major features that are characteristic of each stage. As illustrated in the figure, the first three stages of evolution apply

	STAGE 1: Establishing start-up	STAGE 2: Carrying out mandate satisfactorily	STAGE 3: Fulfilling basic mandate in a 'superior way'	STAGE 4: Extending basic mandate – low risk moves	STAGE 5: Extending basic mandate – strategic development	STAGE 6: Becoming strategic centre for the MNE	STAGE 7: Becoming strategic pivot for the MNE	STAGE 8: Becoming strategic apex for the MNE
Strategic importance to corporation	*LOW*			*MODERATE*		*HIGH*		*VERY HIGH*
Operational performance	*IMMATURE*	*SATISFACTORY*	*SUPERIOR*					
Strategic focus	*OPERATIONAL STABILITY*		*OPERATIONAL EXCELLENCE*	*LOW RISK MANDATE EXTENSIONS*	*STRATEGIC MANDATE EXTENSIONS*		*CONSOLIDATE STRATEGIC POSITION*	*DETERMINE CORPORATE STRATEGY*

Figure 3.1 Stages of subsidiary evolution and their characteristics (adapted from Delany, 2000)

when the subsidiary is fulfilling the core tasks that it has been established to execute (i.e., its *basic mandate*). The focus during these stages is on steadily improving its effectiveness in fulfilling these initial responsibilities.

- **Stage 1: Establishing start-up**. In this start-up stage, the on-site assistance of managers from elsewhere in the company may be needed to support the operation. Even with this help, operational performance may still be patchy.
- **Stage 2: Carrying out the basic mandate satisfactorily**. Basic operational performance is now at a level where it attracts little criticism, although not yet to the point where the location would be considered a reference site, or particularly innovative.
- **Stage 3: Fulfilling the basic mandate in a 'superior way'**. Achievement of basic operational metrics exceeds expectations to the level where the site is seen as a reference point for other sites. Subsidiary responsibilities are still limited to the original mandate.

In the next two stages, the subsidiary begins to extend beyond the original scope for which it was established.

- **Stage 4: Extending the basic mandate through low-risk moves**. This is a critical stage where the subsidiary begins to use its reputation as a superior performer to push its boundaries, albeit in a relatively low-key way since sponsors are unlikely to accept high-risk moves at this point. The strategic initiatives undertaken during this stage are likely to be into areas that are a natural extension of current responsibilities, or which have future potential that is not considered the territory of another subsidiary. The basic mandate must continue to be fulfilled in a superior manner if the subsidiary is to earn the right to do this.
- **Stage 5: Extending the basic mandate with strategic development.** This stage continues to build on the success and reputation achieved in previous stages, but now seeks to move into areas of greater strategic importance to the corporation. Some of the moves made in Stage 4 can provide a springboard for this. The basic mandate must continue to be performed to a superior level, but it can be extended into areas of greater value. An acid test for a subsidiary's position in this phase is whether its closure would represent a significant loss of competence for the parent.

In the final three stages of evolution, the subsidiary earns increasing levels of strategic importance to the company. The number of strategic centres in any organisation is limited, and therefore, these final stages will only ever be achieved by a few subsidiaries.

- **Stage 6: Becoming a strategic centre for the corporation**. Basic responsibilities must continue to be performed at a high level, but boundaries have been pushed to the level where the subsidiary has a significant position in relation to the global operations of the company. This stage will typically involve genuinely strategic mandates such as R&D or process design. The subsidiary will also contribute to wider corporate strategy formulation in its areas of scope. Closure of subsidiaries at this stage of evolution would represent a major loss to their corporations.
- **Stage 7: Becoming a strategic pivot for the corporation for key activities**. This stage involves the superior performance of original mandates and their subsequent enhancements. The subsidiary is recognised as one of the few global locations of major strategic importance and investment in the company. It is likely to have a broad breadth of responsibility across its areas of functional interest (e.g., R&D, sales, P&L and strategy).
- **Stage 8: Becoming the strategic apex for the corporation**. Subsidiaries at this level effectively operate as the head office for their functional remit and are recognised as having responsibility for all major decisions.

Delany acknowledges that not every subsidiary will have a story that neatly fits into this multi-stage framework. There are examples of start-ups that will already have strategic importance for a parent and may even have responsibility for strategy-setting. Such an example may therefore have elements of Stages 1 and 6. Similarly mixed positions across the stages can occur when there are transfers of responsibility from another site, or in the case of an acquisition. Such cases will be allowed a period of forbearance by the parent before their performance and degree of strategic influence align.

It is understandable that a subsidiary might take advantage of any opportunity to extend its mandate, even if this pushes it beyond what would be a strict interpretation of its current maturity stage. An example could be where the subsidiary has the opportunity to move into areas of strategic importance to the corporation (Stage 5) even though it is still getting to grips with its initial mandate (Stage 2). While the motivation to 'seize the day' is very understandable, the risks need to be managed – particularly if there is a large spread between the stages that are represented in the subsidiary. Expectations need to be set and external stakeholders should be carefully managed – ideally so that they feel a shared ownership of any risks. However, even if a subsidiary has elements of more than one stage, when planning strategic moves it is advisable to be realistic about which stage is most representative of the subsidiary's overall maturity at this point.

Evolve What?

When working with subsidiary leadership teams, my experience has been that they continue to find Delany's stages of subsidiary evolution very useful. It helps them to recognise their current positioning within their corporations, to trace their evolution to this point and to consider how they might move to future stages in the model.

However, Delany regards all subsidiaries as cohesive business units, each with a well-defined and singular mandate. The company examples that he provides to illustrate the model are all manufacturing and distribution subsidiaries, indicating that it was these types of businesses that provided the primary basis for his research. This is not fully representative of the more fragmented nature of many current subsidiaries and particularly those involved in services that do not require a critical mass of employees in one location, as is generally the case for manufacturing and distribution operations. At the time of Delany's research, the internet was not as fully developed. The companies studied would not have been exposed to the highly networked, cross-location teams that are commonplace today.

Particularly for services functions that do not require economies of scale, subsidiaries now often operate as a loose confederation of teams that share local infrastructure. Although they are co-located, they often operate as part of separate internationally integrated business functions in their corporations, and sub-units within the subsidiary may report through different management lines to the parent. For example, the IBM Technology Campus in west Dublin hosts software development functions, digital sales, large deal consulting services, IT outsourcing services and many other international functions that all report through different corporate divisions. Even for local operations that are more cohesive than this, the subsidiary may also incorporate small teams performing peripheral, but important work. Consider, for example, a highly cohesive large-scale manufacturing operation that shares facilities with smaller, but strategically important teams whose day-to-day operations are integrated with corporate functions outside the manufacturing line (e.g., Marketing and R&D).

The reality that subsidiaries may now be more fragmented than in the past does not negate the usefulness of Delany's model. Indeed, some of these disparate functions can be considered as fitting nicely within the model, as they can be viewed as low-risk moves that form part of Stage 4, or more assertive strategic moves as part of later stages. But there are also cases where the portfolio of responsibilities that a subsidiary now holds has not evolved as part of any deliberate strategic process. Sometimes an opportunistic divide-and-conquer approach by the subsidiary leaders can allow them to win a broad mix of responsibilities, based only on the desire to increase employment and share costs at their location. Alternatively, a corporation may view the subsidiary as a catcher for any functions that they feel may benefit from the resources that the site has to offer. In the case of the IBM Dublin Technology Campus, the corporation judged the city to be an attractive location given the available skills and government incentives. Grant agreements covering a range of possible job types were made between the government agency responsible for encouraging FDI (IDA Ireland), and IBM corporate HQ, which then acted as a broker in encouraging its divisions to take advantage of the location's benefits for their growth and restructuring needs.

In cases where the functions within the legal entity of the subsidiary are disparate, a Country Manager will often be appointed by the corporation to act as a figurehead when dealing with local stakeholders and as a resolution point for issues experienced locally by individual sub-units. This can cover common needs such as liaising with government bodies, developing relationships with universities or other companies operating in the sector, considering common hiring needs across sub-units, or even solving day-to-day issues with buildings or other infrastructure. I recall one such site leader joking that the most emotive responsibility of the role was to mediate disputes for car parking spaces. Seldom, is that local leader explicitly given responsibility to plan for the strategic development of the portfolio of teams that make up the subsidiary – although the more far-sighted leaders take it on themselves to assume this responsibility.

A question that then arises for the subsidiary management team is at what level of integration should strategic planning for the subsidiary take place across its current portfolio of responsibilities? Should it be for every sub-unit incorporated in the legal entity, or only those that have a logical associa-tion with each other? Can Heads of sub-units opt-out or only engage to a limited extent? What level of sacrifice can be expected of any sub-unit for the greater good of the wider subsidiary teams (e.g., cost sharing, resource sharing, operational management time sacrificed to contribute to subsidiary strategy planning discussions)?

These are questions that require mature discussion, and they should not be fudged. It should be recognised that the personal career progression and compensation of individual sub-unit managers may be decided through their corporate line, and they will need to balance this against the needs of the subsidiary as a whole. Priorities will of course differ between a man-ager who is a local employee and whose career trajectory will be within the region, and a manager assigned from elsewhere in the corporation to lead the sub-unit for a set period, but who will continue to pursue their career in another part of the company. In either case, it is a lot to expect of a sub-unit manager to make sacrifices that benefit a peer sub-unit even if they are in dire need (e.g., by accepting a greater share of infrastructural cost or by giving up some critical skills). Even if it can hide such local sup-ports from corporate sponsors, a sub-unit that aims to earn more autonomy from its divisional management will not want this autonomy constrained by then having to strictly adhere to a local strategic agenda. As we will discuss later, strategy requires choices and trade-offs. The need for a sub-unit leader to balance the requirements of the subsidiary and their corporate division should be respected by peer managers.

Having said all this about the factors that might discourage a sub-unit from engaging in broader subsidiary strategy planning, there are undoubted benefits from seeking to make the subsidiary whole greater than the sum of its parts. Some of these relate back to the motivating factors that were dis-cussed earlier in this chapter (e.g., wider career opportunities for staff). In a competitive internal market, there is also the benefit of having local allies within a safe harbour for sharing ideas, debating challenges and providing operational support in times of need.

It should be clear from this discussion that early agreement is needed within the subsidiary management team on what will be the scope of any strategic planning and what will be the rules-of-the-game. It is also good practice to agree on a governance process, covering details such as the frequency of meetings, boundaries for what is up for discussion, levels of representation in strategic planning and the resolution process for any disagreements.

A final consideration on this question of what the focus for subsidiary evolution will be is the question of what to do about any external functions upon which the subsidiary or one of its sub-units is dependent, but which is not within its direct management control. Examples could include a third-party outsourcer that supports the subsidiary's core activities, or a sister site which shares the responsibility for one of the subsidiary's functions. It is difficult to generalise about these as it depends so much on context and history. However, whether these are to be included in the scope of strategic planning needs to be considered. The most assertive approach is to regard them as dependencies that need to be controlled. The strategy planning should therefore regard them as an inherent part of the landscape. One option is to collaborate with them on strategic planning. An alternative is to improve the subsidiary's relative power-position so that it can exert the required level of control and secure its support. Either way, this will require some careful manoeuvring and stakeholder management as we will cover later.

In summary, the first step in the strategic planning process for a subsidiary is to decide what scope of functions the management team wishes to develop and evolve. Is it a single cohesive mandate or is it a portfolio of elements – each with its own boundaries but expecting that the future for the whole will be stronger than that for the sum of its individual parts? Each of those parts may have tentacles into functions that are managed externally to the subsidiary, but on which it has dependencies.

How to Evolve

Having established the scope for subsidiary strategy, managers can then consider the tactics that should be pursued to move from one stage of maturity to the next. This question will be explored more fully in the following chapters. However, four points are worth considering as a precursor to this.

1. Fulfilling existing responsibilities satisfactorily is generally a qualifier for moving forward to any future stage. If operational performance is unsatisfactory, this needs to be resolved first. If operational performance declines later, this needs to be addressed before moving on.
2. The nature of the tactics that will be employed when making any strategic moves should be carefully considered to maintain stakeholder support. We will return to this in Part III.

3. The intended result from any strategic moves should be understood – specifically in relation to whether they are designed to win a new mandate which must then be operationalised, or to develop a competence that can become a platform for making the case to HQ that a new mandate should be formally allocated.
4. Even if the evolution of the subsidiary can be considered in terms of its development within the internal market of the MNE, we should not forget that subsidiaries also operate within local and global markets. The externalities associated with these markets should also remain in focus so that their influence on the evolution of the subsidiary can be optimised.

Below, we will investigate these dimensions of how evolution from any stage to the next can be pursued.

Manage Perceptions of Performance

As has already been emphasised, a subsidiary cannot hope to move from any stage of maturity to the next unless it continues to carry out its current mandates in a superior manner. Minor or temporary under-performance shortfalls may be tolerated, but the *snakes and ladders* analogy should be remembered. If there are widespread perceptions that the subsidiary is unable to cope with current responsibilities, this can lead to a slippage backwards through one or more evolutionary stages.

Therefore, maintaining operational performance is the price-of-entry to the game at all stages of maturity. However, particularly in the first three stages, steadily improving operational performance should be the sole focus of the management team. The only exceptions might be (a) where the opportunity to extend a mandate arises and this cannot be ignored, or (b) where winning an additional mandate can noticeably improve efficiency by allowing fixed costs to be shared. Nevertheless, as stated above, extending responsibilities while still bedding-in an original mandate is a risky tactic. It can be exhausting for a management team that is likely to be already thinly spread, and it will demand skills and resources that may already be in short supply. The safer option is to use these stages to develop operational skills and management competence that will deliver a good foundational reputation for the subsidiary and a solid platform for later development.

If we accept that superior performance is a criterion for moving to Delany's Stage 4 (low-risk moves), this raises the question of what is meant by superior. In cases where outputs are very well defined and measurable, and where there are established performance benchmarks, this may be clear-cut. However, outputs are not always so quantifiable, and performance perceptions can vary between stakeholders based on their interpretations of the results and the conditions under which these were achieved. These perceptions can be influenced, so subsidiary leaders should also be proactive in ensuring that performance is favourably represented. In a highly competitive environment, there may even be external players who will portray the subsidiary's performance negatively for their own gain, or because they have rose-tinted recollections of how things used to be.

Perceptions are reality, so they need to be actively managed. Managing perceptions is an often-underestimated skill that requires foresight and vigilance. A prerequisite to this is an investment in relationships that maintain two-way lines of communication and can be drawn on in times of difficulty to earn the 'benefit of the doubt'. Managers who are skilled in managing perceptions will be adept at communicating good news, but not to the extent that they get a reputation for self-promotion, embellishment or manipulation.

To influence stakeholder perceptions of performance and value, it is useful to think of this as the difference between *expectations* of what should be delivered and the *experience* of what was delivered.[6] If the experience of subsidiary performance exceeds expectations, then stakeholders will be satisfied. Otherwise, they will not. Of course, this is just another way of expressing the old maxim goes, it is important to 'under-promise and over-deliver'. However, it is important here to recognise that both expectations and perceptions of experiences can be influenced – and it is part of the subsidiary management role to do this.

Expectations can be set by agreeing operational targets for KPIs, cost etc. in advance and ensuring that the measurement process for these is clear. Even if the organisation is not being held to strict targets in the early stages, it is good to have these defined so that there are consistent expectations set across all stakeholders. If the subsidiary is taking responsibility for a transfer of activity from another site, it is useful to ensure that historical performance benchmarks over an extended period are documented. These will provide an important reference point if disputes arise later about whether performance is at an acceptable level. Staff training and assessment materials should be approved by stakeholder representatives so that expectations can be set about what level of performance can be expected of new staff with this level of training. All new operations need time to get up-to-speed, so expectations should also be set with stakeholders on the glidepath to get to the desired levels. This may all seem like overkill if sponsors of the subsidiary are reasonably relaxed about the performance that is expected. However, when the early enthusiasm for a new venture fades, the benefit of carefully setting expectations in advance will become apparent.

Managing expectations should be an important on-going focus for managers, but equal focus should be given to influencing perceptions of how performance is experienced by stakeholders. If KPIs are very measurable and transparent, this may appear straightforward. But there will still be opportunities to manage perceptions by explaining reasons for shortfalls, highlighting wins, communicating success stories etc. This needs to be done judiciously so that the subsidiary does not get a reputation for constant bragging or excuse-making. However, feeding good news to supportive stakeholders gives them ammunition when they are defending performance in forums where the subsidiary is not represented.

Achieving hard KPI targets is important, but subsidiary leaders should recognise that there is opportunity to shape how stakeholders experience these measurements. By engaging, explaining and emphasising, the relationship between expectations and experience can be influenced so that perceptions of superior performance are managed.

Adopt Scout or Subversive Strategies

As the maturity level progresses past Stage 3, more deliberate actions can be taken to push the boundaries of subsidiary mandates. The later chapters will go into some depth on the factors that will need to be considered and tactics that can be employed to make such moves. Suffice it to say at this point that such actions can be undertaken with or without the knowledge and endorsement of HQ sponsors. In his article on subsidiary evolution and in an earlier publication co-authored with his colleague Eddie Molloy,[7] Delany refers to the alternative approaches as *Scout and Subversive behaviours* (where the term 'Scout' refers to a member of a Scout Association, committed to always being well-behaved and dedicated to doing good deeds). Subsidiaries following Scout strategies will be careful to follow the rules set by their sponsors and only push boundaries when they have explicit approval to do so. Subversive strategies are engaged in without the knowledge of HQ. This is not to imply that the subversive approach is dysfunctional to the corporation. These strategies are regarded as subversive because subsidiary leaders judge that HQ will prefer if they focus solely on their set mandate and to do anything else causes them to feel subversive. Under such circumstances, it is better to remain low-key and accept that sometimes it is easier to ask for forgiveness than permission.

A careful mix of Scout and Subversive behaviours is also possible, depending on the stakes. Decisions on which option to pursue will be influenced by the power-balance between the subsidiary and HQ, recognising that this is dynamic and changes over time.[8] If the subsidiary has the resources and the power to withstand any backlash that might result from a solo-run, a subversive investment may be warranted. If it will be easy to get this agreement, then there is no point in risking an action that may lead to an erosion of trust and power now.

Develop Charters and Capabilities

In 1998, Birkinshaw and Hood published their model of subsidiary evolution. This proposed that subsidiary development can, at its most fundamental level, be understood as being driven by change across two dimensions. The first of these covers changes in the mandates that are assigned by HQ (which they refer to as *Charters*). The second dimension relates to changes in the subsidiary's ability to fulfil current and new responsibilities (which they refer to as *Capabilities*).[9] The model, which is reproduced in Figure 3.2, proposes that a subsidiary can evolve either by:

1. Being assigned a new charter by HQ and then developing the capability to deliver this new responsibility, or
2. By developing a capability that will position the subsidiary to be formally awarded a new charter to take advantage of this competence later.

A premise of the model is that charters and capabilities will seldom neatly align during an evolutionary phase, and one will lead or lag the other. Importantly, this framework also proposes how a subsidiary's importance within its network can decline or improve.

Although they adopt different perspectives, the Birkinshaw and Hood model can be seen as complementary to Delany's model which was published two years later. Whereas Delany focused on the stages of evolution as a sequence over time, Birkinshaw and Hood identified how changes in charters and capabilities interact to show how a subsidiary's role can rise and fall. For our purposes, this provides a useful alternative viewpoint

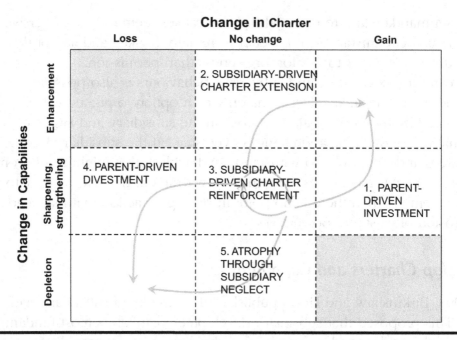

Figure 3.2   Subsidiary evolution as a function of Charter and Capability Change (Birkinshaw and Hood, 1998. Reproduced with permission)

into how movement from one stage to the next in Delany's model can be achieved.

In the chapters that follow, we will use this perspective on charter development and capability development as major planks in the structure that will frame a subsidiary strategy. The Delany model will remain a very useful reference point, as it helps us to position the subsidiary in terms of its maturity and its opportunity to push boundaries. The Birkinshaw and Hood model provides a framework and vocabulary that we can use when considering how these boundaries may be pushed at any stage of evolution, through a symbiosis of charter extension and capability development. Note that from herein the term *charter* will be used interchangeably with *mandate* when referring to any formal allocation of responsibilities by a HQ to a subsidiary.

The alternative routes to growth and decline that are described in the Birkinshaw and Hood model merit some elaboration here. Five pathways are proposed:

1. **Parent-Driven Investment**. This is simply where the subsidiary is assigned a new responsibility by HQ, even if it does not yet have the capability to fully deliver on this. Relating this to the Delany model, it

is a case where the subsidiary is pushed beyond a strict interpretation of its current evolutionary stage. Time for transition will be allowed by the parent and there will be some forbearance as performance levels improve to the required levels. Over time, the capability will be developed, and the subsidiary will be positioned to deliver the new charter at a satisfactory, or even superior level.

2. **Subsidiary-Driven Charter Extension**. This is a somewhat more subversive pathway whereby the subsidiary has ambitions to extend its charter, but it has not yet been allocated the responsibility by HQ. The strategy adopted is to develop the required capability to a level where it can be demonstrated to stakeholders, and in doing so convince them that formally awarding a charter extension is justified. When I consider this pathway, I am reminded of times working with colleagues in India who were always impressive in their ability to integrate with groups working in other time-zones. They were particularly astute at identifying their strongest employees who could attract roles from other locations when staffing gaps emerged. These individual roles could then act as a Trojan Horse, by building other supports and staff members around them until a level of critical mass was reached. In this way, a charter extension could be earned by building around individual capabilities in a deliberate but non-threatening manner.

3. **Subsidiary-Driven Charter Reinforcement**. This pathway recognises that choosing the right time for strategic moves is an important part of any organisation's development. There will be times when it is best to 'stick to the knitting', work on performance improvement and await the best opportunity for negotiating a charter extension or for developing a new capability. This is not about standing still, but rather it is about bedding-in existing capabilities and sharpening focus. It can be equated to the first three stags in Delany's model, but it also applies in later stages when a new responsibility must be more solidly delivered before the next move is made.

4. **Parent-Driven Divestment**. In this case the subsidiary has maintained an acceptable level of competence in its delivery, but the parent decides to de-scope the charter. This could be because of changes in corporate strategy direction, or wider business issues that drive a need for internal restructuring. When the scope of responsibility is reduced it is difficult to maintain the same level of capability. Attrition, staff redundancies, or other mandated cost actions will cause the competence to quickly erode unless suitable replacement work can be found. There may be no

fault with subsidiary management when this happens. That is, except where this may have been predictable and mitigating actions could have been developed in anticipation of such risks.

5. **Atrophy Through Subsidiary Neglect**. This pathway to the decline of the subsidiary is the one that reflects most poorly on subsidiary leaders. Capabilities are allowed to erode to the extent that they are no longer sufficient to deliver on existing responsibilities in full, so the charter is then reduced in scope or withdrawn completely. It may be that the neglect that drives this route is caused by the parent – for example, through a historical lack of investment in facilities or staff that eventually makes it impossible for the subsidiary to fulfil the charter satisfactorily. Economic pressures or staff shortages in the local market could also drive depletion in capabilities when compared to past cost-competitiveness and competence levels. It is important in this case to recognise that reductions in capability are often relative to what is available from other sources. That is, the level of competence of the subsidiary may have been stable over time, but it falls behind that available from alternative providers at a lower cost. Alternatively, it may not have kept up with the latest production processes or substitute technologies. While such outside factors are difficult to control, it is arguable that the subsidiary leadership team should have recognised the trends and taken strategic actions to reduce the risk that this would ultimately lead to the loss of a charter.

The attraction of the Birkinshaw and Hood model is that it provides a very simple perspective on how the development and decline of subsidiaries can be understood in terms of the interplay between two elements – charter changes and capability changes. These will provide useful anchor points when we discuss how subsidiary strategy can be designed and put into effect in the following chapters.

Factor-In External Influences

The previous section discussed how changes in the market within which the subsidiary operates can impact its position relative to alternative providers. This could be because labour rates in the local market increase, making it more difficult to attract and retain staff at previous cost levels. New global competitors could also emerge, or new technologies could offer a replacement for some of the functions provided by the subsidiary. Externalities such as these can be a source of opportunity as well as risk, and subsidiary leaders should remain cognisant of how they may influence the evolution potential of their organisation.

Government incentives such as capital grants, employment and training grants and favourable tax regimes can provide additional supports for the subsidiary's evolution. Equally, their absence relative to other locations can present a threat. Research has also shown that subsidiaries can channel additional value to their corporations, sourced from their local business networks.[10] This can include value from university relationships, supplier networks, industry associations and positioning within clusters of subsidiaries operating in related industry sectors.

This shows us that a very broad view of capabilities should be adopted when considering the opportunities for using these as a platform for charter extension. We will return to this point in Chapter 5 but suffice to say at this stage that the development of capabilities is not confined to resources controlled by the subsidiary's internal management hierarchy. Equally, depletion of a capability can result from the loss of certain local network connections or government supports coming to the end of their term.

Wider resources that can strengthen capabilities should therefore remain on the radar for subsidiary leaders.

Summary

In this chapter we first considered the motivating factors that will provide impetus for a subsidiary strategy. We will return to the subject of motivation later, but it is important even at this early stage to sow some seeds in our thinking on what will drive this journey and who will be motivated to participate.

Delany's model of subsidiary evolution was then explored as a structure for reflecting on the current maturity stage of a subsidiary and how this might continue to evolve. This acknowledges that aspects of more than one maturity stage may be evident, particularly in subsidiaries that have been assigned a portfolio of responsibilities.

Readers were then encouraged to think carefully about the scope and boundaries of their subsidiary strategy. That is, what functions should it include, how should local and corporate agendas be balanced, what level of buy-in can be expected from disparate participating sub-units, and what should the governance process look like?

In the last section of the chapter several factors that are relevant to the question of HOW to evolve the subsidiary were introduced. These include the need to continually manage performance and external perceptions of this performance as a precursor to strategic advances. The types of strategic behaviour that may be appropriate when pursuing strategic initiatives were also discussed – across the spectrum of scout and subversive extremes. The opportunity to evolve by extending charters before capabilities, or capabilities before charters, was then outlined using the Birkinshaw and Hood model that provides a broad structure for the following two chapters. Lastly, the need to avoid a totally inwardly focused posture was stressed, and the opportunity to take advantage of external supports was emphasised.

Notes

1. Martin Christopher, "The Agile Supply Chain: Competing in Volatile Markets," *Industrial Marketing Management* 29, no. 1 (2000).
2. J. Birkinshaw and T. Pedersen, "Strategy and Management in Mne Subsidiaries," in *The Oxford Handbook of International Business Studies*, ed. A. Rugman (Oxford: Oxford University Press, 2009).
3. L.W. Sargeant, "Strategic Planning in a Subsidiary," *Long Range Planning* 23, no. 2 (1990).
4. J. Birkinshaw, "Foreign-Owned Subsidiaries and Regional Development: The Case of Sweden," in *Multinational Corporate Evolution and Subsidiary Development*, ed. J. Birkinshaw and N. Hood (Basingstoke: Macmillan Press, 1998).
5. Delany, "Strategic Development of the Multinational Subsidiary through Subsidiary Initiative-Taking."; ibid.
6. Paul Lyons and Louis Brennan, "Assessing Value from Business-to-Business Services Relationships: Temporality, Tangibility, Temperament, and Trade-Offs," *Journal of Service Research* 24, no. 1 (2019).
7. Edmond Molloy and Edward Delany, "Strategic Leadership of Multi-National Subsidiaries: An Overview for Senior Executives," ed. M.D.L. Management Consultants Ltd (Quantum International, 1998).
8. Bjorn Ambos, Kazuhiro Asakawa, and Tina C. Ambos, "A Dynamic Perspective on Subsidiary Autonomy," *Global Strategy Journal* 1 (2011).
9. J. Birkinshaw and N. Hood, "Multinational Subsidiary Evolution: Capability and Charter Change in Foreign-Owned Subsidiary Companies," *Academy of Management Review* 23, no. 4 (1998).
10. Ulf Andersson, Mats Forsgren, and Ulf Holm, "Balancing Subsidiary Influence in the Federative Mnc: A Business Network View," *Journal of International Business Studies* 38 (2007).

INTROSPECTION AND ANALYSIS

Having laid some foundations in Part I to aid understanding of how corporations and their subsidiaries evolve, we can now move on to the more practical matter of how a subsidiary can structure and develop its strategy. Busy managers are hardwired to perform speedy evaluations and to make decisions quickly. This style is not effective for strategy formulation, where a more in-depth assessment of current status and opportunities is advisable before decisions are made on where to invest time, effort and reputation. The emphasis in this part of the book is on slowing the reader's thinking, to consider all dimensions, to objectively look at the data and to question the preconceptions that our minds naturally bring to the fore.[1] Chapters 4 and 5 follow the Birkinshaw and Hood model by providing guidance on how to analyse *Charters* and *Capabilities*, respectively. Chapter 6 focuses on the broader environment within which the subsidiary operates and provides perspectives on how to consider the impact of factors such as competition, industry turbulence and geopolitical influences on strategic planning.

The steps and models that are proposed in this part may appear quite formulaic, but readers should remember that there is no one-size-fits-all in strategy formulation. While it is intended that these models should guide your thinking, it is important to keep the emphasis on the *substance* of your discussions, rather than be blinded by the *form* of the models that are

DOI: 10.4324/9781003425502-5

provided to stimulate your thinking. That is, readers should be selective on what works best for them and feel free to adjust the models or develop alternatives to achieve the same ends.

Note

1. Daniel Kahneman, *Thinking, Fast and Slow* (Penguin Random House, 2011).

Chapter 4

What We Do: Analysing Our Charters

In his book *Good Strategy, Bad Strategy: The Difference and Why It Matters*,[1] Richard Rumelt, the renowned thinker on business strategy, rebuts the commonly held perception that strategy is centred around themes of organisational ambition, leadership, visioning and planning. While having an ambitious vision may be the mark of a charismatic leader and may be highly motivational for organisational stakeholders, unless this is grounded in a realistic analysis of the current environment and backed-up by achievable actions, this is not a strategy.

Rumelt asserts that "the core of strategy work is always the same: discovering the critical factors in a situation and designing a way of coordinating and focusing actions to deal with these factors."[2] He emphasises that discovering these critical factors must begin with a diagnosis of what is really going on. This should include a detailed and objective assessment of the current state of the business and its offerings, in terms of competitive positioning, customer perspectives, strengths and weaknesses. Obstacles should be clearly identified so that the strategic actions will include initiatives to overcome them. Challenges and opportunities should be considered from a range of alternative viewpoints to question preconceptions and ensure that all dimensions are understood. Strategic direction should be based on carefully considered choices and should avoid trying to accommodate all perspectives just to be popular. The sources of power that must be harnessed to realise the strategy should also be identified and actions to direct these sources must be well thought-out.

DOI: 10.4324/9781003425502-6

Fundamentally, a business strategy should begin with deep diagnosis of the current state, be clear in how it will deal with obstacles and articulate precise actions to build on strengths. In doing so it should create value that will be appreciated by customers and other stakeholders, while strengthening the uniqueness of the organisation.

As stated in the introduction to this part of the book, this chapter and the following two are intended to slow down the reader's thought processes and to discourage you from jumping to conclusions or solutions at this early stage. This is intrinsic to the diagnosis phase that Rumelt recommends should be the foundation of every strategy. This begins with the focus in this chapter on the analysis of the current responsibilities that are assigned to the subsidiary. This process of reflection may also trigger initial ideas on early-stage opportunities that may have future potential. These can be noted and returned to later when all aspects of the diagnosis phase are completed.

In many subsidiaries, the parent organisation will assign a range of responsibilities to the subsidiary – either across multiple product and service offerings or across multiple supply chain stages in the same offering. In other cases, the charter allocated by headquarters (HQ) may be very narrow and concentrated on a single offering or process element. Even in these more specialised cases, subsidiary leaders may see the potential to widen the scope of the organisation and to spread the risk by winning responsibility for new offerings, customer segments, territories or process elements. Therefore, in this chapter, we assume that the subsidiary may encompass a portfolio of current responsibilities and future opportunities, where each of these should be considered separately to analyse their contribution to the value that the subsidiary offers to the parent, now or in the future.

In the previous chapter, we discussed some of the considerations that arise when a subsidiary is comprised of a range of charters, each of which may have with different sponsoring organisations within the corporation. Each such sub-unit is likely to be managed within the subsidiary by executives who identify with these remote sponsors and have dependencies on them for their own career progression and that of their employees. That discussion concluded that in these cases, a mature debate is required between executives to agree on the ground-rules for strategy planning – on the assumption that this may at some point require trade-offs between individual subsidiary charters and a local strategic agenda. This is particularly relevant in the context of the diagnosis of charters and their strategic positioning that is begun in this chapter.

It is fair to say that expecting sub-unit executives to prioritise the broader strategic potential of the subsidiary over the needs of their part of the organisation is easier said than done. Open discussions in which judgements are expressed by peers on the strengths, weaknesses and potential of one's own sub-unit can lead to defensiveness, conflict and even retaliation when the discussion later turns to the evaluation of peers' sub-units. Objective evaluations of charter positioning are a necessary part of the process, but there is a danger that this may be interpreted as a criticism of how the charter has been managed to this point. Agreeing with a negative assessment can feel like the proverbial turkey voting for Christmas. In a worst-case scenario, this debate on charter positioning could be so contentious that it gets the whole strategy formulation process off to a bad start that can be difficult to recover from.

The person chairing these discussions should remain sensitive to these issues and should be sufficiently respected and strong to arbitrate and find common ground. This person need not necessarily be the leader of the subsidiary. In some instances, it may be useful for the leader to delegate or rotate the role of Chair so that they can voice their own views without compromising the role of independent facilitator and arbitrator. Depending on the culture of the organisation, it may be appropriate to agree in advance what is on and off the table and to agree a process for dealing with disputes.

BOX 1
INTRODUCING THE HETSOL CORPORATION
(FICTITIOUS EXAMPLE)

The Higher Education Technology Solutions Corporation (trading as HETSol) provides software solutions and associated services to the third-level education sector. The company was founded in the USA in 2005 and immediately experienced a period of rapid growth as its products proved very popular with US universities. Building on this success, it began its expansion into Europe in 2012 and into Asia in 2015.

The corporation now provides a range of software products to assist universities in the design of courses, lecture materials and student assessment including the recording of grades and timetabling. Some exciting new products and services are now in the early stages of customer testing. These provide software tools for the analysis of student grades and trends, including remote and onsite services which will be provided by HETSol to assist academic communities in fine-tuning their offerings to improve student outcomes.

HETSol Corporation is organised in a divisional structure, with major units focusing on R&D, Product Development and Distribution, Fee-earning Services, Customer Support, Sales and Marketing, Talent, and Finance. The corporation currently employs over 4,000 people worldwide.

To enable its expansion into the European Union market, in 2012, the corporation established HETSol Support Labs in an EU country. HETSol received financial support from the government of that country in return for a commitment to create an initial 100 jobs. In the start-up phase, the subsidiary quickly grew beyond this job creation target, leading the government agency to offer additional grants up to 500 employees.

The first responsibility assigned to the operation was to provide multi-lingual technical support to HETSol customers in Europe. Responsibilities subsequently expanded to include some pre-sales technical support to sales teams, product testing services and more recently some small software development teams acting as a satellite of HETSol's product laboratories in Pennsylvania and Ottawa. The subsidiary has recently contributed resources to a global effort to develop skills in advanced data analytics as part of a proposed new service offering that is currently undergoing feasibility studies with some established customers.

The HETSol Support Labs subsidiary now employs 260 people. This number has remained largely static for the past 18 months as the corporation has focused additional investments in a further new laboratory in Sofia, Bulgaria, which is the ancestral home of one of the company founders.

At a corporate level, there is recognition that some level of reinvention of the company is needed to remain innovative in the face of the financial pressures on the university sector and the increasing market penetration of some emerging niche competitors. The HETSol Support Labs subsidiary would like to contribute to this effort.

Some of the concepts and models that are described here and in later chapters are easier to relate to when illustrated by an example. For this reason, a fictitious subsidiary – The HETSol Corporation – is introduced in Box 1. As we progress, this case study will be built-upon to demonstrate how the ideas presented can be applied to a particular case.

The remainder of the chapter describes four steps to identify and analyse the charters that comprise the subsidiary's responsibilities:

1. Firstly, we discuss the basic task of identifying the subsidiary's current charters.
2. The second step builds on Delany's model of subsidiary evolution as discussed in Chapter 3, to facilitate discussion on the current level of maturity of each charter and its future potential.
3. The third step is influenced by the Boston Consulting Group's Growth Share Matrix.[3] It enables an evaluation of each charter in terms of positioning within the overall portfolio of charters.
4. Finally, focus is recommended on the opportunities for innovative charter development, either by building on existing responsibilities or identifying opportunities to extend into new areas of value to the parent.

The recommended approach is that these steps should be completed by the subsidiary management team working collaboratively. Such open debate is a good way of ensuring that a wide range of perspectives is drawn-upon, but this will also play an important part in ensuring buy-in for any conclusions that are reached. The approach assumes that all members of the management team are prepared to invest the time, effort and open-mindedness required to make this a meaningful exercise. The process is likely to continue over an extended period, but irregular involvement by participants in these discussions can be as problematic as no participation. In some cases, the subsidiary leader may conclude that for political, time-pressure or immaturity reasons it is not feasible to complete this satisfactorily as a team. In these exceptional cases, the steps can be completed by the leader acting alone, but careful thought will need to be given to how to secure real buy-in to the conclusions and resulting actions later.

When the steps are completed by a team, it should be anticipated that these initial discussions on charters may not be fully conclusive. It is likely that a management team will return to them later as part of the iterative process of strategy formulation. Their value is mainly derived from the discussions that take place as the team, as they use the models that are presented in the remainder of this chapter to explore the charters from different angles. It is therefore recommended that notes should be made of key points raised in these discussions, even if there is no unanimous agreement on these points.

Remember always that this is part of a diagnosis phase, intended to get everything on the table, explore alternative perspectives and build early experience with the strategy process.

Charter Identification

A first step in this stage of the process is to agree on the list of charters that should be categorised and analysed. This may be straightforward in some cases, but in highly integrated subsidiaries it may be difficult to determine the boundaries between responsibilities. Sub-units within the subsidiary may appear relatively cohesive (e.g., production and quality control), but it may still be wise to analyse them separately in this diagnosis phase so that the positioning and strategic potential for each can be focused upon separately.

The following factors can be considered when deciding whether a sub-unit warrants being treated as a separate charter:

- Is it the subject of a separate memorandum of understanding with a sponsoring organisation?
- Does it report upwards through a separate management line?
- Does it have a critical mass within the subsidiary?
- Does it relate to different product or service offerings, or different supply chain stages?
- Is it subject to separate planning and resource allocation processes within the company?
- Is it recognised outside the subsidiary as having a unique identity?
- Do those managing the charter agree that it should be included in a portfolio-oriented strategic process?

If the answer to any of the above questions is "Yes," then it may be worth considering the sub-unit separately at this early stage. It can always be re-integrated back into the whole later.

Box 2 illustrates how this exercise was completed by the HETSol Support Labs management team.

BOX 2
HETSOL SUPPORT LABS
CHARTER IDENTIFICATION

The HETSol Support Labs management team developed the box below to identify the charters to be included in its strategy formulation process:

Charter	Estab.	Reports To	Description	People
Technical Support	2012	Customer Support	First-level support of European customer email, webchat and phone queries. Identification of product bugs before passing to US-based software development teams for resolution.	125
Product Testing	2016	Product Development and Distribution	One of several global sites performing structured testing and usability verification on new product releases and major bug fixes.	60
Sales Support	2018	Sales and Marketing	Provides technical consultancy to sales teams as part of bid processes. Supports pre-sales customer queries arising from their technical feasibility studies.	30
Software Engineering	2019	Product Development and Distribution	Acts as a satellite of product development teams by providing supplementary coders.	40
Analytics Services	2021	Fee-earning Services	Developing specialised skills in the areas of data analytics as part of emerging services offerings.	5

Analysis of Charter Evolution

When the initial list of charters has been identified, the next step is to draw on Delany's model to reflect on the evolutionary stage that each one has achieved to this point. To add further depth to this part of the diagnosis phase, it is useful to then consider the potential that each may have to progress their evolution over the *strategic timeframe*. This immediately raises the question of how long this strategic timeframe should be. Depending on the speed of movement in an industry, this could range from 1 to 10 years or more. In deciding the timeframe that should apply to strategy planning, such industry norms should be considered, but it is also important to set a timeframe that finds a balance between the time needed to achieve noticeable results, and a period within which the current management team is likely to remain in position and cohesive. There is little point in setting aiming a strategy at a period that is too short to achieve results or too long to achieve a meaningful level of ownership as the players change. The likely tenure of the subsidiary leader is particularly relevant to the setting of the strategic timeframe, unless there is confidence that the next leader will assume a similar level of ownership for the strategic ambitions resulting from this process. When balancing these considerations, in most cases, the strategic timeframe will be in the range of three to five years.

Figure 4.1 provides a template for documenting the evolutionary stage of current charters and their potential to further evolve in the timeframe set for

CURRENT TIMEFRAME: _____   FUTURE TIMEFRAME: _____

CURRENT CHARTERS:	STAGE 1: Establishing start-up	STAGE 2: Carrying out mandate satisfactorily	STAGE 3: Fulfilling basic mandate in a 'superior way'	STAGE 4: Extending basic mandate – low risk moves	STAGE 5: Extending basic mandate – strategic development	STAGE 6: Becoming strategic centre for the MNE	STAGE 7: Becoming strategic pivot for the MNE	STAGE 8: Becoming strategic apex for the MNE

Figure 4.1   Charter evolution analysis (adapted from Delany, 2000)

the strategy. The stages are as defined by Delany (see Figure 3.1). Using this template, the current stage of each charter should be analysed first, before considering their future potential. It may be useful to allow time for each team member to privately consider their views so that they are not overly influenced by more vocal colleagues when this is opened for debate.

For each charter listed in the rows of the table, the current evolutionary stage should be noted by entering a 'C' in the appropriate column. When the maturity stage of all current charters is agreed, the future stage that may be achievable for each should be debated and the consensus recorded by entering an 'F' in the appropriate cell. In some cases, the current and future stages may be the same, and in others, the future stage may even be at a lower level of evolution than the current (remembering that the evolution of subsidiary charters can be like a game of snakes and ladders). Categorisations should fall clearly within one cell or other in the table, and participants should avoid the temptation to 'fudge the issue' by selecting half-way positions. To minimise 'groupthink' as part of this exercise, it is also useful to specifically challenge the group on whether external stake-holders would agree with these categorisations. One way of doing this is to assign secondary roles to team members, whereby one person is asked to represent the likely perspective of the HQ sponsor in relation to the stage of evolution, with others representing internal customers, external customers, peer sites etc.

As stated previously, the value in this exercise is as much in the discussion that ensues as it is in the output. It allows team members to voice any fundamental perceptions that they have developed about individual charters and provides a space for these to be debated and challenged. It also gets any strongly held views on the potential to develop existing charters out on the table, even if there will be some way to go yet to determine whether these are the most valid opportunities and whether they should be prioritised in a strategy.

In some ways, this exercise can act as a valve to release any pent-up ideas that are held about the direction that the subsidiary should take. It clears the air and gets the team into the mode of strategic discussion, while also beginning a realistic diagnosis of the subsidiary's status within the corporation. It is therefore important to allow sufficient time and not to rush to judgement on individual categorisations. Notes should be taken on perspectives and opportunities that emerge as part of the discussion. Having said this, to avoid getting bogged-down or side-tracked, it may also be necessary to record ideas that can be returned to later, so that the discussion can move on. Making notes in this way has the added benefit of giving participants reassurance that the process will at some point progress to solutioning – just not yet.

Box 3 shows how this exercise was completed by the HETSol Support Labs subsidiary management team.

BOX 3
HETSOL SUPPORT LABS
CHARTER EVOLUTION ANALYSIS

In May 2023, the management team began their discussions on a subsidiary strategy. They agreed that a reasonable future timeframe for their planning was the end of 2026 (while recognising that they may revise this as their strategy discussions developed). Having individually considered the evolutionary stages of each of their current charters, they opened this for discussion and began to debate the *Current* stage that was appropriate for each. Some colleagues were asked to play the roles of divisional sponsors for each charter, and in doing so they raised some valid questions to challenge initial perceptions of the evolutionary stages. After some useful discussion, the team progressed to consider the *Future* stage that each charter could reasonably aspire to in the strategic timeframe. The completed template and accompanying notes are shown below.

CURRENT TIMEFRAME: 2023   FUTURE TIMEFRAME: 4Q26

CURRENT CHARTERS:	STAGE 1: Establishing start-up	STAGE 2: Carrying out mandate satisfactorily	STAGE 3: Fulfilling basic mandate in a 'superior way'	STAGE 4: Extending basic mandate – low risk moves	STAGE 5: Extending basic mandate – strategic development	STAGE 6: Becoming strategic centre for the MNE	STAGE 7: Becoming strategic pivot for the MNE	STAGE 8: Becoming strategic apex for the MNE
Technical Support			C	F				
Product Testing			C F					
Sales Support		C		F				
Software Engineering		C			F			
Analytics Services	C			F				

■ **Technical support**: As the most long-standing charter, this is now being fulfilled in a superior manner. There may be an opportunity to extend the charter by developing data bases of technical solutions that could be made available directly to customers as self-service options.

- **Product testing**: This function is being fulfilled very satisfactorily, but it is difficult to see how the responsibility can be extended in the immediate timeframe.
- **Sales support**: This is a developing responsibility that provides a valuable outlet for some of the subsidiary's best technical skills. In the longer term, this could be extended by earning sales leadership responsibility for some prospective European deals.
- **Software engineering**: Although this is still a developing responsibility, the availability of deep technical skills in the local labour market indicates that it is a prospect for longer-term strategic development – particularly since such skills are in short supply globally.
- **Analytics services**: This responsibility is in the very early stages and it is not yet clear whether it will be developed as a service in the longer term by the corporation. If it is, the local team has the opportunity to push the boundaries on this and to be at the forefront of its development as a strategic offering for the company.

Analysis of Charter Strategic Positioning

The next step in analysing the status of the subsidiary's charters is concerned with their strategic positioning within the parent organisation. Although the previous exercise provided a perspective on the maturity of each charter and the potential for this to continue to evolve over a given period, the strategic choices that will be faced later will need to consider whether this evolution is worth pursuing. Becoming a strategic pivot or apex for any charter is less worthwhile if that function will not remain strategically important to the parent. There is also the question of how easy or difficult it will be to push the boundaries of a charter in the face of internal or external competition. A further limitation of the charter evolution analysis is that it does not focus on opportunities that are not yet part of the set of charters assigned to the subsidiary, but which could be nurtured to develop into something which will become strategically important in the future.

To probe these questions, we need to consider each charter in terms of its strategic importance to the parent, and the degree to which the subsidiary has an exclusive responsibility in this area. Having done this for each charter individually, we can consider the portfolio as a whole. This is done to assess the overall cohesion of the portfolio of charters and the extent to which the charters when considered together provide a secure platform for the subsidiary, but with the potential to stretch boundaries and grow in size or in depth of responsibility.

Figure 4.2 presents a model adapted from the Boston Consulting Group Growth Share Matrix. The model helps in analysing the strategic positioning of each charter in the portfolio. It requires each charter to be categorised across two dimensions:

1. **Exclusivity as a provider**: For certain charters, the subsidiary will be the only one with this responsibility, whereas for other charters there will be other subsidiaries or third parties who also deliver the function. Exclusivity is binary, so this should be categorised as either High or Low. Note that certain functions may still be regarded as being exclusively delivered, even if another organisation performs the same function for a different product or a different territory. This assumes that this other provider could not easily expand to take over the scope covered by our subsidiary. For example, if a subsidiary is the only one providing distribution logistics management for Europe, it can be regarded as having exclusive responsibility, even if similar responsibilities are assigned to subsidiaries or other partners in North America or Asia. This is because it would not be feasible for North American or Asian providers to manage this function in Europe. However, if our subsidiary manages logistics for some countries in Europe and other European subsidiaries manage others, this may not be considered an exclusive responsibility

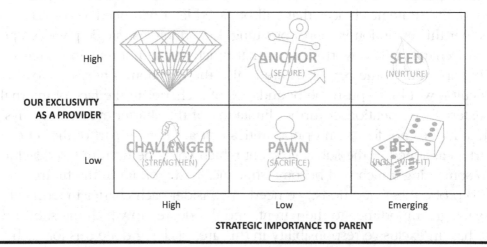

Figure 4.2   **Charter portfolio analysis (influenced by the BCG Growth Matrix)**

as it would not be complicated to switch providers. Equally, if an alternative technology or process exists that can substitute for the subsidiary's services in some circumstances, the responsibility cannot be regarded as exclusively delivered. So, although the question of exclusivity may initially appear simple, there are some nuances that may need to be considered.

2. **Strategic importance to the parent**: Certain functions will clearly be of high importance to the stated strategy of the parent, whereas others may be necessary, but of lower strategic importance. This categorisation is relevant because sponsors will likely be more amenable to investments in areas that are of high strategic importance, whereas those that are not may be seen as 'necessary evils' that are often the subject of cost-cutting actions. Areas of high strategic importance are also less likely to be considered as options for re-location or outsourcing, given the risks involved. This categorisation also allows for the identification of emerging opportunities, whose strategic importance is not yet firmly established.

As shown in Figure 4.2, analysing current and potential new charters across these two dimensions allows them to be categorised into one of six groups:

- **Jewel** *(High exclusivity; High strategic importance)*: These charters are highly valuable to the parent and the subsidiary. The subsidiary should avoid complacency by protecting their security while continuing to improve and polish them.
- **Anchor** *(High exclusivity; Low strategic importance)*: While these charters may not be ranked highly by the parent in terms of their strategic importance, their exclusivity is likely to provide a source of stability and security to the subsidiary. Their low strategic importance to the parent could make them a target for an alternative sourcing strategy and therefore they should continue to be secured.
- **Seed** *(High exclusivity; Emerging strategic importance)*: These opportunities may present a valuable source of future growth and security for the subsidiary. They should therefore be carefully monitored and nurtured.
- **Challenger** *(Low exclusivity; High strategic importance)*: These charters will be part of a battleground for future investment within the internal supply chain of the company. Although the parent may be concerned about dysfunctional competition between sites which may limit

collaboration in a strategically important area, rivalry is likely to exist as sites seek to earn more control over this function. The subsidiary should strengthen its contribution in the face of this competition and recognise that other providers are likely to be doing the same. In this case, differentiators are critical.

■ **Pawn** *(Low exclusivity; Low strategic importance)*: These are responsibilities that are shared across several sites and are not of strong strategic importance to the parent. This does not imply that they are worthless as they may make an important contribution to the subsidiary in terms of reputation, critical mass or skills development. However, where more strategically important opportunities exist, these may be judiciously sacrificed by reducing the skills or resources that are allocated to them.

■ **Bet** *(Low exclusivity; Emerging strategic importance)*: These are charters that show promise for the future, but this promise is recognised by other sites that are also investing resources in this area. Like the *Challenger* category, this is a battleground for competition, but in this case the future strategic importance of the function to the parent is less assured. The subsidiary may need to 'roll with the punches', by keeping a close watch on how this area develops, monitoring relative strengths compared to other sites and making assertive resource investments as required.

Categorising charters in this way can be provocative and emotive for a management team, especially when it comes to hearing peers' judgements on one's own area of responsibility. The exercise requires maturity and openness that some teams or individuals may not be ready for.

As in the previous exercise, it may be useful to assign roles of external stakeholders to participants so that external perspectives are considered. This may also help to remove some of the emotion from the debate. Again, the role of the meeting chair is critical in finding common ground, knowing when to record consensus (or the lack thereof) and moving on, but also in ensuring that difficult issues are recognised and debated. Some groups may find it challenging to rate the strategic importance of a charter to the parent, if the parent's strategies are not well-articulated or they are subject to regular change. In these cases, the debate itself will be useful if it helps the team reach a consensus on how the strategy of the parent is likely to develop. As has been emphasised previously, the value in this case is as much in the debate as it is in the output.

When completing this exercise, it is recommended that the six-box model be reproduced on a whiteboard, a flipchart, or an electronic equivalent. Charters can be documented on sticky notes. They can be placed on the model and moved as the discussion progresses. Management teams usually find that this kind of physically active participation in these discussions keeps all team members involved and provides a good level of energy for the debate that follows.

Box 4 shows the portfolio analysis exercise was completed by the HETSol Support Labs team.

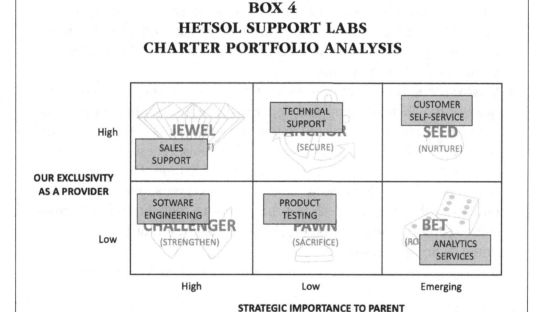

BOX 4
HETSOL SUPPORT LABS
CHARTER PORTFOLIO ANALYSIS

- **Technical support** (anchor): The subsidiary is the exclusive provider of this function in Europe, although HETSol has a strategy to improve product reliability in order to reduce customer requirements for post-sale technical support. Therefore, in its current form, this function is unlikely to be regarded as strategically important by the parent.
- **Product testing** (pawn): There are several sites performing this function for the software engineering function. It is perceived internally as a necessary evil, with little strategic relevance.
- **Sales support** (jewel): HETSol Support Labs has developed the model of how technical skills can support pre-sales engagements and avoid

the cost of developing deep technical skills within regional sales teams. Sales will remain strategically important for HETSol, and as products become more complex, the strategic importance of providing technical input to sales processes will increase.

■ **Software engineering** (challenger): High-quality software engineering will always be strategically important to HETSol's offerings. These skills are in much demand globally, leading to the farming-out of work from the US labs to HETSol subsidiaries across the globe when they can offer these skills.

■ **Analytics services** (bet): There is debate internally as to whether these proposed services will be valued by customers sufficiently to make it a viable fee-earning opportunity. Like other subsidiaries, HETSol Support Labs has responded to the call for skills in this area while feasibility is assessed.

■ **Customer self-service** (seed): In the course of the discussion, the head of the Technical Support department proposed that some of the data bases and tools created internally to improve efficiency could be developed into customer self-service tools. These could reduce the need for traditional technical support over time. Developing such tools could have global value and could become strategically important given the strategic desire of the parent to reduce post-sales costs. Although not a current charter, the group agreed that this should be noted as an opportunity.

Charter Innovation

The analysis of charter strategic positioning as described in the previous section will have identified some emerging areas of strategic importance and categorised these as *seeds* or *bets* based on the degree of exclusivity that the subsidiary has in these areas. These may be the most obvious emerging opportunities that are currently on the radar. However, some additional innovative thinking may be needed to identify less obvious opportunities.

Few corporations are ever satisfied with their cultures of creativity, as evidenced by regular pleas to their business units to be more innovative. Subsidiaries that are removed from the rigidity of headquarters structures, and closer to customers, have the opportunity to step-up to this expectation. However, there is of course a difference between the desire to be innovative in charter development and the ability to overcome innovation blockers, such as the protection of existing silos in case these may be cannibalised, fears of failure and change, recollections of when similar ideas were tried and failed before, short-term horizons for success, an absence of ownership for innovation and the lack of time and money.[4] Despite their best intentions, corporations that developed in stable industry sectors may simply not be environments that foster innovation. Subsidiaries that have evolved under the watchful control of headquarters may never have been afforded the scope to innovate. Countering this legacy can be challenging for subsidiaries seeking to extend mandates into creative new areas. This requires a realistic reflection on the innovative capabilities of the subsidiary and explicit efforts to promote innovation.

Rita McGrath and her colleagues developed an *Innovation Proficiency Scale* to facilitate self-analysis on the ability of an organisation to innovate and change.[5] The scale has eight levels:

1. **Extreme bias towards exploitation**: The organisation operates in a market that has a strong history of stability, regulation, and bureaucracy. The status quo is taken for granted as the way things are done. There is a strong emphasis on sustaining existing advantages, and innovation is generally perceived as being risky.

2. **Innovation theatre**: There are initial efforts to introduce some innovative thinking to an otherwise conservative organisation. This happens in isolated pockets. While there may be increased talk about innovation, there is little general support or sustained effort.

3. **Localised innovation**: Innovation is more sustained than before, but still tends to be episodic and occurring only in isolated parts of the organisation. Innovation is not appreciated as an important cross-organisational discipline.

4. **Opportunistic innovation**: Previous innovation efforts have shown some results and are attracting greater appreciation. Where opportunities for growth become apparent, the organisation is prepared to support innovative ideas to exploit these. Specific investment is made in innovation projects, but the body of the organisation continues to operate as before.

5. **Emergent proficiency**: Executive sponsorship and dedicated resources are forthcoming for innovation initiatives. This will include early signs of governance around innovation and metrics to monitor its contributions to the business and returns on investment.

6. **Maturing proficiency**: There is strong commitment and resource investment in innovation supported across the executive team. Innovation contributes to executive compensation and factors into executive promotions. Best practices guide innovation activities, including tools, pan-organisational connections, and efforts to reach out to external sources of ideas.

7. **Strategic innovation**: Innovation is a clear part of the organisation's ethos as communicated externally by the most senior leaders. All steps in the product life cycle are expected to continually explore opportunities for innovation. Employees recognise their responsibilities to innovate and feel empowered to do so. The governance, funding and measurement of innovation outputs are core parts of the organisation's management system.

8. **Innovation mastery**: The organisation benefits from having cadres of highly proficient innovators and track records of wins resulting from their initiatives. The organisation is recognised as a role model for innovation and a source of best practices.

It is a useful exercise to consider where on this scale the corporation as a whole is placed and then the level of innovation proficiency of the subsidiary. The relative positions of these two assessments can be revealing in relation to how open the parent may be to innovative charter development, as well as providing an assessment of how well positioned the subsidiary is to develop new opportunities. This may also highlight the potential for the subsidiary to become an innovation leader, including some pointers on how to develop innovation capability to the next level in the scale.

This thought process may lead to additional ideas on how to develop the *seeds* and *bets* that were identified in the charter portfolio analysis. It may even trigger additional ideas. It should not be expected that innovations will always be revolutionary or earth-shattering. In his excellent book *How Innovation Works*, Matt Ridley explores a range of the most impactful innovations of our time.[6] He provides convincing evidence that innovations usually build on existing ideas and involve the search and recombination of existing technologies into new forms (consider how the smartphone combines digital cameras, sat nav systems, email, credit cards etc.). Innovation often takes advantage of technological advances, but when these advances reach a plateau, the innovation can come from using the technology in new settings (e.g., Amazon pioneered internet selling of books, but when this sales and distribution model was optimised, it was expanded by them and others to many other sales applications). Innovations are not always oriented around products and can often be aimed at new areas of value-add in the supply chain (e.g., companies like Deliveroo inserted themselves into the takeaway food sector). Fundamentally, innovation is usually incremental, going through a series of steps before an idea reaches its mature form (e.g., the first movies were recordings of stage plays, without taking advantage of the new opportunities for staging and editing that the medium enabled).

Innovations are there, waiting to be discovered. The analysis of existing charters can be extended to consider opportunities for innovation that may provide new sources of value. This may even help in building a strong innovation capability in the subsidiary, and one which can even position the subsidiary as a centre of competence for innovation within the corporation.

Summary

The four steps that are described in this chapter provide focal points for analysing and debating different dimensions of the subsidiary's current responsibilities and exploring opportunities for additional responsibility. While each step focuses on individual charters in sequence, it is also critical to adopt a more wholistic approach by considering the total portfolio in terms of its maturity and mix. Discussing the portfolio as a whole is important, as the mix of responsibilities may itself be a sign of strength or weakness. For example, although charters that have been categorised as *Pawns* and *Anchors* may not have the greatest strategic potential, it can still be highly important to maintain these as sources of resources that enable them to maintain critical mass and continue to build its reputation, while beginning to make strategic moves into areas of future potential. Remember that these steps are only part of the diagnosis phase and are designed to develop a common understanding of the current positioning of charters and to flush out any issues. They are also intended to encourage the management team into the mode of strategic thinking.

While the main emphasis of this phase is on the present, the templates allow for some initial discussion on the future – through their consideration of the potential for charters to continue to mature and where innovative charter development could contribute to the parent's strategic objectives. Having emphasised in the introduction to this part of the book the need to slow down during this diagnosis phase and to avoid jumping to conclusions, it may seem incongruous to then encourage discussion on future potential.

However, it is difficult to complete an objective analysis of the current status of a charter without questioning how this positions it for the future. Also, there are likely to be some pent-up ambitions within a management team and it is useful to provide an outlet where these can be vented, even at this early point in the process. It may transpire that some of these preconceived ideas are flawed, although others might spark ideas that are worth returning to later. As long as everyone recognises these as possible inputs to future conclusions, rather than firm agreements at this point, this can be helpful to the ongoing discussion.

Open-mindedness should continue as the analysis proceeds to the next diagnostic phase – which involves analysing the capabilities that the subsidiary can draw upon and develop.

Notes

1. R.P. Rumelt, *Good Strategy, Bad Strategy: The Difference and Why It Matters* (New York: Crown Business, 2011).
2. Ibid., p. 2.
3. Sandy Moose, "The Growth Share Matrix Revisited—a Ted Animation," Boston Consulting Group, https://www.bcg.com/publications/2014/corporate-strategy -growth-share-matrix-revisited-ted-animation.
4. Rita McGrath, *Seeing around Corners: How to Spot Inflection Points in Business before They Happen* (New York: Mariner Books, 2021), p. 154.
5. Ibid., pp. 156–58.
6. Matt Ridley, *How Innovation Works* (London: 4th Estate, 2020).

Chapter 5

How We Do It: Analysing Our Capabilities

Following the two dimensions of subsidiary development that are identified in the Birkinshaw and Hood model (Figure 3.2), our next focus should be on the analysis of capabilities that are available to the subsidiary. These capabilities are resources that the subsidiary can draw upon and develop in support of any strategic objectives.

It is important in this phase of our diagnosis to take a wide perspective on capabilities. Whilst the term may most obviously apply to the strength of skills and process effectiveness that exists in the subsidiary, there are several other dimensions to capabilities that we need to identify and critically evaluate. Some well-regarded writers on business strategy distinguish between resources and the capabilities that are enabled by these resources as separate contributors that require equal focus.[1] For our purposes and to maintain consistency with the Birkinshaw and Hood model, when we refer to capabilities this also includes the resources that are "productive assets, owned by the firm, whether they be tangible, intangible, or human."[2]

Also, when we talk of capabilities there is a tendency to focus on those that are an asset to the organisation – as an indicator of "what we are capable of." In a diagnosis phase, we need to give equal focus to those that represent a weakness or even an absence. As in other areas of our discussion so far, it is not sufficient to only identify the existence of these capabilities, whether they be strong or weak. It is also very important to assess how they are perceived by stakeholders in decision-making positions. A strong capability that is not widely recognised by stakeholders may be less influential

DOI: 10.4324/9781003425502-7

than one that we know to be weak, and where stakeholders are aware of this weakness.

A very important consideration when we think about capabilities is to reflect on which are a source of uniqueness and competitive advantage to the organisation. Clearly, while there may be benefits in developing capabilities that are commonplace within a corporation, these will not provide differentiation which will be a source of strategic advantage. Recognising this, we begin the chapter with a review of *sustained competitive advantage* and the characteristics of capabilities that provide a basis for long-term differentiation in a competitive internal market. Two steps are then recommended in the process of identifying and analysing capabilities that may be a source of such advantage:

1. First, existing or absent capabilities should be identified. To facilitate this, a set of headings is provided under which capabilities can be considered. This is to ensure that a broad perspective on the identification of capabilities is adopted.
2. Then these capabilities should each be assessed using a model based around the Strengths, Weaknesses, Opportunities, Threats (SWOT) framework. This is designed to encourage a deep critical analysis of each of the capabilities that was identified in the previous step.

Sustained Competitive Advantage

Jay Barney is credited with introducing the concept of sustained competitive advantage[3] and with leading the development of thinking on how lasting competitive advantage can be created and protected by firms.[4] This led to the theory of the *Resource-Based View of the Firm*, which, at its most fundamental level, proposes that companies operating in the same market will differ from each other in terms of the resources that they control and how they integrate these resources when serving customers. Firms are different in the eyes of customers because of the resources that they have developed.

For example, Amazon and ASOS both operate as online retailers, with some overlap in the products that they sell. Amazon differentiates itself by developing online marketing and distribution systems that provide customers with access to a huge range of products, complemented by services intended to enhance customer loyalty (e.g., Amazon Prime). ASOS concentrates on fashion products with an emphasis on "no-questions-asked" return policies if the customer does not like the product that is delivered. Both are very successful and competitive, but both seek to differentiate themselves as the portal of choice for online shoppers. Both also put a lot of effort into developing those resources (or capabilities) that make them different, and in promoting the benefits of these differences to shoppers. Even in highly commoditised markets firms will seek to differentiate themselves by developing their brand image as a resource that customers will value.

One of Barney's most important contributions was his identification of four characteristics that not only provide a source of competitive advantage but also one that will last. These four characteristics – which we will explore in some detail in this section – are value, rarity, being difficult to imitate and being difficult to substitute. Barney's argument was that sources of competitive advantage will be transient unless they (a) remain valuable to customers over an extended period, (b) they are not widely available to other firms, (c) they are difficult for others to copy in the short term and (d) they are not easy to substitute with some alternative product or service that satisfies the same need. Developing capabilities that meet these four criteria should be a central plank of any organisation's strategy.

In the remainder of this section, we will consider each of these in more detail, and we will focus particularly on how they apply to the capabilities of subsidiaries seeking to develop sustained competitive advantage within competitive internal markets.

Valuable

For a capability to be a source of sustained competitive advantage, it must be valued by customers and this value should be appreciated over an extended period. A firm that makes novelty toys may experience an advantage over its competitors if it produces a spinning top that becomes the "must-have" toy at Christmas. However, as toys can be fads, this may not be a lasting advantage once the novelty of the product wears off or a new novelty comes along. The real source of sustained competitive advantage in this case is not the ability to manufacture and distribute the spinning top, but the creative capability to conceive and design such novelties that will satisfy gaps in the market. A capability that is truly valuable from a sustained competitive advantage perspective is one that is either directly appreciated by customers (e.g., haute couture fashion tailoring) or which enables the organisation to deliver something that provides subsequent value to customers or the firm (e.g., processes that enable low-cost manufacturing, lower prices and higher profits).

In the subsidiary context, value is assessed by stakeholders such as corporate sponsors, internal customers or external customers. The key is in understanding the criteria that stakeholders will use when judging the value that the subsidiary's capabilities deliver. Customer value judgments are often described as a trade-off between the benefits that are delivered (e.g., level of quality and service) and the sacrifices that are made in return for these benefits (e.g., costs incurred).[5] As referenced in Chapter 3, value assessment has also been found to be based on the difference between the expectations of the customer and their subsequent experience (i.e., where experience exceeds expectations customers will feel that they have had value).[6] Perceptions of benefits, sacrifices, expectations and experiences can all be influenced either positively or negatively. Therefore perceptions of value can also be volatile and transient.

When judging how any capability contributes to the sustained competitive advantage of a subsidiary through the value that it creates, we need to put ourselves in the shoes of stakeholders. Is the capability really valued or does it provide something that delivers downstream value to them? What is their current perception of this value and can this be improved by emphasising the benefits that the capability enables, by rationalising the sacrifices (costs) that it entails, by managing expectations and by promoting positive experiences? We also need to consider whether this value will continue to be important over time. For example, the ability of a subsidiary to provide the parent with a short-term cost–benefit by availing of government grants will no doubt be appreciated at that time. However, as the 17th-century English churchman Thomas Fuller said, "eaten bread is soon forgotten." Unless the cost–benefit continues in the next planning cycle, the capability to take advantage of grants was not a source of lasting value – except through any residual appreciation that the stakeholder may have or if it was invested wisely to achieve a longer-term cost–benefit.

Rare

It is self-evident that if something is to be a competitive differentiator it should not be widely available from other competitors in a market. All supermarket chains offer products such as bread and milk at broadly similar prices. Providing these types of products is a qualifier for entry to the supermarket sector, not a differentiator. The German retailer Lidl, and its compatriot Aldi, disrupted the grocery retail market by continuing to offer the basics, but complementing this with a more limited range of good quality products from unfamiliar brands, but at lower prices than were available from established supermarket chains such as Tesco. Lidl differentiated the shopper's experience by also offering "middle aisle" ranges with everything from chainsaws to wetsuits. Their model of multiple smaller stores, each with a similar layout and located close to residential areas, challenged the large out-of-town megastore model that dominated the grocery retail sector until then. Lidl's ability to offer this alternative shopping experience was certainly valued by customers, but it was also rare. This rareness was more than just an eccentric idiosyncrasy. It was supported by an aggressive real estate strategy, a highly thoughtful sourcing strategy for products, a fine-tuned supply chain to keep their large numbers of outlets stocked (albeit with a more limited range) and creative planning processes to determine what new "middle-aisle" products would attract more customers. It is also important to note that this rareness was not exclusive as Aldi adopted a similar model. However, it did persist for an extended period, and it continues despite efforts by some competitors to respond to aspects of their uniqueness (e.g., the Tesco Metro sub-brand of smaller stores that are located within town centres).

In an open market such as grocery retailing, firms have more opportunity to develop rareness than will be available to subsidiaries within internal markets where the rules are set by the parent. In open markets, even firms selling commoditised products, such as oil or batteries, will invest in their marketing and brand image to create perceptions of uniqueness relative to competitors. In contrast, corporate parents will rightly promote consistency of operations across their subsidiary networks and will expect that best practices and skills should be shared for the good of the organisation as a whole. Against that background, subsidiary leaders may feel that there is little that they can do to develop differentiated capabilities, unless they act very subversively.

However, even under conditions where sites share a charter, there may be opportunities to develop rare and differentiated capabilities. If the parent organisation is strict on the principle of openness and sharing of best practices and skills, then a subsidiary could become an exemplar in playing to this expectation. If there are other sites that appear to be better in any area, then it is reasonable to ask them to share their secrets. They may not be as open as you would like, but it will be difficult for them to refuse and any suspicions of reticence on their part will cast them in a bad light. On-site visits are much more effective in this case than remote discussions. In this sense, the openness to investigate and learn develops as a strong capability of the subsidiary. This is one that is often more rare than one might think – especially across more mature sites.

Subsidiaries can also aspire to be the site that others use as a reference point, as in Delany's Stage 3 (Figure 3.1). Even if best practices will have to be shared, the capability to develop these practices can be seen as a differentiator for the subsidiary. To achieve this, it is useful to identify those areas where the subsidiary has some autonomy in developing rare capabilities. Examples could be in recruitment practices or staff development initiatives. Even in a highly standardised global network of subsidiaries and third parties, there will be opportunities to be recognised as best-in-class.

To illustrate these points, I will digress to discuss how my colleague David Cornick and I sought to achieve differentiation for the IBM subsidiary that we established in Dublin to deliver call centre technical support services to Personal Computer customers. The site was part of a network of such centres supporting the US market, where a caller could be answered by the next available agent across similarly configured IBM centres in Raleigh, Toronto and Dublin, or from a third-party outsourced centre in Florida. As the least experienced site, we realised that our initial differentiator as a low-cost location while supported by government start-up grants was temporary. We were fortunate to be able to hire highly capable employees, so we identified agent skills as our long-term differentiator. Although we were subject to rigid financial controls in this low-margin business, we recognised that we had full autonomy for recruitment and staff training. We focused on competency-based employee selection and we devoted some of our most highly skilled employees to our training department. We were proud of the fact that whenever we were pressurised to make cost reductions, we resisted the temptation to reduce investment in training. As well as improving our achievement of key performance indicators (KPIs), good training proved to be an important benefit for staff and it improved retention. When the third-party outsourcer in Florida was commissioned by headquarters (HQ), we initially saw this as a threat. However, we quickly realised that it was another opportunity to learn, so we requested a site visit and gained some great insights into how they operated and supported their other customers. Our ambition and enthusiasm to develop the subsidiary became an asset that made us different from the more established sites that seemed less open to change. This difference was greatly appreciated by our HQ sponsors.

Difficult to Copy

Rareness can be temporary if it is easy for others to replicate. Therefore, those capabilities that are most difficult to copy will be a stronger source of sustained competitive advantage. The case of Lidl provides a good example of this, where although Tesco eventually copied some aspects of their distribution systems they could not replicate the entire model – and indeed would not want to do so as this would compromise their entire brand and value proposition.

Ryanair is another interesting example. The history of the company shows that it struggled to survive in its early days as it tried to compete with established national carriers such as British Airways, by offering similar services that even included a business class option. It was only when they studied the model adopted by Southwest Airlines in the USA that they saw an opportunity to become differentiated in the eyes of customers. Ryanair was not Europe's first low-cost airline, but by copying the Southwest Airlines model diligently it grew to be the largest carrier in the region in terms of fleet size and passengers carried. It was able to do so because it had little to sacrifice in reshaping itself as Europe's most successful "no frills low-cost airline." For many years, national carriers in Europe found it impossible to compete with Ryanair on price as they were burdened by their legacy cost bases and work practices. By the time that these national carriers accepted that the market had shifted and they were able to radically address their cost structures, Ryanair had used the strength of their model to develop a route network that made competition difficult even for new carriers who adopted a similar approach. Ryanair, Easyjet, Vuelling, Eurowings and others have shown that it was not impossible to copy the Southwest Airlines model (or indeed the further developments of this that were pioneered by Ryanair). However, it was particularly difficult to do so for carriers burdened with existing brand images and cost structures that were underpinned by the customer expectations embedded in these brands. Ryanair showed that developing capabilities that are difficult to copy is not always about keeping processes secret. It is often about recognising where the conditions that have shaped a market can be disrupted, and planning how players who have grown their businesses in response to these conditions can be wrong-footed and slow to react.

The challenges that subsidiaries face in developing capabilities that are difficult to copy are very similar to those faced when seeking to develop rare capabilities. In an open internal market, it is not possible to use patent legislation or to secure intellectual property protection to make something difficult to copy. Indeed, the onus may be on a subsidiary to assist other subsidiaries, or even outsource partners, in copying best practices. But it is not always easy to copy a talent, even when this is clearly demonstrated. Any amateur golfer who has seen an analysis of Tiger Wood's swing when in his prime will recognise the difference between knowing and doing. Again, the objective should be to become a role model and to learn ways of developing capabilities that may be clear to see, but still difficult for other organisations to emulate.

Difficult to Substitute

In the context of sustained competitive advantage, substitution is different to copying. If two coffee shops are located side by side they can be considered *copies* of each other as they provide very similar ways of satisfying a customer's need for refreshment. For example, if a customer's reason for going to a coffee shop is to socialise with friends, then going to the cinema or a bar is a form of *substitute* that threatens the coffee shop's business – even though coffee shops and cinemas would not usually be considered direct competitors.

The early innovators of digital cameras, satnav devices and portable music players had a relatively short tenure when the technology was developed to enable smartphones to substitute for all of these products. Steve Jobs and the team at Apple recognised that the underlying need in consumer electronics was for the portability and attractiveness of products. They pushed the technology to satisfy this need so that smartphones could eventually provide a platform to satisfy all of these diverse application requirements. There were few customers who could have recognised that their mobile phone would become such a multipurpose tool, but Apple understood deeper needs that the customer could not even envisage. Jobs liked to reference the quote attributed to Henry Ford that "If I had asked people what they wanted, they would have said faster horses." (even though there is some dispute as to whether Ford ever actually said these words).[7] These days smartphones also substitute for TVs, radios, credit cards, cash, wallets, printed tickets, newspapers and more. It is hard to envisage what might eventually substitute for our smartphones, but no doubt that day will come.

A subsidiary's capabilities can be substituted by a new technology or process that is more effective in fulfilling the need. Some call centre services have been substituted by chatbots and voice recognition systems. Some IT systems management services have been substituted by cloud-based infrastructure. Equally, there may be opportunities for subsidiaries to substitute for an existing solution by reinterpreting the need. Many international shared services subsidiaries have shown how they can provide an alternative to the model of providing services such as Finance, Procurement and HR locally and in a distributed manner. Centralised shared services may not be as popular with some end-users, but they can deliver cost effectiveness and standardisation that is attractive to a large organisation. Ambitious subsidiary leaders may come up with innovative applications of the capabilities that the subsidiary offers to substitute for an existing solution to company needs.

The most important point here is that subsidiary leaders should be open-minded and creative when considering where the capabilities that they provide (and indeed the charters that these capabilities support) may be replaced by substitute solutions, or where they can offer an alternative answer to an existing need elsewhere in the company. The instinct may be to dismiss the potential that one of the subsidiary's capabilities could be replaced, by convincing oneself that this would not do everything that the current solution delivers, or that it has been tried before. This is understandable but may ultimately prove futile.

For a capability to be a source of sustained competitive advantage in the internal market, it should be difficult to replace it with an alternative solution to the same problem, however creative this may be. The bravest subsidiary leaders may even challenge themselves and their teams to devise substitutes for their existing capabilities. It is better to lead the thinking on possible alternatives, rather than be led by it.

From the sub-sections above and the examples that are given, it should be clear that not all of the four characteristics must be achieved in order to make a capability a source of sustained competitive advantage (with the emphasis here on *sustained*). It should also be clear that these four characteristics are not mutually exclusive. The lines sometimes overlap between a capability that is, for example, rare and also difficult to copy, or valuable because it is difficult to substitute. Sustained competitive advantage is not binary and will vary in strength depending on how these factors combine "in the round" under the particular conditions that prevail in the internal market.

We can now go on to consider the headings under which capabilities can be identified, and then assessed, to determine their contribution to sustained competitive advantage.

Identifying Capabilities

In the article in which Birkinshaw and Hood propose their charter and capability model of subsidiary evolution,[8] they define capabilities as the capacity that the subsidiary has to deploy resources "to effect a desired end." They emphasise that capabilities emerge over time. Although some capabilities may be shared across subsidiaries, they tend to be difficult to transfer from one subsidiary to another. In vibrant subsidiaries, new capabilities are constantly being developed, but these typically emerge on the margins of existing capabilities.

To assess a subsidiary's capabilities, it is advisable to adopt a very broad view on where these might exist or be absent. The nature of capabilities means that sometimes they are so ingrained that they can be difficult to identify, and they are often taken for granted.[9]

To ensure that the identification of capabilities adopts a broadly based and investigative perspective, they can be considered under the headings which make up the CREST mnemonic: Contractual, Relational, Emotion-driven, Structural, Talent-oriented. At this stage in the process of analysing capabilities, it is not important to make judgments on the contribution of each. The intention is merely to identify capabilities that are relevant so that their robustness and potential importance to a future strategy can be assessed later.

Contractual Capabilities

Contractual capabilities are those that are underpinned by a formal agreement describing commitments between the parties involved. These could include a grant agreement between the company and a government agency, customer contracts for the provision of services, or internal memoranda of understanding between business units outlining their respective responsibilities and commitments to each other over a given period. Local regulatory obligations can also be considered under this heading. For example, if the law places restrictions on the termination of employment contracts without compensation, this can be regarded as a contractual capability that may not be available to subsidiaries operating in other jurisdictions.

The contracts identified may have different durations, degrees of commitment and even levels of enforceability. The subsidiary may not even be a direct signatory to some of them, but they can still be a source of stability which is an asset and can therefore be regarded as a capability for our purposes.

Identifying capabilities under this heading is important as it will encourage discussion on whether these contracts are being utilised to the full extent possible (e.g., are government grant agreements being fully drawn down?). When identifying such capabilities, it is also important to identify areas where this level of contractual cover is not in place, but where this would be beneficial. For example, the subsidiary may be devoting valuable skills to a new project, without any firm commitment that this will continue, or without any formally agreed termination conditions.

Relational Capabilities

The relationships that the subsidiary has developed can also be regarded as a capability that may prove important to strategy planning. These include relationships with corporate sponsors, customers, peer subsidiaries, suppliers, trades unions, external bodies such as universities, and ecosystems of other organisations operating in the same sector (e.g., industry associations). These relationships can provide important sources of support and intelligence, so they should not be underestimated.

The identification of relationships, given their nebulous nature, is a subjective exercise. A good approach is to consider all the connections that the subsidiary has with its internal and external stakeholders (customers, suppliers, partners, employees, sponsors), and in each case to identify relevant relationships, even if these are weak or non-existent.

Emotion-Driven Capabilities

Emotion-driven capabilities are those that relate to perceptions about the subsidiary or reputations that have been formed. It can be particularly difficult to identify capabilities under this heading as perceptions and reputations are so individually held and often not openly expressed by people outside the subsidiary. And yet, emotions drive decision-making, so they need to be monitored and influenced.

At this point in the process, the objective is to identify those emotion-driven perceptions that combine to form the reputation of the subsidiary. Of course, not all stakeholders that matter will share a common perspective on each of these elements. The strength or otherwise of these elements across stakeholders will be assessed in the next step. For now, it is sufficient to identify the dimensions of the subsidiary's reputation that are subject to individual and emotional judgments. This may include elements such as trustworthiness, reliability, flexibility, work-ethic, selflessness, creativity and ambition. Not all of these may apply and there may be others that are more important to the corporate culture of your company.

Structural Capabilities

This heading covers those capabilities that provide infrastructural under-pinning for the subsidiary. This includes elements such as facility leases or ownership, sunk investment costs that require return on investment and regulatory benefits that are important to the parent (e.g., corporate tax benefits). There can be some overlap here with the Contractual heading, but this area merits separate focus as not all structural capabilities will be supported by explicit contracts. An example could include production processes that are embedded in the fabric of the subsidiary, and which may be difficult to replicate elsewhere.

Structural capabilities are those that make it painful for the parent to exit, but this can also identify structures that could be further optimised as a source of strategic strength (e.g., can the existing facility be more widely utilised to provide a better return for the parent?).

Talent-Oriented Capabilities

These capabilities cover the skills of the people within the subsidiary and how these contribute to the parent's business. They include professional skills across the disciplines that are important to each of the subsidiary's charters, management skills, process design skills, business support skills and planning skills. How individual elements combine into the overall intellectual capital of the organisations is also important to consider. The recruitment and training infrastructure that enables these skills can also be included here. It may also be relevant to identify softer skills relating to the work-ethic, motivation and commitment levels of employees.

It may be more straightforward to identify capabilities under this heading as managers tend to feel proud of their employees and their skills. However, it is also important to consider where desirable skills may be weak or absent. Of course, until the subsidiary fully develops its strategy, it will be difficult to know where shortfalls in specific skills must be addressed.

Managers should appreciate that this step represents a first pass at the identification of talent capabilities as part of this diagnostic phase. The list can be reviewed and revised in later iterations.

Figure 5.1 provides a table that can be used to list the capabilities of a subsidiary and to assess each as a source of sustained competitive advantage. A column is included to show the type of capability under the CREST framework. This is to encourage consideration of each heading under this framework, and where no capabilities can be identified under any heading, questions should be asked about whether the category is being considered sufficiently deeply and creatively.

The table also provides for an initial assessment of each capability under the four headings that contribute to sustained competitive advantage. It is likely that each capability will be considered *valued* at some level, as otherwise it would not have been identified as a capability. However, those that are not also rare, difficult to copy or difficult to substitute will often simply be qualifiers for entry to the internal markets in which the subsidiary is competing. This is certainly not intended to suggest that capabilities that are valued, but not rare, difficulty to copy or difficult to substitute should be ignored or underplayed. This could lead to capability atrophy leading to charter loss that Birkinshaw and Hood warn about in their model (see Figure 3.2). However, unless these capabilities can be developed to make

CAPABILITY	CREST CATEGORY	VALUED	RARE	DIFFICULT TO COPY	DIFFICULT TO SUB

Figure 5.1   Capability identification and assessment of sustained competitive advantage

them more differentiated, they will have a different degree of strategic importance and opportunity, when compared to those that also rate under the other sustained competitive advantage headings.

The example in Box 5 illustrates how the HETSol Support Labs management team identified their core capabilities and the initial assessment of sustained competitive advantage that they completed as part of this exercise.

BOX 5
HETSOL SUPPORT LABS
CAPABILITY IDENTIFICATION AND ASSESSMENT

CAPABILITY	CREST CATEGORY	VALUED	RARE	DIFFICULT TO COPY	DIFFICULT TO SUB.
Gov't grant agreement: Grants available up to 400 jobs	C	x	x	x	
Memoranda of Understanding with all sponsors	C	x			
Relationships with Divisional Senior VPs	R	x			
Local university relationship	R	x	x	x	
Membership of local industry cluster organisation	R	x	x	x	x
Reputation for trustworthiness, reliability and flexibility	E	x			x
Reputation for technical skills and creativity	E	x			x
Building lease:10-year agreement	S				
Process embeddedness: Organisational skills and processes	S	x		x	x
Software design and engineering skills	T	x		x	x
Data analytics skills	T	x	x	x	x
Product testing skills	T	x			
Customer support skills	T	x	x	x	x

Notes:

As input to the deeper analysis of these capabilities in the next diagnostic step, the group stepped back from this list and noted some overall reflections.

■ It was agreed that commitments from HETSol Corporation underpinning operations are weak, but this is typical of how the corporation operates. Under-utilised government grant commitments up to 500 employees could provide an opportunity for growth propositions for HETSol corporation.

■ Relational capital is variable across corporate sponsors, but some strong relationships in the local market and with local universities could offer opportunities.

■ The overall reputation of the subsidiary is positive in terms of key factors such as flexibility and trustworthiness, although some recent operational challenges may have dented perceptions of reliability.

■ Structural underpinnings of the organisation are weak as the lease on the building has flexible exit criteria. However, it would be operationally challenging to move processes elsewhere, and this would require some payback of government grants if this happened in the next three years.

■ Talent, while continuing to develop, is patchy in some key areas. Recent attrition levels in an active labour market are a particular concern.

Analysing Capabilities

Although an initial identification and categorisation is performed in the previous step, a deeper analysis is required to understand those capabilities that may have strategic potential, or which need to be addressed as part of strategic planning. To achieve this, we can use the adapted version of the SWOT framework that is shown in Figure 5.2.

Readers will no doubt be familiar with SWOT analysis and will have used it in other contexts. The emphasis in this case is on capabilities and specifically those that are real strengths for the subsidiary, those that are important weaknesses, those that may be a source of future opportunity and those that are under threat. The model recommends a second level of categorisation under each SWOT heading, to help in the identification of the factors that are most deserving of attention in future steps:

■ **Capability strengths**: In the context of analysing capabilities, strengths are most influential when they are a source of sustained

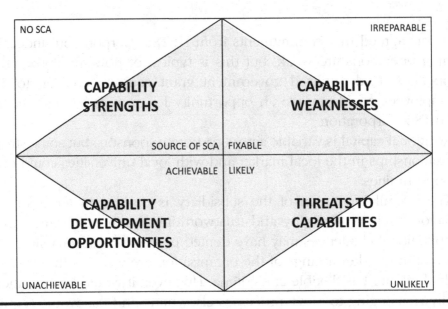

Figure 5.2 Analysing capabilities using the SWOT framework

competitive advantage (abbreviated as SCA in the figure). Again, this is not to suggest that strong capabilities that do not contribute to sustained competitive advantage are unimportant. If these are valued as qualifiers for participation in the internal market then they should be monitored and maintained, preferably to a level where they become differentiators that are difficult to copy or substitute.

■ **Capability weaknesses**: All organisations have weaknesses, and it is important to redress these where possible. However, if a weakness cannot be fixed in a reasonable timeframe, then it may be better to expend efforts elsewhere, while taking actions to mitigate the weakness. For this reason, this adapted SWOT model recommends that when capability weaknesses are recognised, a further level of analysis is needed to determine whether these can be fixed or not in the strategic timeframe.

■ **Capability development opportunities**: Some capabilities offer an opportunity to develop into a strength that can become a source of sustained competitive advantage. However, as with weaknesses, it is important to be realistic about whether this is achievable in the time available. If it is not easily achievable, discussions should follow about what can be done to make it achievable, and whether this effort is merited given the benefits that the capability could deliver.

■ **Threats to capabilities**: Underlying factors in the operating environment may present a threat to strong capabilities or those that are a
source of future opportunity. Equally, such threats may make capability
weaknesses even worse. It is important to critically analyse the sources
of such threats. A good approach is to review each of the capabilities
that have been noted as strengths, weaknesses or opportunities, and to
step back and consider how these might be threatened. As indicated in
the model, this should include an assessment of how likely or unlikely
these threats may be.

To complete this exercise, using sticky notes on a whiteboard, flipchart or
electronic equivalent will enable debate as elements are moved from one
categorisation to another. As with all SWOT exercises, the same capability may be categorised in more than one quadrant (e.g., where a current
strength could become a source of complacency and weakness or where
a new opportunity threatens the relevance of an incumbent capability). Such duplication is not a problem at this stage. It is more important
to ensure that all views are heard so that the diagnosis of capabilities is
comprehensive.

Having completed the exercise the group should feel that an insightful analysis of capabilities has been completed, including a categorisation
of strengths that provide real sources of sustained competitive advantage,
weaknesses that can and should be repaired, achievable opportunities to
develop new capabilities and likely threats to capabilities. It can also be
useful to step back from this analysis of individual capabilities and to consider linkages between capabilities, or dependencies on other capabilities
that have not been highlighted. For example, having a robust set of documented operational processes is only beneficial if strong management systems are also in place to ensure consistent monitoring and measurement
of these processes. This reflects the view that individual capabilities often
do not represent sources of sustained competitive advantage until they are
knitted together with others. It is this combination within a *strategic capabilities architecture* that creates the source of advantage and differentiation
that competitors find difficult to replicate.[10] Therefore, considering these
overall synergies between capabilities can reveal additional insights into the
strengths of the subsidiary.

Box 6 provides an example of how this SWOT model was used by the
HETSol Support Labs team when analysing their capabilities.

BOX 6
HETSOL SUPPORT LABS
CAPABILITY ANALYSIS USING SWOT

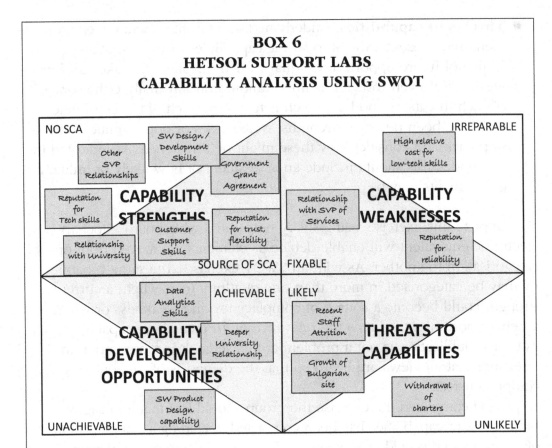

Notes:

■ The team recognised that they have a number of important strengths, although some – such as technical skills and good relationships with most of the divisional senior vice presidents (SVPs) – were not particularly differentiating. Some unique strengths such as the availability of further government grants and the reputation of the subsidiary for trust and flexibility are a real asset.

■ It was noted that the relationship with the SVP of revenue-earning services was weak as this individual is new to the company. However, this could be improved with effort. Some recent operational issues have negatively impacted external perceptions of reliability and this requires attention. The subsidiary is no longer able to offer low-cost skills due to changes in the employment market. This can be offset in the short term by government grants, but cannot be fixed longer term.

■ The emerging area of data analytics was recognised as a skills opportunity that could be further developed with investment. The potential
to develop the relationship with the local university which has deep
data analytics and other technical skills was also recognised. There
was some discussion on the potential to move into software product
design but this was felt to be very challenging for the foreseeable
future.
■ Staff attrition and the growth of the new Bulgarian site were recognised as threats, although it was not felt that charters were in immediate danger because of this.

Summary

In this chapter, a number of concepts and tools were presented to assist
subsidiary leadership teams in identifying and categorising organisational
capabilities that are likely to have future strategic importance. The degree
of importance will be influenced by the extent to which these capabilities
offer a source of sustained competitive advantage – a concept that is usually
considered in market-based systems and which we re-interpreted here for
the internal markets within which subsidiaries operate. Thinking of capabilities in this way enables initial perspectives to be formed on their importance
relative to each other. Then, a refinement of the SWOT analysis framework
was provided as a tool for identifying those strong capabilities that can be
a source of sustained competitive advantage, weaknesses that can be fixed,
opportunities that can be developed and threats that warrant mitigating
actions.

Our focus at this stage remains on diagnosis so that any future strategy
that is formed is based on a deep foundation of understanding. Nevertheless,
it is inevitable that during the process participants may jump forward occa-
sionally to solutioning. Cutting off such discussions may prove frustrating for
team members who are anxious to "cut to the chase," so some space should
be allowed even at this stage for such brainstorming. Notes can be made of
ideas that may be returned to later.

However, the team should remain cognisant that a final part of the diagnostic puzzle must be considered before decisions can be made on the
right focus for any strategy. That step requires consideration of the external

environment within which the subsidiary operates, and this is the focus of our next chapter.

Notes

1. Robert M. Grant, *Contemporary Strategy Analysis*, 8th ed. (Blackwell, 2013).
2. Vaughan Evans, *25 Need to Know Strategy Tools* (Harlow: Pearson Education Limited, 2014), p. 51.
3. Jay Barney, "Firm Resources and Sustained Competitive Advantage," *Journal of Management* 17, no. 1 (1991).
4. Jay Barney and Delwyn N. Clark, *Resource-Based Theory: Creating and Sustaining Competitive Advantage* (Oxford University Press, 2007).
5. K.B. Monroe, *Pricing—Making Profitable Decisions* (New York, NY: McGraw Hill, 1991).
6. Lyons and Brennan, "Assessing Value from Business-to-Business Services Relationships: Temporality, Tangibility, Temperament, and Trade-Offs."
7. Patrick Vlaskovits, "Henry Ford, Innovation, and That 'Faster Horse' Quote," *Harvard Business Review online* (2011).
8. Birkinshaw and Hood, "Multinational Subsidiary Evolution: Capability and Charter Change in Foreign-Owned Subsidiary Companies," p. 781.
9. Cristina Mele and Valentina Della Corte, "Resource-Based View and Service-Dominant Logic: Similarities, Differences and Further Research," *Journal of Business Market Management* 6, no. 4 (2013).
10. William R. King, "Creating a Strategic Capabilities Architecture," *Strategic Planning* Winter 1995 (1995).

Chapter 6

Where We Do It: Analysing Our Environment

A limitation of both charter analysis and capability analysis as described in the previous two chapters is that these are largely introspective processes. Introspection has its benefits if by forcing ourselves to look from the outside-in we can uncover things that are too close for us to see from our normal day-to-day perspective. But no organisation has the luxury of working in a vacuum, so to fully understand the backdrop against which a strategy should be formulated we must also look from the inside-out, and in doing so critically assess the wider environment within which the subsidiary works – now and in the future. We will refer to this as the *macro environment*.

Macro environmental considerations not only determine how charters are delivered and capabilities are developed. They will also influence any strategic potential and shape how this potential can be most successfully fulfilled through strategic actions. This chapter identifies the different dimensions of this macro environment and details how each of these dimensions can be analysed to assess their potential impacts on strategic choices.

Failure to deeply understand the environment surrounding a strategic action can have fatal consequences, even when there is a sound rationale behind the strategy itself. The American online services provider AOL discovered this to its cost when it purchased the social media company Bebo in 2008 for $850m. Although at the time this looked like a smart way of entering the social media market, AOL failed to think through how it would counter the growing popularity of Facebook as a formidable competitor in this space. Either they did not plan for the additional product development

DOI: 10.4324/9781003425502-8

and marketing investment that this would require or they did not anticipate how the developing global financial crisis would limit their ability to follow through on any planned investments. AOL sold Bebo for a reported $10m two years later to Criterion Capital Partners, who subsequently sold back to one of the original Bebo founders in 2013 for just $1m.[1] Arguably, a more realistic assessment of the competitive and investment macro environment could have saved AOL $840m and perhaps even prevented the ultimate demise of Bebo.

Assessing the macro environment can of course reveal opportunities as well as problems, not least in the case of subsidiaries. In the late 1990s, there was much hype about the so-called *Y2K bug*, with many companies fearing the impacts on their systems if date formats and calculations embedded in their code could not cater for the change from years beginning with "19," to those that would soon start with "20." The Indian subsidiaries of multinational enterprises (MNEs) such as IBM recognised this as an opportunity to offer high volumes of low-cost software engineering skills that could supplement those in developed economies at this time of high demand. Although India had already begun to open as a source of offshore resources, it was an unknown quantity as a service provider at that time and was still judged with some nervousness by Western executives. But by recognising the pressure that established subsidiaries were under to deal with this challenge, and by proactively promoting their readiness to assist, Indian teams were able to seize the opportunity and establish their credentials as a reliable source of technical and project management skills. Indian subsidiaries could have viewed the turbulence caused by the unknown impacts of Y2K as a reason for biding their time and awaiting a more stable climate for attracting foreign direct investment (FDI) projects. Instead, they grasped the opportunity and used this stress in the macro environment as a foundation for the many subsequent investment projects that followed.

Although the previous two phases were mainly positioned as dispassionate self-analysis – aimed at slowing down thought processes and challenging preconceptions – they will also hopefully have proved effective in uncovering major elements that are likely to form the scaffolding for a future strategy. Specifically, the concepts and frameworks that were outlined enabled the identification of charters that provide opportunities for the future and capabilities that can be exploited as sources of sustainable competitive advantage. Therefore, at this point, in the strategy development process, it is understandable if those involved already feel that they have enough content to work on, and they may feel weary about being faced with this further level of diagnosis in the macro environment. There may even be privately held concerns about "paralysis by analysis."

It is natural for busy managers to want to "cut to the chase" and to move on to a phase of solutioning the ideas that have come to the surface thus far. Paradoxically, although the chaotic pressures of day-to-day operations may have contributed to a consensus that the subsidiary needs to gain some control by developing a strategy, the investment of time required to do this properly may sometimes feel like "fiddling while Rome burns." The exercises to date may already have identified more opportunities that can realistically be pursued, so priorities will have to be agreed and choices will have to be made. However, those involved in the strategy process should be reminded that making such choices will require consideration of the climate that will surround strategic actions. Where will this climate create the opportunity to push boundaries and develop new capabilities and responsibilities? Also, where will it present challenges that require mitigating actions, or where may it even appear so challenging that an alternative strategic target should be chosen? This explains the importance of this final diagnostic phase as discussed in this chapter. Good strategy requires a realistic assessment of the operating environment, with an analysis of environmental factors that will present *headwinds* to be buffeted, or *tailwinds* to be caught and capitalised upon.

Framing the Macro Environment

The subsidiary's operating environment is multifaceted and shaped by a hierarchy of related conditions. The dimensions of the macro environment that applies to subsidiaries are represented in Figure 6.1 as a series of concentric ovals. The first and innermost factor is the operating environment of the subsidiary itself, which has already been the subject of much reflection through the ideas and frameworks discussed in the previous two chapters. The subsidiary's internal operating environment is in the first instance also shaped by two often unrelated sets of external influences. The first is the region where the subsidiary is located, as this will dictate regulatory, economic and labour market factors. The subsidiary also operates within the internal market of the parent and will therefore be influenced by its strategies, organisation structures and politics. As the figure also illustrates, both initial sets of influences that exist outside the boundaries of the subsidiary are also subject to marketplace forces driven by customer needs and

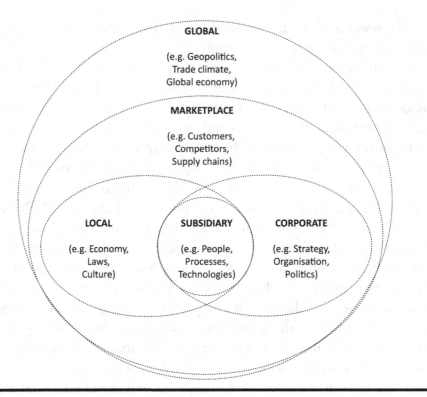

Figure 6.1 Forces shaping the subsidiary's macro environment

competition. Finally, all the above influences are shaped by broader global factors that determine how supply chains are developed or readjusted based on the impacts of geopolitics, economic forces and appetites for risk.

Environmental Change

The following sections in this chapter will explore each of the concentric ovals in Figure 6.1 in turn. Frameworks will be suggested as aids to assessing factors that may be relevant in each case. Before we do so, let us consider how we should view changes happening in each of these environments, based on their speed, magnitude and direction. Of course, change is a constant in business, and if you reflect on your career to date, I doubt you will be able to identify many extended periods of calm and constancy. Even the most powerful firms frequently operate in highly turbulent environments in which they remain busy by creating markets, exploiting opportunities and protecting their position. Assessing the macro environment is therefore important not only to develop a better common understanding of current

external influences on the subsidiary but also to reflect on how these influences might change, and the potential impacts and opportunities that may
result from these changes.

The Russian American academic Igor Ansoff is credited with triggering
a wider debate on whether strategy planning is feasible in highly turbulent business environments.[2,3] Ansoff defined environmental turbulence as
"numerous, frequent, rapidly developing events that are discontinuous from
the past, difficult to anticipate, and difficult to respond to." His strong view
was that the factors driving environmental turbulence should be treated as
strategic issues that need to be managed, as they will have a future positive
or negative effect on business performance.

Henry Mintzberg – another highly respected writer on business strategy –
disagreed. He argued that in turbulent environments, formal strategic planning (much like what is covered in this book) is pointless. This is because
detailed strategic plans cannot possibly cater to the unpredictability that will
inevitably be encountered in such circumstances. Mintzberg was not against
strategy development, but he contended that when faced with extreme turbulence, it is better to remain flexible and to rely on management intuition
to pursue a broad strategic direction, rather than following plans that were
conceived without detailed knowledge of the nature of the turbulence that
will dictate the operating environment.[4] While he disagreed with Ansoff
on the usefulness of detailed strategic planning when faced with volatile
conditions, he agreed that turbulence could present sources of opportunity.[5] Mintzberg's central point was that this opportunity is more likely to be
exploited by leaders who adopt intuitive responses to turbulent conditions,
guided by a broad, but clear strategic ambition. Ansoff counter-argued that
the potential impacts of turbulence, and the actions required to mitigate and
exploit it, should be factored into a strategic plan so that an organisation is
well-prepared.

While the debate between Ansoff and Mintzberg may be seen as a
case of two academic heavyweights trading theoretical punches through a
series of journal articles, it highlights a question that is fundamental to the
focus of this book. Can, and should, subsidiaries develop detailed strategic
plans in turbulent environments – particularly when the environmental turbulence experienced by subsidiaries also includes local and corporate factors that can amplify global and marketplace volatility? We will return to this
debate in the concluding section of this chapter. However, much depends
on the degree of turbulence that is experienced. One of Ansoff's contributions was his categorisation of levels of turbulence, ranging from repetitive

and predictable changes to those that are irregular and difficult to anticipate. He defined five levels – from relative calmness to full-scale disruption:

1. **Repetitive**: At this lowest level of turbulence, changes to the firm's environment are not very frequent, and they do not significantly alter the conditions within which the organisation operates. Upcoming changes are also relatively predictable. Therefore, at this level, the operating environment is calm and constant.

2. **Expanding**: At this level, changes to the operating environment are a factor for management, but they tend to be slow and incremental, enabling firms to cater to change without major issues. Historical changes allow extrapolation of the nature of future changes. Change is a factor, but it is slow and predictable.

3. **Changing**: The scope and frequency of changes are notable features of the operating environment at this level of turbulence. Change is faster than before, but still predictable to a level where well-managed organisations can anticipate and respond.

4. **Discontinuous**: Changes are characteristic of a clear transition from one phase in a business operating environment to the next, with the business climate going through a state of flux as it adjusts to this transition. Organisations struggle to cope with the frequency of change and particularly with its increasing unpredictability.

5. **Unpredictable**: Change is widespread, irregular in its frequency and unexpected in its consequences. Organisations are regularly caught by surprise. They find it extremely difficult to respond to emerging changes and to anticipate where the next changes will come from.

The following sections discuss each dimension of the market environment illustrated in Figure 6.1 in turn, starting with the outermost oval – the Global environment. For each dimension, methods are suggested for considering the potential areas of impact. Figure 6.2 integrates the concepts that have been discussed above into a template that can be used to capture relevant information about each force that may either help or hinder strategic action (i.e., tailwinds and headwinds). Tailwinds are environmental factors that present sources of opportunity; for example gaps in offerings that have been exposed by competitor actions and require investment by the parent. Headwinds include factors such as economic pressures that will limit investment budgets, or internal political issues that may slow decision-making.

Environmental Factor	Source G=Global; M=Marketplace; L=Local; C=Corporate.	Level of Turbulence 1=Repetitive; 2=Expanding; 3=Changing; 4=Discontinuous; 5=Unpredictable	Effect of Turbulence ← = Headwind; → = Tailwind
Examples ...			
Brexit: Additional paperwork / admin	G	5	←
Business growth / irregular demand	M	4	→
Labour shortages / attrition	L	3	←
Constrained investment climate	C	1	←
Inexperienced but ambitious employees	S	2	→

Figure 6.2   Assessment template for environmental changes

The Global Environment

All businesses are likely to be impacted by the prevailing global world order (or disorder). In an MNE context, this will be more relevant as the corporations in question have global aspirations and dependencies. The PESTEL framework provides a useful checklist for considering the sources of turbulence in the global business environment. PESTEL is a mnemonic covering six types of factors – Political, Economic, Social, Technological, Environmental and Legal. It is an extension of the original four (i.e., PEST) factors that were previously thought to cover all factors that characterise the climate within which firms pursue their interests.[6] This was before it was widely accepted that environmental and legal considerations have an increasing influence in globalised business contexts.

- **Political**: This covers the policy directions of governments and multilateral groups such as the EU. It also relates to trade agreements and other political alliances that are formed between governments. For example, in recent years, Brexit, America First and increasing nationalism in Russia have signalled shifts in political agendas away from the previous broad support for open-market economic connections. The resulting political turbulence in the global environment may have impacts that will be felt at the subsidiary level.

- **Economic**: Although many regional economies are linked, they will also have their own strengths, weaknesses and other nuances. These economic factors – whether they be within the home country of the parent, or across the markets in which it operates – may trickle down to the subsidiary. If so, they should be noted as sources of turbulence that may vary in their magnitude and in whether they are sources of potential or harm.

- **Social**: These factors incorporate the impact of cultural changes across different markets and operating units. Social changes may also be driven by demographic movements, shifts in sources of skills and changes in customer preferences or buying patterns. Changes in recent years from high-street to online retail in the fashion sector is an example of how social changes in buying behaviour (enabled by technological advances) have reshaped how successful businesses are required to operate.

- **Technological**: Since the start of the industrial revolution – and arguably even before this – innovations in technology have altered and disrupted industries. In our globalised economies, emerging technologies such as robotics, artificial intelligence and speech recognition may emerge from a range of sources around the world and cause ripple effects in global markets. Technologies can enable product and service alternatives, but they can also revolutionise supply chains, causing disruptive effects on established industries.

- **Environmental**: The impacts of climate change, and the increasing regulatory and moral obligations on businesses to pursue sustainable strategies, require radical new thinking by global businesses. Weather events present new threats to supply chains. The urgent need for solutions is also creating new markets and opportunities that may overthrow existing practices. The turbulence that this may cause to corporations, customers, competitors and subsidiaries merits due consideration.

- **Legal**: Even in our globalised world, laws vary from region to region. As evidenced by Brexit, it cannot be assumed that existing trading standards and regulatory environments will continue indefinitely. An area that is relevant to many subsidiaries is the example of corporate taxation regimes. The harmonisation of tax rates across countries that has been promoted by the Organisation for Economic Co-operation and Development (OECD) for many years[7] finally won some consensus in 2021. This has the potential to reduce the influence that variations in rates between countries will have on FDI decisions, while increasing the overall amount of tax paid by corporations. This may present opportunities for subsidiaries operating from some countries and threats for others.

The individual elements of PESTEL provide a good checklist for considering global factors that may influence a subsidiary's strategic choices and how these are likely to change. There is some overlap between the elements, and some sources of turbulence may be driven by more than one element. It is also likely that some of the PESTEL headings may not be a source of change that will impact significantly a subsidiary or its strategic direction. If consideration of that element does not quickly trigger a consensus on its potential to have an impact on subsidiary strategies, then the discussion should move on.

It should also be noted that the PESTEL framework has traditionally been regarded as a tool for identifying threats arising in the macro environment. In our case, we should also consider where the changes that these factors drive may also be a source of opportunity – either through the disruption that they cause or because our subsidiary is better positioned than its rivals to deal with this change. There may even be instances where a source of turbulence could potentially represent either a headwind or a tailwind, depending on how it is grasped and managed.

The Marketplace

The marketplace that impacts the subsidiary will include the competitive environment for the parent's products and the supply chain that the subsidiary partakes in to fulfil these products. Shifts in customer expectations, improvements in competitive offerings or impacts on how products are brought to market may all cause pressures that ultimately affect the subsidiary. Until now, we have considered the subsidiary to be operating within the internal market of the parent, where it competes against other units for resources and responsibilities. However, there may also be emerging practices or offerings in the external market that could be an attractive alternative to what the subsidiary currently provides. This is why the marketplace factors that are considered potential sources of impact and change should include the external markets (if any) for the supply chain elements that the subsidiary contributes.

Michael Porter's *5-Forces Model* has achieved popular acceptance as a tool for analysing the ingredients that combine to determine the competitiveness of a market.[8] It is popular because it is relatable and intuitive. Like the PESTEL framework, for our purposes, it also has the advantage that it may already be familiar to any manager who has previously taken an undergraduate module in business studies. The five forces identified by Porter are:

- **Extent of competitive rivalry**: This force covers the general extent and aggressiveness of competition in a market. It is often driven by the number of competitors that have chosen to participate, and how competent and well financed they are. Higher levels of competition will result in greater choices for customers and alternative sources of revenue for suppliers. Participating companies are likely to be more innovative in their offerings and routes to market. Each of these factors can lead to higher levels of turbulence that may be sources of challenge or opportunity.

- **Potential for new entrants**: Attractive markets will encourage new entrants, but the prerequisites for entry may act as a deterrent. For example, if high levels of investment are required for entry, or if existing customer loyalties will be hard to shift, then new entrants may find it difficult to get a foothold. Alternatively, if it is relatively easy for new entrants to participate, this may add to the level of turbulence experienced by incumbents. This can particularly be the case where an absence of intellectual property protections may make it easier for a company that is new to a market to learn from the experiences of incumbents and to develop the next iteration of an offering.

- **Power of suppliers**: When the availability of inputs is constrained – either in its quality or quantity – suppliers will clearly be in a more powerful position. Supplier power can be tempered by investments in relationships, or contractual agreements. However, suppliers will generally work to optimise their power position so that they can maintain flexibility and optimise prices. When supplier power is a dominant force, it can lead to macro environmental turbulence as their actions can become unpredictable and difficult to control.

- **Power of customers**: Customer power is a function of how much opportunity they have to switch to another provider. Other factors include their ability to exert harm through their enforcement of contractual terms and conditions, or reputational harm through their external communications in the marketplace. For example, in the restaurant sector, customer power has been significantly enhanced by the ability to submit online reviews, whereas in the past the reach of customers was limited to word of mouth within their personal networks. Dependencies which providers have on customer endorsements and repeat business can create turbulence that ultimately impacts the subsidiary.

■ **Threat of substitutes**: As has been discussed previously, substitutes are alternatives that are available to customers in place of existing product selections. Close substitutes can be similar products or services. However, a substitute can also be an alternative way of satisfying the same need. Substitutes that are dissimilar to existing offerings can be very difficult to predict. For example, before Airbnb, most hotel operators would have viewed other hotel chains as the most likely source of substitutes for their customers. They would not have anticipated a new disruptive competitor like Airbnb that does not itself own accommodations anywhere. The leisure accommodation industry is not the only sector that has been disrupted by substitutes enabled by the internet (consider Netflix in the case of TV broadcasting and Amazon in retail for example). Even in very mature sectors such as retail banking, the emergence of niche players such as Revolut and Monzo provides telling examples of how a deeper understanding of customer needs can allow a substitute product to be disruptive. Such substitutes can overcome traditional barriers to entry by exploiting a niche and taking advantage of the inability to respond by established players who are burdened by their existing processes and infrastructure.[9] Anticipating the threat of substitutes requires deep reflection on customer needs, including their ability to do without.

Subsidiary managers who are involved in the strategy development process will have a lot of industry experience to apply to the assessment of the current state of the marketplace under the above 5-Forces headings. However, much additional insight can be gained from talking directly to customers and also to front-line employees who are dealing with customer issues daily. The most difficult customers and the most demanding employees can often provide the greatest sources of insights that challenge preconceptions. Pope Francis emphasised that we can perceive a situation most accurately when it is viewed from the margins rather than from the centre.[10] Similarly, it has been argued that the changes that will trigger disruptive change begin at the periphery, as "snow melts from the edges."[11] Therefore, stretching yourself to go beyond the usual sources of information can provide new perspectives on what is happening, or about to happen, in the marketplace. An additional benefit of nurturing these front-line and customer contacts is that the knowledge gained can prove very powerful when talking to executives up the line. They are often far removed from the coalface and will value providers of information who feed them with success stories and keep them in touch with reality.

Considering each of the 5-Forces in turn as potential sources of variability may help to identify challenges or opportunities in the marketplace that must be factored into strategy planning. The forces cover different elements of the supply chain, but it may also be useful to consider where the supply chain may itself be variable and unpredictable, with the potential for restructuring. Fashions for supply chain integration or disintegration should be considered – such as the trend towards fine-slicing as discussed in Chapter 2.

The Local Environment

Subsidiaries also have important dependencies within the region in which they are located, where they compete for talent and other resources and are subject to the local environmental conditions that prevail. In highly integrated economies that are home to many subsidiaries, the local environment will inherit many features of the global environment. But while local economic conditions may reflect global trends, the effects may manifest differently in different economies (e.g., through their impacts on the local labour and housing or energy markets). Subsidiaries located in the EU should take a broad perspective on what is meant by "local" since much of the regulatory environment and rules for government support are set at an overall EU level. For example, the EU is increasingly signalling its intent to limit the market activities of any subsidiaries with non-EU parents that are judged to have benefitted from "unfair" subsidies in their home countries.[12]

The PESTEL framework can again be used to reflect on the degree of environmental turbulence caused by these factors, and to consider whether the potential impacts of these should be accommodated in strategic planning. Of course, a regional perspective should be adopted in this case, to consider whether localised political changes, economic impacts, social stability and so on are factors that may present headwinds or tailwinds. When assessing these factors, it may be insightful to refer to publicly available reports by companies such as EY which regularly produce detailed assessments of the relative attractiveness of FDI markets and the challenges that participation in these markets can entail.[13]

Also, in this context, it is worthwhile to give additional consideration to the availability of government grants and other FDI incentives. Although this question may already have been explored when analysing current and future capabilities, it is worth assessing how these compare to incentives available to the parent in other global regions, and whether this represents a threat or opportunity to subsidiaries operating in the local environment.[14,15]

The Corporate Environment

The factors shaping the internal market of the parent will of course have a direct effect on the options available to the subsidiary when pursuing a strategy. In Chapter 2, the point was made that, while we use the term "market" here to reflect the fact that there are customers and competition, the trading climate within corporations does not satisfy all the conditions of an open market. Specifically, subsidiaries competing for increased responsibility do not have full control over how they invest, how outputs are specified or the priorities set when allocating resources. So, while there is some merit in using Porter's 5-Forces model to consider some of the factors at play in the internal market, the model was not designed for this purpose. Using this model as a lens for examining the internal market may reveal additional insights on levels of turbulence when subsidiaries jockey for power (competitive rivalry), the potential for investments by the parent in new subsidiaries (threat of new entrants), the influence of upstream partners in the supply chain (power of suppliers), the extent of autonomous decision-making by internal service users and sponsors (power of customers) and any threats that may arise from alternative delivery models such as outsourcing (threat of substitutes).

However, this does not capture the full picture of the internal market. In this context, powerful personalities and their agendas should also be assessed, as covered by the following two considerations:

■ **Politics**: Politics is inevitable in organisations, whether they be large or small. In the subsidiary world, where agendas can incorporate a mix of functional, regional and personal objectives, politics is all the more likely to be part of the landscape. Politics is often assumed to be dysfunctional to organisational goals and is associated with deceitfulness, mistrust and facetiousness. However, those involved in political manoeuvrings often do not recognise them as such. If they do, they will probably rationalise these as being for the greater good of the corporation – since they will appreciate the importance of their agenda over all others. One of Mintzberg's reservations about detailed strategic planning was his assertion that internal politics will always disrupt the orderly world of planning. However, much depends on politics is really disruptive or whether it is just part of the background noise in an organisation. The extent to which clandestine political activity is tolerated within the culture of the organisation is also a factor. If we accept that some level of political activity is inevitable, the major questions are whether this must be influenced, and if so, how?

■ **People**: Politically motivated actions are executed by people, and the power of these actions will be determined by their direct organisational responsibilities and the strength of their networks of connections to others in powerful positions. The status and volatility of relationships with key individuals can therefore have a significant impact on the macro environment within which the subsidiary operates. In Chapter 8, we will give more in-depth focus to stakeholder management – which includes the making of an inventory of people who are in a position to give impetus to or inhibit planned strategic actions, and planning how these people should be brought on-side. However, even at this early stage, it is useful to consider whether the corporate environment includes individuals or collectives who will need such management attention.

A further potential limitation, or source of opportunity, is driven by the fact that in the corporate internal market the subsidiary does not always have the freedom to define its own operating environment with a view to maximising efficiency and effectiveness. Specifically, the following features of the operating environment are usually inherited from the corporate environment:

■ **Processes**: Well-defined operating procedures should mitigate turbulence in an operating environment. That is, unless these procedures are not fit for purpose – in which case they can make the situation worse. Those who own and design processes on behalf of the parent can exert a great degree of influence over the operating environment.

■ **Technology**: The effectiveness of modern corporations is frequently determined by the functionality and stability of their IT systems. Frequently, when we hear of organisations pursuing business transformation projects, this is synonymous with a major retooling of their systems and the sunsetting of fragmented applications architectures that have evolved organically over many years. This can be a source of turbulence that, at least in the immediate term, works counter to the flexibility and agility that such systems transformations are often aimed to enable.

As with the other dimensions of the macro environment, using the 5-Forces model and the above headings to reflect on corporate sources of resistance and support may or may not identify additional factors that will need to be incorporated into a strategic plan.

Box 7 shows how the template provided earlier in this chapter was used by the HETSol Support Labs leadership team to capture the most important factors shaping their macro environment.

BOX 7
HETSOL SUPPORT LABS
MACRO ENVIRONMENTAL ANALYSIS

Environmental Factor	Source G=Global; M=Marketplace; L=Local; C=Corporate.	Level of Turbulence 1=Repetitive; 2=Expanding; 3=Changing; 4=Discontinuous; 5=Unpredictable	Effect of Turbulence ← = Headwind; → = Tailwind
Geopolitical issues impacting product-line expansion into Russia/Asia	G	4	←
Global economic pressures may limit new customer acquisition.	G	4	←
Competitor offerings catching-up	M	2	→
Offshore outsourcers becoming increasingly attractive in the market	M	3	←
High staff attrition, limited compensation budgets	L	2	←
Government need to protect FDI, and corp. tax given global economic outlook	L	4	→
Competition for R&D budgets between SW Eng. and Services divisions	C	3	→
Founder appears to favour new investments in Bulgaria Lab	C	3	←
Corporate investment planning is slow and lacking engagement.	C	1	←

Notes:

- **Global**: Sanctions against Russia and continuing tensions between Western countries and China have stalled HETSol Corp's momentum in extending into these markets. This will put pressure on year-on-year revenue growth plans. Even in existing markets, growing economic pressures and other demands on government finances may limit university spending on new technologies such as those offered by HETSol.
- **Marketplace**: Some new niche competitive products are continuing to emerge, but this has the plus side that HETSol will need to invest in new offerings to remain ahead of the market. They may, however, look to offshore providers for some of the software engineering resources, given the inflation in labour costs in the United States and EU.
- **Local**: Technical skills are in high demand in the market, leading to staff retention challenges. However, this is recognised by the government, and new incentives are being offered to upskill the existing labour force and to attract higher-value FDI projects.
- **Corporate**: An internal battle for R&D budgets is underway between the SW Engineering Division and the new Revenue-earning Services division. Whichever wins, HETSol Support Labs can be positioned to quickly staff available roles. However, the family connections of one of the founders with Bulgaria will lead to a desire to direct new investments there, so that this subsidiary quickly gets to critical mass. The planning process in the corporation remains laborious, which may slow decision-making. An added challenge is that subsidiaries tend not to be given the opportunity to directly input into these annual planning processes.

Anticipating Inflection Points

Analysing each dimension of the macro environment using the methods described in the previous sections will identify those aspects of the subsidiary's operating climate that are currently most volatile. However, this will not necessarily highlight areas where there may be impending environmental changes that will exacerbate challenges or create openings for new opportunities. Subsidiaries can gain an advantage by being among the first to anticipate such changes, so it is important to be open-minded and to encourage creative thinking into the potential sources of any such impending changes.

In her book, *Seeing Around Corners: How to Spot Inflection Points in Business Before They Happen*,[16] Rita McGrath builds on the observation of Andy Grove, former Intel CEO, that markets can demonstrate *strategic inflection points* which signal that the fundamentals underpinning a sector are about to change exponentially.[17] She describes how significant changes in business environments usually happen slowly at first, but then accelerate quickly. Her thesis is that these inflection points can be inferred by observing signals in a market, and the organisations that are successful in doing this can take advantage of innovations that shape the next phase in a market. McGrath does not suggest that managers can accurately predict the future – even if reading the signals can reveal some of its possibilities. But she recommends that organisations seeking to build game-changing innovations should develop a list of potential upcoming inflection points. They should create strategies that keep their options open to take advantage of these, while also knowing when to rule these out if events indicate that they are no longer likely. She refers to this as *discovery-driven planning*, designed to continually anticipate and re-evaluate potential inflection points while preparing for the possibilities that these may unleash.

This chapter cannot do justice to the body of contributions from authors who investigate how inflection points can be anticipated and how they can be exploited to fuel disruptive innovations. McGrath's book provides an excellent synopsis of the thought processes, but readers who have a deeper interest in this aspect of strategy-making will find some additional sources in the endnotes.[18,19,20] Predicting environmental changes that may or may not prove to be a source of disruption can be a very speculative exercise. Even if the subsidiary has the skills and the access to market intelligence to do this well, there is a danger that it may shift the focus of the strategy to cater for events that are possible, but not inevitable.

Despite those cautionary words, it is nonetheless useful to step back from the analysis of current changes in the macro environment (Figure 6.2) and to reflect on whether any of the dimensions of this environment may be subject to an upcoming change that has not yet fully registered its impact.

Following McGrath's concept of *discovery-driven planning*, the objective here is not to plan rigidly for all possibilities, but it is at least worthwhile to identify these possibilities so that the subsequent subsidiary strategy can be positioned to accommodate the most likely of them. Having considered the current level of volatility in each dimension of the macro environment and remembering that turbulent change tends to start slow and then accelerate exponentially, it is useful to brainstorm on whether there are signals that a more impactful degree of change may be on the horizon. Any such changes can be categorised using the matrix in Figure 6.3 to identify those that are most likely and will have the highest impact.

Potential environmental changes that are judged to be likely and which will have a high impact on the subsidiary and/or the parent should be prioritised for further investigation and should be given special attention in the subsidiary's strategy. Those that are likely, but with a lesser impact, should be accommodated, including regular reviews of their continuing likelihood and impact assessment. Those that less likely, but which would have a high impact were they to happen should be the subject of ongoing monitoring – particularly in relation to their likelihood in the short-to-medium term. This categorisation will also show which of the environmental changes that have been identified through this brainstorming can be ignored, if they are judged to be unlikely to occur and in any event, they would have a relatively low impact.

Box 8 shows how the HETSol Support Labs team completed their identification and categorisation of potential changes that may occur in their macro environment.

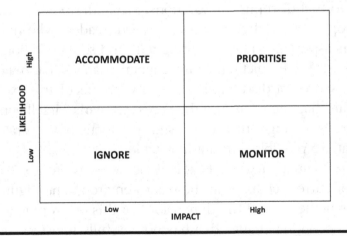

Figure 6.3 Macro environmental impact analysis

BOX 8
HETSOL SUPPORT LABS
CATEGORISATION OF POTENTIAL ENVIRONMENTAL CHANGES

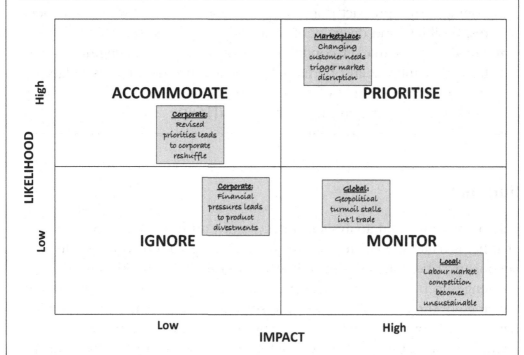

Notes:

- **Global**: There is a possibility that current global tensions could further escalate into a worldwide conflict. While the impact of this would be significant, it is not judged to be a strong likelihood at this point (MONITOR).
- **Marketplace**: Indications from the market generally, and from specific technical support requests received, are that customer needs have significantly shifted in the aftermath of the COVID-19 pandemic. Student expectations of remote learning have altered how courses are delivered. This has also changed how student performance is assessed, exacerbated by the increasing proliferation of "essay mills" and AI technologies which dishonest students can commission to complete their coursework when studying remotely. Using online tools to merely replicate the traditional classroom environment is no longer sustainable and new solutions will be needed (PRIORITISE).

- **Corporate**: Current political tensions at the corporate level are likely to lead to a reorganisation, but this should not threaten local charters (ACCOMMODATE). Financial pressures may lead to some continuing honing of the product portfolio, but the local operation has sufficient responsibility and diversity of charters to withstand this (IGNORE).
- **Local**: Labour market conditions continue to be challenging. This is likely to continue and perhaps accelerate. However, this is judged to be manageable in light of current budget outlooks and the availability of skilled new hires in the market (MONITOR).

Summary

Macro environmental analysis is a necessary part of the strategy process as it helps us to appreciate the prevailing climate within which strategic actions must be pursued – including where this presents opportunities, challenges to be overcome or even insurmountable roadblocks that require a change of direction. If we view the subsidiary as a small boat trying to navigate choppy waters while not being blown off course, the weather conditions cannot be controlled, so it is critical to anticipate where head-winds need to be buffeted and where tailwinds can be exploited. At the risk of over-extending this metaphor, in highly turbulent waters, there may even be an argument for returning to a safe port and awaiting better conditions. This is the essence of the debate between Ansoff and Mintzberg, where Ansoff argues that environmental challenges should be recognised and planned for in order to survive. Mintzberg's counterargument is that intuition and flexibility are more reliable assets when faced with extreme turbulence so that leaders are not held back by the shackles of a strategic plan that was conceived without knowledge of the conditions that would confront it.

However, as we have seen, environmental turbulence for a subsidiary can exist across several dimensions of the operating environment and can be experienced at different levels of severity. It is hard to disagree that when the cumulative environmental turbulence becomes too volatile to predict, *adaptive strategic behaviour* is required to supplement existing strategic plans with higher levels of creativity and flexibility. However, at lower levels of turbulence, it makes sense to manage the conditions and weather the storm.

In complex macro environments, managers may already be preoccupied with coping with the impacts of turbulence – whether that be in the global, marketplace, corporate or local environments. However, if a strategic process is to be forward-looking, it should also anticipate where changes to the environment may be imminent. Taking time to look for signals of these upcoming changes and considering the extent to which these are likely and impactful is a very worthwhile exercise. While we may not be able to reliably predict future events, we can at least anticipate the range of possibilities, and we should make deliberate provision for the most likely and significant of these in our planning.

So the strategy development process should include an objective assessment of the environment, not least to assess how current and anticipated environmental turbulence should influence planning. The approach outlined in this chapter provides a structure for doing this in a subsidiary context. Completion of the templates provided will enable an overall assessment of turbulence, and how this could develop. This may lead to the conclusion that the conditions are currently too volatile to risk a concerted strategic push. Or, for example, it could conclude that actions that are dependent on stability in the global environment should be temporarily sacrificed in favour of those that can rely on a higher level of stability in the local environment. The methods discussed in this chapter are intended to bring issues to the fore and facilitate such judgments.

The sections that discussed the dimensions of the subsidiary's macro environment outlined models that can be used to objectively assess the conditions at play in each (i.e., PESTEL and 5-Forces). These are intended as checklists that should trigger consensus on the most influential factors. With the possible exception of threats of substitutes (which usually require more thoughtful reflection), if the headings suggested do not quickly bring something to mind then it is better to move on. Also, it should not be expected that every source of change and turbulence can be predicted. After all, few strategic plans could have allowed for the impacts of the COVID-19 pandemic (although the best ones may have had some contingency in place for a high-impact, but unknowable event). This is where intuition and iteration of planning comes in, and it re-emphasises why the strategy formulation process should always allow the opportunity for revaluation and the revisiting of assumptions as the situation evolves.

Notes

1. Donna Tam, "Remember Bebo? Yeah. That's Why the Founder Is Killing the Site," *CNET*, https://www.cnet.com/tech/services-and-software/remember-bebo-yeah-thats-why-the-founder-is-killing-the-site/.
2. H.I. Ansoff, *Strategic Management* (London: Macmillan, 1979).
3. "Conceptual Underpinnings of Systematic Strategic Management," *European Journal of Operational Research* 19, no. 1 (1985).
4. Henry Mintzberg, *The Rise and Fall of Strategic Planning* (New York: Free Press, 1994).
5. "That's Not 'Turbulence,' Chicken Little, It's Really Opportunity," *Planning Review* 22, no. 6 (1994).
6. Francis Aguilar, *Scanning the Business Environment* (New York: Macmillan, 1967).
7. Chris Giles, "Oecd Drafts Principles for $100bn Global Tax Revolution," *Financial Times*, October 12 2020.
8. Michael E. Porter, *Competitive Strategy: Techniques for Analyzing Industries and Competitors* (New York: Free Press, 2008).
9. T. Bradshaw, "'Tech Debt': Why Badly Written Code Can Haunt Companies for Decades," *Financial Times Magazine*, 27 November 2019.
10. Mark Carney, *Value(s): Building a Better World for All* (London: HarperCollins Publishers, 2021), p. 371.
11. Andrew S. Grove, *Only the Paranoid Survive: How to Exploit the Crisis Points That Challenge Every Company and Career* (New York: Doubleday, 1996).
12. Alan Beatie, "Brussels Sharpens a Weapon That Might End up Spearing Its Friends," *Financial Times*, July 18 2022.
13. EY, "How Will Europe Compete for Investment Amid Ongoing Turbulence: Ey Attractiveness Survey Europe. May 2022," ed. Marc Lhermitte (2022).
14. Brian Smith, "How Europe, India and Africa Are Incentivizing Foreign Investment," (EY, 2021).
15. Douglas van den Berghe, "A Guide to Fdi: What Is the Point of Incentives?," *Investment Monitor*, https://www.investmentmonitor.ai/investment-promotion/guide-to-fdi-what-is-the-point-of-incentives.
16. McGrath, *Seeing around Corners: How to Spot Inflection Points in Business before They Happen.*
17. Grove, *Only the Paranoid Survive: How to Exploit the Crisis Points That Challenge Every Company and Career.*
18. Clayton M. Christensen, Scott D. Anthony, and Erik A. Roth, *Seeing What's Next: Using the Theories of Innovation to Predict Industry Change* (Boston: Harvard Business School Press, 2004).
19. Rita Gunther McGrath and Ian C. MacMillan, *The Entrepreneurial Mindset: Strategies for Continuously Creating Opportunities in an Age of Uncertainty* (Boston: Harvard Business School Press, 2000).
20. Zenas Block and Ian C. MacMillan, *Corporate Venturing: Creating New Businesses within the Firm* (Boston: Harvard Business School Press, 1993).

CHOICES AND ENABLERS

It is likely that the steps and frameworks described in Part II will already have triggered ideas on focus areas for the subsidiary strategy. Part III concentrates on translating these sets of ideas into an achievable strategic plan and identifying the actions necessary to execute it – including the need to seek support and influence decision makers. Chapter 7 discusses how the final contents of the strategy can be chosen, how the plan can be structured and the options for how it can be communicated internally. Chapter 8 encourages readers to think about the need to gain support for the plan from decision makers and other stakeholders. The issues associated with exerting influence to secure support for the subsidiary strategy are explored in this chapter. Chapter 9 then provides a brief outline of the governance processes that will be required to maintain focus on the execution of the strategy, while keeping its objectives and contents under review as conditions continue to develop. Chapter 10 concludes this final part of the book by discussing the responsibilities of parent organisations in encouraging subsidiaries to fulfil their potential and ensuring the smooth running of the network.

DOI: 10.4324/9781003425502-9

11

CHOICES AND ENABLERS

Chapter 7

Making Strategic Choices

Throughout the previous chapters, my use of the word *strategy* assumes that readers have a shared view of what is meant by this term and what a strategy should include. I accept that given the differences between subsidiaries, their business models and the norms that apply within their parent organisations, managers will have varying perceptions of what a strategy should look like. I also acknowledge that while many parents may be encouraged to see ambitious subsidiaries seeking to extend their mandates by finding ways to add more value, others may have reservations about their subsidiaries developing local strategies, for fear that this will lead to dysfunctional internal competition or the prioritisation of selfish local agendas over broader corporate objectives. These alternative perspectives will influence how a subsidiary strategy initiative should be positioned. So there is no single best way of framing the strategy, as so much depends on context.

This complicates the task of proposing how the ideas that will have emerged from the diagnosis phase described in Part II can be transformed into a plan that will be appropriate to any given setting. Therefore, the approach taken in this chapter is to explore a range of options and to allow you to consider which are the best fits for the specifics of your environment. To avoid being too open-ended in this exploration, we can at least agree on some guiding principles based on what has been discussed so far.

1. Strategy is more than just a statement of objectives or vision (we will return to the concept of *vision* later in this chapter). A good strategy should be founded on three core elements: a diagnosis, a guiding

DOI: 10.4324/9781003425502-10

policy (or vision) and coherent but achievable action.[1] If the diagnosis, the clear ambition or the action plans are missing, the strategy will be incomplete. To quote John Lonergan, former Governor of Dublin's Mountjoy Prison, "Vision without action is a daydream. Action without vision is a nightmare."[2]

2. Strategy is not a static concept. While it provides a "North Star" to guide the subsidiary's direction, it should remain under review as conditions develop. Particularly in a turbulent climate, pursuing a strategic direction should be a blend of what was originally intended, what needs to be adjusted in the light of changing circumstances and what may even have to be postponed or abandoned.[3]

3. A strategy should be aimed at creating value that will distinguish the organisation from others – particularly in the eyes of customers and other stakeholders. As Jack Welsh said, "the first step of making strategy real is figuring out the big 'aha' to gain sustained competitive advantage – in other words, a significant, meaningful insight about how to win."[4]

4. The strategic timeframe should be long enough to allow real changes to be affected, but it should also recognise the likely tenure of the leadership team. It can be difficult for a strategy to survive the transfer from one set of leaders to the next – particularly at the top of the organisation where new leaders will usually want to put their own stamp on things.

5. Strategy involves choices on what to do, but also what not to do. If everyone immediately signs up to every aspect of a strategy, this usually implies that the strategy is founded on compromise, and difficult choices and trade-offs have not been made.[5]

Taking these principles as read, the remainder of this chapter explores the options for developing a subsidiary strategy by considering the following questions:

■ Why are we doing this?
■ What do we want to be famous for?
■ How should we position our strategy?
■ What will success look like?
■ How can we get there?
■ What support are we looking for, and when?

Why Are We Doing This?

We began our discussion on subsidiary development in Chapter 3 by considering the factors that typically motivate the desire to develop and pursue a strategy (see the sub-section titled "Why Bother?"). It is worthwhile to reflect on these again now, to remind yourself of the main drivers that apply in your case. Your perspective on these may even have changed as your thinking has continued to develop.

The motivators that were identified can be broadly categorised under the headings of:

■ Those that are oriented around *employee* needs.
■ Those that are centred on responding to the needs of the *parent*.
■ Those that are concerned with optimising the security and further development of the *subsidiary* within the internal market of the parent.

Of course, there are overlaps between these headings, where some of the motivators align with more than one of these agendas. To aid additional reflection on the main motivators in your case, Figure 7.1 presents them again – this time as a Venn diagram to illustrate the overlaps between agendas.

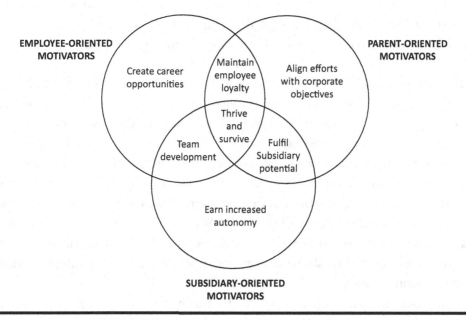

Figure 7.1   Strategy development motivators

The motivation to make an important contribution, and therefore to continue to exist (*Thrive and survive*), should be shared by employees, the subsidiary itself and the parent. Parents and employees share the objective to build their value propositions to each other so that employees maximise their efforts within the subsidiary structure and the parent can rely on their commitment to contributing to its success (*Maintain employee loyalty*). Employees should also benefit from the contribution that being part of a subsidiary strategy initiative makes to their personal professional development. This will also add to the overall organisational capabilities of the subsidiary (*Team development*). The desire of the subsidiary organisation to maximise its potential to contribute to corporate success should also be shared by the parent so that it gets adequate returns for its investment in the subsidiary (*Fulfil subsidiary potential*). The other motivators are more solely aligned with the agendas of employees (*Create career opportunities*), the parent (*Align with corporate objectives*) and the subsidiary (*Earn increased autonomy*).

While the categorisation shown in this figure is relatively loose and open to argument, considering the range of motivators from this perspective may provide additional clarity on why a subsidiary strategy process is being followed in the first place. Specifically, it can give some clarity on whether employee, parent or subsidiary priorities are more important in your case. Where choices are required between potential targets for strategic focus, it may help the decision-making process to consider the extent to which an objective may contribute to each motivator or a combination of them.

Of course, one of the options open to the subsidiary is to do nothing other than to continue to focus on day-to-day operational demands. There may be arguments for this if the environment is currently extremely turbulent and the best option appears to be to "baton down the hatches" until the macro environment grows more stable or the operational performance of the subsidiary provides a more solid foundation for moving forward. If this is the shared judgment of the leadership team, it will still be useful to reflect on the motivators identified in Figure 7.1. Will the lack of response to any of these result in problems that will be difficult to rectify in the future? Is some interim action needed to shore up one or more of these motivators, pending a fuller response later?

In all cases, having a clear view of the motivators for action or inaction will assist the process of making difficult choices.

What Do We Want to Be Famous For?

To be known, appreciated and admired, a subsidiary should be differentiated from its peers and deliver high value to its sponsors. To give security
to the subsidiary, these differentiators should also be lasting. In Chapter 5,
we used Barney's breakdown of the characteristics of sustained competitive
advantage (valuable, rare, difficult to copy, difficult to substitute) as a lens for
analysing capabilities. However, as a way of identifying what the subsidiary
wants to be famous for over an extended period, these concepts can also
be applied to the intersection of capabilities and charters. That is, the best-
positioned subsidiaries will be those that are responsible for charters delivering high value, that are differentiated and difficult to replicate or replace and
delivered using strong capabilities that are not commonly available.

To achieve this requires choices on the charters and capabilities that
should be focused upon, while taking account of the headwinds or tailwinds
that are present in the macro environment. A range of potential focus areas
will already have emerged from the exercises described in the earlier chapters, and it may be challenging to bring these together into a single place
where choices can be made. Figure 7.2 provides a template designed to

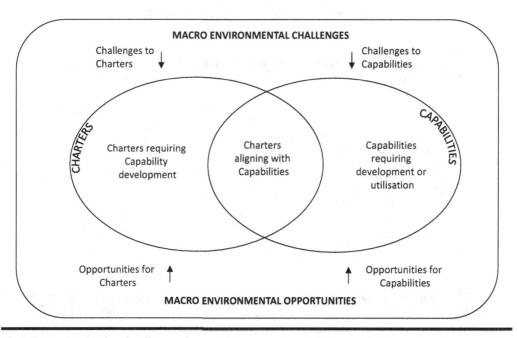

**Figure 7.2   Bringing it all together - Charters, Capabilities and Macro Environmental
Influences**

assist in doing this. This can be used to identify charters that require capability development, capabilities that require development or are currently under-utilised and areas where charters and capabilities are strongly aligned. It also allows the main areas of macro environmental opportunity and challenge to be captured so that their impacts on current and future charters and capabilities can be evaluated.

The process of populating this template may allow some of the outputs from the charter, capability and macro environment analysis to be consolidated or otherwise netted down into a more manageable set of possibilities. Opportunities that were not already identified may also come to the fore now when the team considers charters and capabilities in the light of their macro environmental analysis.

Box 9 shows how the above framework was used by the HETSol Support Labs team to provide a consolidated analysis of the key outputs from their diagnosis phase, including notes on how this should influence their further strategic thinking.

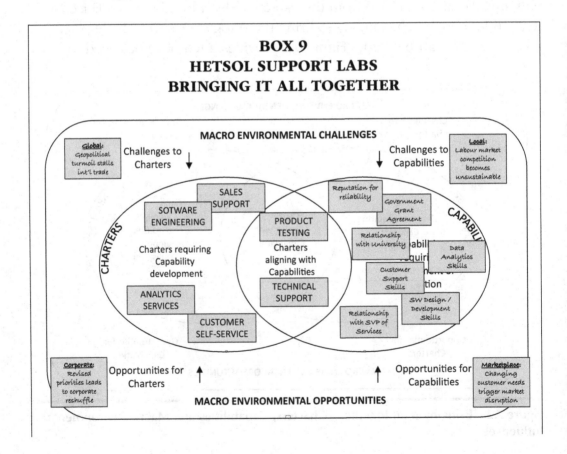

Notes:

Product Testing and Technical Support responsibilities provide a foundation for the subsidiary's contribution to the parent, although they offer limited strategic benefits to the subsidiary as standalone functions. To improve the positioning of HETSol Support Labs within corporate structures, the development of higher value-adding charters and capabilities is required. The skills developed through Product Testing and Technical Support are good feeders for this, as confirmed by the success in redeploying the best of these skills to Software Engineering, Sales Support and Analytics Services. Currently, there is under-utilisation of the insights that all of these functions provide into the strengths and weaknesses of HETSol's product portfolio, and how current offerings cater to the latest needs of customers.

The anticipated corporate reshuffle is likely to place more emphasis on cost reduction and new revenue-earning services. There is an opportunity to develop relationships with senior vice presidents (SVPs) who will now be in more powerful positions, but who will also be subject to more pressure to deliver. SVPs in charge of Product Testing and Technical Support functions are also likely to require new thinking to meet more aggressive cost budgets.

The insights gained from Technical Support and Sales Support functions have highlighted changes in the requirements of university clients in the wake of the Covid-19 pandemic. Specifically, new solutions are needed to improve the student online learning experience and to enable more robust assessment tools for remote students. HETSol Support Labs is uniquely positioned to draw attention to these market changes. There is also an opportunity to build a deeper relationship with the local university for collaboration on future needs in the sector and for the testing of prototypes. This, coupled with the opportunity to build on the existing foundation of skills, may provide a focus for a subsidiary strategy that will increase the ability to add value.

When this consolidated picture is captured, further choices will likely still be required to prioritise those areas that offer the best prospects of sustained competitive advantage. There is no rigidly defined process for making these choices and for making the leap between a range of relatively unstructured possibilities to a set that is cohesive, achievable and worthwhile.

However, as input to making this leap, let us again consider charters and capabilities in turn so that the possibilities consolidated into the Figure 7.2 framework can be further netted down to those final choices that should form the kernel of the strategy.

Selecting Charter Focus Areas

It is intuitive to conclude that the activities that should be most sought-after and protected within the subsidiary's portfolio will be those that add most value to the parent's business. This begs questions about how this value can be assessed and how the value delivered by different subsidiary charters can be compared. Stan Shih who was CEO of Acer – the Taiwanese personal computer company – offered his perspective on which activities within their global value (or supply) chain offered most value to that corporation.[6] A generalisation of Shih's perspective – which became known as the *Smiley Curve* – is shown in Figure 7.3.

As illustrated in the Smiley Curve, Shih's conclusion was that in the personal computer market, the activities that differentiated the company from competitors were those at the start of the product development cycle (R&D, design, commercialisation of designs) and those closest to the customer (sales, marketing, brand management, logistics, services). This is not to suggest that the activities in between (manufacturing, business support services) are not valuable, as clearly the company could not operate without the efficient operation of these functions. But they are not the most important

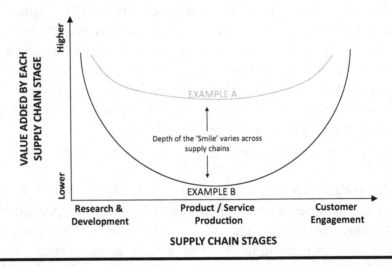

Figure 7.3 The Smiley Curve of global value chains (adapted from Shih, 1996)

differentiators and therefore Shih judged them to be lesser value-add. By implication, the locations that fulfilled the functions to the left and right of the curve can be assumed to be more critical to the company, while those locations delivering functions in the centre are less differentiated and more replaceable. Although Shih was giving his assessment on sources of greatest value from the perspective of the parent organisation, it is reasonable to conclude that the same activities maximise the value to subsidiaries, as they provide a source of greater security and investment. Employees should also benefit from their involvement in higher-value activities as these roles are likely to be better remunerated.

Shih's Smiley Curve has been found to be generally applicable across a range of industry sectors, and it continues to have credence today. Consider, for example, how Apple differentiates itself by designing innovative and desirable consumer electronics products, and by marketing and supporting these products in a unique way through its branding, advertising, retail stores, online presence and customer support structures. Much of the manufacturing and logistics that comprise the central part of Apple's supply chain are outsourced to third parties who are judged to have more competence in these areas. Therefore, any Apple subsidiaries that remain involved in these latter activities might justifiably feel less valued than those involved in R&D or marketing.

Academic studies that have confirmed the validity of the Smiley Curve across industries have also found that the depth of the curve can vary between sectors and over time.[7] When production technologies are improved, the outer ends of the smile are pulled up and the middle is driven down. This reflects the more knowledge-intensive orientation of process designs and the fact that production effectiveness is a function of the technology and standardisation, rather than the unique attributes of the production location. Specific locations are therefore perceived to be adding less incremental value in these cases. If production involves customisation that cannot be catered for through standardised procedures, then the middle of the curve will add more value, leading to a shallower profile.

I introduced the Smiley Curve to a workshop of subsidiary managers in 2019, intending that this should provoke some discussion and knowing that many of this group were involved in activities at the centre of the supply chain. There was indeed a reaction, with one of the participants taking strong issue with me for implying that functions such as those delivered by that subsidiary were not delivering value. Of course, this was not my intention, but I stood by the assertion that also in that industry, the activities at the start and end of the supply chain added more value. There will be exceptions to this, such as industries with highly specialised production processes that are dependent on specialised manufacturing technology or deep technical skills (e.g., medical devices and software product development). Nevertheless, the Smiley Curve remains a useful tool to provoke discussion on where the most value-add is delivered. For supply chain functions that are highly standardised, the curve provides a framework for considering whether there are opportunities to increase the subsidiary's value-add by extending up or down the supply chain. We will explore this further later in the chapter when we get to the question: *How can we get there?*

Extending the scope of the subsidiary's responsibilities across the parent's supply chain is just one way of increasing competitive advantage. The other possibility is to increase the impact of the subsidiary through additional scale in its operations. Increasing scale involves doing more of the same thing and getting a greater share of the pie. This can be attractive as increasing the size of the subsidiary's operations can bring economies of scale, as well as providing more career opportunities for employees and better opportunities for the subsidiary to develop increased depths of expertise. Also, with a greater share of the workload comes an increased dependence by the parent, and this can also make it more difficult to transfer workload elsewhere without the risk of operational disruption.

The scope and scale options described above relate to individual charters. However, as emphasised in Chapter 4, it must also be appreciated that the strength of the subsidiary can be a function of its portfolio of charters, including how these resonate with each other so that the whole is greater than the sum of the parts. The charter portfolio analysis that was facilitated through the framework in Figure 4.2 (Charter portfolio analysis) will have highlighted the potential for each existing charter and those that are in their formative stages. While this may have identified charters that have a questionable long-term outlook unless they become more aligned with the corporation's strategic objectives, this does not necessarily mean that they should be allowed to wither on the vine. They may provide valuable sources of skill development, network access or customer insight. However, the contribution that they can make to the overall subsidiary strategy needs to be evaluated so that their ability to support wider ambitions can be fully understood.

Selecting Capability Focus Areas

The capabilities to be nurtured by the strategy will obviously be influenced by the charter outlook. These should also deliver clarity of purpose in terms of where the subsidiary wants to focus its contributions to the parent, and what it wants to be famous for.

It is important to take stock of capabilities that may be eroding over time, as will have come apparent in the capability SWOT analysis (Figure 5.2). Remember that the strength of capabilities is also open to perception and is relative to perceptions of what is available elsewhere. The macro environmental analysis may have uncovered additional threats that may accelerate the erosion of capabilities or indeed increased the opportunity to develop and leverage existing capabilities even when these are relatively weak. Recognising where there is a need to move to higher ground in the capabilities offered can be an important plank of strategy.

For example, while researching this book, I interviewed a subsidiary manager who worked mainly from home, coordinating production activities that were previously executed in his local subsidiary but had since been transferred to Eastern European sites. This manager was satisfied with the senior level that was allocated to his role in the corporation. He did not see any disadvantage to him from no longer having production activities within the local subsidiary. He felt that his time was better spent using his professional management skills to coordinate other locations, rather than pointlessly defending local functions against the significantly lower labour costs that were available in Eastern Europe. This was a recognition of the reality of the macro environment in this case and an acceptance that in such circumstances subsidiaries in more developed countries must move to higher-value capabilities if they are to survive, even if this decreases local headcount. Effectively, this represented a shift to a higher stage of maturity in the Delany model of subsidiary evolution (see Figure 3.1). It was apparent that the manager in question felt secure as he was now acting in a quasi-headquarters (HQ) role. The independent oversight that this gave to HQ was a source of value to them. Even if the need for this capability is reduced, it would take some time for the newer subsidiaries to develop these skills.

This change in scope and scale appears to have been a necessary survival strategy for that local subsidiary, and one that secured the career options for this manager for the foreseeable future. However, it was not clear whether this helped the longer-term development of his subsidiary. When the capability is centred on the skills of individuals it can have limited strategic benefit unless it can be transformed into an organisational competence.

How Should We Position Our Strategy?

When a subsidiary leadership team reaches clarity on its general ambition and the focus areas that can be developed through strategic initiatives, there will be a need to seek wider support for this direction. External stakeholders and employees will need to be sufficiently motivated by the strategic aspirations if they are to support the allocation of resources and accept any associated risk. Although the ambition of a strategy may be exciting to those who were involved so far in its development, others may be suspicious of its intentions or pessimistic about its likelihood of success. Early resistance can lead to entrenched positions that can be difficult to reverse later.

It is therefore imperative to give some thought to how strategic aspirations should be positioned for this wider audience. Referring back to the Birkinshaw and Hood model (Figure 3.2), should the emphasis be on the opportunity for new charter acquisition as a way of contributing more value, on new capability development or on some combination of the two? This emphasises the distinction between positioning the proposed direction as primarily an *acquisition* strategy that is focused on targeting specific new markets or wider responsibilities, and a *competency development* strategy that may lead to the expansion of charters later.

Rita McGrath quotes from an interview with a CEO who characterised strategy as a straightforward process that is centred on "who are we serving, what problem are we solving, and what is our unique competitive advantage."[8] From the perspective of this CEO, strategy is not defined by a longer-term plan to grow the organisation or to acquire customers in new markets. It is about having a clear and ambitious sense of purpose, that will guide the organisation, and if fulfilled will attract more customers and result in continuing business success. This is a "build it and they will come" approach that is centred on a clarity of purpose which is more a statement of *who we want to be*, rather than *what we want to achieve*. In fast-changing markets, there is something to be said for focusing on what the organisation can do best for customers, on the assumption that this will give more assurance of success than becoming preoccupied with a specific strategic market opportunity.

A strategy that emphasises organisational capability development will often be more palatable to stakeholders than one that is explicit about charter development ambitions. The latter can be perceived as being territorial and even predatory. Publicly voicing such ambitions can make them a subject of private criticism elsewhere in the organisation. It can encourage accusations that the subsidiary is getting above its station and should "stick to its knitting" by focusing instead on current operational problems. There is also of course the risk that naming a charter acquisition objective will make it a target for others and a demotivator for employees if it is not quickly achieved.

Positioning the strategy as one of competency development does not mean that the subsidiary may not still have specific areas of increased responsibility in its sights. But in most cases, it will be more politically astute to put the communications emphasis on the developmental objectives, where these represent a clear statement of where the subsidiary intends to deliver maximum value to the parent.

Indeed, in some companies, it may be better to downplay the word *strategy* when referring to the subsidiary's ambitions, for fear that this raises questions about whether a subsidiary should have its own strategy and how this aligns with parent strategies. It may be more astute to use a term like *purpose* to put the emphasis on the desire to deliver capabilities that are of most value to the parent, now and in the future. Positioning the subsidiaries' ambitions in this way can provide a useful topic for discussion with stakeholders on their expectations, and it can help to achieve early buy-in from them to the subsidiary's desired direction. It may even lay some seeds with stakeholders on how the achievement of these capability ambitions could enable charter extensions.

What Will Success Look Like?

A traditional starting point for a company strategy is to define a vision, comprised of *BHAGs* (Big, Hairy, Audacious Goals) which capture the core ideology of the organisation and represent an envisioned future that is vivid and inspirational.[9] The intent is that such vision statements should motivate the organisation towards an ambitious future state, while providing clarity on the core purpose of the organisation. Vision statements should be *graphic* in their description, they should set a clear *direction*, they should establish *focus* for the organisation, the goals that the vision incorporates should be *feasible*, the achievement of these goals should be *desirable* to stakeholders and the vision should be *easy to communicate*.[10]

The process of setting vision statements has had mixed reviews over the years. When the concept was first developed, the recommendation was that such a statement should cover a 10-to-30-year horizon. This seems difficult to contemplate now given the unpredictability that has impacted markets in recent times. Some vision statements are effective in capturing the central purpose of the organisation, however ambitious this may seem at the time when the vision is set. Good examples of how such visions can inspire focus and purpose across an organisation are that of the Alzheimer's Association of America ("A world without Alzheimer's disease") and Microsoft's vision shortly after it was founded ("A computer on every desk in every home"). Other vision statements are arguably little more than aspirational marketing tag lines, such as that of Uber ("We ignite opportunity by setting the world in motion") and Disney ("To make people happy").

For some subsidiaries, it may be useful to develop a vision statement if the process of creating one brings the management team together with a cohesive sense of purpose that stretches the boundaries of what the organisation can ultimately aim to achieve. Such vision statements can also be useful for inspiring employees around the longer-term ambition. However, if a subsidiary vision is to be communicated within the organisation, it should of course be consistent with whatever corporate vision or strategy exists and it should be clear on how it supports that view of the future. This may be complicated if the subsidiary's charters are fulfilled on behalf of several corporate sponsors, who each have discrete longer-term ambitions. There may also be difficulties reconciling the strategic timeframe assumed in the corporate vision with the timeframe in which the subsidiary needs to achieve its own objectives. That all needs to be achieved while avoiding the common pitfalls in vision setting – such as making them so aspirational that they are unachievable, or so vague that they are meaningless.

So the feasibility and usefulness of developing and communicating a vision will vary from subsidiary to subsidiary. Even if the decision is made not to have an explicit vision statement, debate is still required on what the future should look like and what will determine success. Of course, this can be approached through open discussion, but there are also some methods that can be used to elicit ideas and ensure that all views are heard:

■ An exercise can be carried out in which each individual writes down an imaginary future headline about the subsidiary from the business pages of a national newspaper. This can generate some fun as each person shares their headline, but it can help to identify what should be the success criteria for any strategy (i.e., scale, scope, influence – or some combination of these).

■ An individual, or a sub-group of the team, can draft an aspirational case study of the subsidiary, imagining that it is looking back from the end of the strategic timeframe and charting how the story developed. Again, this can be written as a piece from the business section of a newspaper, or as a case study for an academic audience. An alternative is to write this from the point of view of the parent, such as a page from the corporate intranet as it may exist in the future, highlighting the subsidiary as a role model in its development and contribution to the corporation's success.

■ It can also be helpful to talk with supportive corporate stakeholders to get their inputs on the optimum future direction. Seeking the views of stakeholders can build affinity with them and secure early buy-in to strategic aspirations.

■ Imagining the likely visions of similar organisations can also provide a source of inspiration. These could be subsidiaries of competitor companies in the region, or peer subsidiaries within the corporation.

■ For subsidiary managers who prefer a more structured approach, agreeing on answers to a set of specific future-oriented questions can draw out the characteristics of a desired future state. Questions should include the following (it may be helpful to reproduce these on a template that can first be completed privately by team members before opening this up for discussion):
  – If we have no externally imposed limitations, what could be our future scale, scope and influence?
  – What words should characterise our future culture?
  – What do we want to be famous for within the corporation?
  – What do we want to be famous for in the market?
  – What can we reasonably achieve in this timeframe?
  – How can we take these reasonable achievement objectives to the next level?

Irrespective of whether or not a formal vision statement is developed, the subsidiary strategy should be founded on a clearly articulated ambition that is shared across the leadership team, who buy-in to its aspirations and have been involved in its construction. The focus of this ambition can be the development of an identity within the corporation (i.e., a clear sense of purpose, supported by capabilities that offer sustained competitive advantage), or a drive to earn increased responsibility and influence. It is also useful to relate this back to the Birkinshaw and Hood model to clarify its focus on charters and/or capabilities and to the Delany model to gauge how it may advance the maturity levels of individual charters.

How Can We Get There?

Irrespective of how a vision is derived and expressed, this is only useful if it creates an impetus for action. It is usually recommended that this is achieved through a sequence of thought processes that flesh out how the vision will be delivered.

- **Vision directs Mission:** Firstly, the long-term vision should enable clarity on the *Mission* for the organisation. There is often confusion on the overlaps between the mission and the vision, but fundamentally the vision should set out the long-term aspiration, whereas the mission should specify the focus areas in which the organisation will concentrate its efforts to get there. For example, Tesla's vision statement sets the aspirational goal to "accelerate the world's transition to sustainable energy." The company's mission statement clarifies that it will concentrate on electric car production as its focus for achieving this vision: "To create the most compelling car company of the 21st century by driving the world's transition to electric vehicles."[11] The vision provides motivation, the mission provides focus. Given the difficulties inherent in establishing a vision statement for a subsidiary, it may be that the mission statement stands alone, but it should at least be guided by a clear longer-term ambition.
- **Mission defines Goals:** If the focus areas of the organisation are clearly defined in a mission statement, short- and long-term *Goals* can be set to achieve this mission. Goals should be timebound and the criteria for their achievement should be clear (e.g., "To be recognised by HQ as the leading internal provider of [a specific competence] by [a specific date])."

- **Goals dictate Actions:** The *Actions* required to achieve each goal should be listed. Actions should be SMART (Specific, Measurable, Assignable, Realistic, Time-bound).[12]
- **Execution should conform with Values:** The *Values* of the subsidiary should sit as an umbrella over the Vision, Mission, Goals and Actions. These values define the culture and ethos of the organisation. They are likely to be largely inherited from the corporate culture of the parent, although they may have some specific nuances or emphasis that differentiates the subsidiary in areas where local management has autonomy (e.g., an innovation culture).

Laying out the mission, goals, actions and values in this way is likely to require some depth of thinking on the route that is required to work towards the subsidiary's ambition, including some exploration of alternative pathways. It may only be feasible to develop a broad outline of the goals and actions at this point, as so much will depend on the ability of the subsidiary to exert influence over stakeholders. This will be the subject of the next chapter. When this is considered, it will probably lead to some iterations of goal setting and action planning.

This model, linking vision to mission, goals and actions, while keeping organisational values in mind, implies a very logical relationship between setting an ambition and executing the necessary strategies to deliver this ambition. However, often the pathway is not so linear. Multiple phases may be required, with beachheads established at each before the next steps can be plotted. That is, it may be necessary to pursue the goals and actions in stages, while keeping the vision, mission and values in sight, but under constant review. This is consistent with the implication of Delany's stages of subsidiary evolution that it is difficult to skip steps, and if the ambition is to achieve a higher evolutionary stage, the path through the interim stages should be planned.

An alternative perspective on the tactics used to acquire higher levels of value-add responsibility within a supply chain network was uncovered through a study of the mobile handset industry published in 2008.[13] This study used the Smiley Curve (remember Figure 7.3) as a lens for investigating the dynamics of how the responsibilities of different locations in the chain can develop as they *catch up* with other locations, or when responsibilities *spill over* when a site can no longer handle the demands placed on it.

The catch-up tactic is used by locations involved in the lower value-add activities to observe what is being done at either end of the curve and work to internalise these competencies. Such initiatives are not only seen in established corporate structures, where ambitious subsidiaries at the centre of the curve acquire the skills that will earn them more responsibility (i.e., like route 2 in the Birkinshaw and Hood model – Figure 3.2 – where subsidiary-driven capability development ultimately leads to charter extension).

Spill-over is a much more opportunistic phenomenon, whereby subsidiaries develop relationships with higher value-adding partners, and over time take on work to assist them when they are under pressure. This is a Trojan Horse tactic designed to enable competency and reputational development that will position the subsidiary for a more formal allocation of responsibility when the time is right.

Catch-up and spill-over tactics may be necessary to bridge the gap between where the subsidiary is now and where it would like to be. These do not happen by accident, and they require specific planning, supported by interim goals and actions which will work the subsidiary towards its desired future positioning.

Box 10 summarises how the HETSol Support Labs team translated their analysis to date into a future strategy for the subsidiary. This conclusion illustrates how in this example, the team made the leap from the preceding detailed diagnosis to a consolidated strategic vision, mission, goals, actions and values. In their case, the vision statement is largely for internal use within the management team. They considered the mission statement to be more suitable for discussion with stakeholders. Its focus on how the subsidiary intends to maximise its value-add was considered less provocative and more likely to secure support. The strategy generally focuses on innovation and customer advocacy as these are areas where the HETSol Support Labs team considered themselves to be uniquely positioned to add value. They see the opportunity to build on the insights that they can gain into future customer needs from their existing technical support and pre-sales support responsibilities. The strategy taps into a conclusion of the diagnostic phase that HETSol has become somewhat complacent in its offerings development and has not fully appreciated the changing needs of customers. HETSol Support Labs aims to add value by becoming a customer champion, but also by developing new university partnerships that will contribute to the need for innovation. It intends to secure financial support from government agencies to offset the investment needed in allocating resources to these new initiatives. The strategy involves some choices, and particularly the recognition that it may be necessary to sacrifice the Product Testing charter to free resources for new responsibilities that require deeper technical skills. Current thinking is that some of this responsibility could be offloaded to the new Bulgarian site as a way of developing a closer operational relationship that may prove valuable later. This will also demonstrate collaboration, teamwork and leadership that should be appreciated by HQ.

BOX 10
HETSOL SUPPORT LABS
SUMMARY OF STRATEGIC DIRECTION

VISION

HETSol Support Labs will be recognised as the European hub for the highest value-adding functions in the company.

MISSION

To deliver the highest levels of value-add to HETSol and our customers through a culture of collaboration, teamwork, innovation and customer advocacy.

GOALS

To work towards the vision, a number of major steps are required:

1. **Socialise and validate**: This step involves the influencing of key internal and external stakeholders to support the intended direction, while also remaining open to their input. The opportunity for government grant-aid in support of an innovation and growth agenda should be assessed, including an understanding of the obligations that this would entail. The potential for a research partnership with the local university should also be investigated. The input and buy-in to this general direction should then be sought from members of the Corporate Senior VP team.
2. **Establish the foundations of an innovation and customer advocacy culture**: Engagement with employee groups on the intended direction should begin, including communication on the expectation that each team member should contribute to innovation and customer advocacy. Forums to ensure focus on these areas should be established as part of HETSol Support Labs' governance processes. Initial ideas should be captured and prioritised.

3. **Allocate resources**: Specific innovation and customer advocacy projects should be agreed and commissioned. These may be funded through a combination of local resource allocations, contributions from corporate sponsors and government grant-aid. Potential targets for these projects include: (1) New digital solutions for customer engagement; (2) Research on new online course-delivery solutions; and (3) Research into new student assessment solutions. A steady move towards increasingly technically oriented roles should be maintained (i.e., SW Engineering, Sales Support and Analytics). Shifts away from Product Testing responsibilities may be necessary to free up skills for new roles. In this case, a closer partnership with the Bulgarian site should be developed, including supporting them in absorbing some of these spill-overs.

ACTIONS

The initial action plan covers the upcoming 90-day period and is focused on the *Socialise and Validate* phase. It includes specific responsibilities and timeframes for engaging with government agencies, university partners and corporate sponsors. Some preparatory activities in support of the later stages are also included.

VALUES

Throughout the execution of this strategy, HETSol Support Labs will remain committed to the values of innovation, customer advocacy, employee engagement and cross-organisational partnership.

What Support Are We Looking For, and When?

Few subsidiary strategy initiatives can ever be fully realised without some form of support from outside the organisation. This may only be in the form of tacit support or acquiescence from stakeholders, if they are satisfied that the initiative can be pursued without diverting attention away from the achievement of core objectives. However, at some point, more tangible commitment may be required from the corporation, or at least there may be a need for an agreement that the subsidiary can use existing budget allocations as the source for any required investment.

Therefore, a critical part of crystallising the strategy is to identify what external supports are needed, and when these will be needed. Associated with any financial support is the risk that the investment will not achieve the expected returns, or worse that the initiative may have unforeseen consequences. This point was clearly articulated to me by Brian Hayes – a highly experienced subsidiary leader and executive mentor. He described subsidiary strategy execution as a triangle, with the objectives at the top, and with capital and risk at the other two points. Capital needs must be quantified, and risks must be clearly identified so that stakeholders have confidence that all requirements and possibilities have been considered. Ideally, the resilience of capital should also be assessed, in terms of its adequacy to cover unforeseen issues and the duration over which it will be required. Risks should not only be identified, but the actions needed to mitigate these risks should be planned. Allowing for these actions, any residual risks should also be realistically identified.

A considered assessment of what is required from outside to enable the execution of the strategy should identify these needs for support, capital investment and risk acceptance. This should also clarify the timing of when this kind of support should be sought – both in terms of when it will be needed to enable action, but also when may be the optimum time to make such requests of stakeholders.

Summary

A downside of completing a very thorough diagnosis phase is that it often results in a volume of considerations that can seem unwieldy when attempting to draw conclusions on the optimum future direction. Even though the various frameworks provided in Part II enable some degree of filtering (e.g., by highlighting weaknesses that are irreparable, strengths that do not provide a sustained competitive advantage or macro environmental factors that can be ignored), it is still necessary to bring all of the remaining considerations together into a manageable format, to step back, to edit these down further and to make the leap from this to a cohesive set of strategy statements. There is no formulaic way of bridging directly from diagnosis to strategic solutions. The diagnosis activities can be seen as "beating the bushes" to ensure that all considerations are uncovered, but the translation of this into a strategic direction requires more creative and wholistic thinking.

The process of making this leap is helped by developing an ambitious but achievable vision, a mission statement providing clarity of purpose by indicating where the organisation will focus to achieve the vision, goals that outline the steps that will be undertaken and the actions needed to deliver the initial goals. Several iterations of this process may be necessary.

It is unlikely that goals and actions can be successfully orchestrated by subsidiary managers acting autonomously. Therefore, a degree of external support will typically be needed – specifically, in relation to capital investment and risk acceptance. Thoughtful planning is needed on how to achieve stakeholder support and how to influence decision-making in this regard. This is the subject of our next chapter.

Notes

1. Rumelt, *Good Strategy, Bad Strategy: The Difference and Why It Matters*, p. 7.
2. J. Lonergan, "Address to Social Care Conference" (Institute of Technology, Tralee, 2006).
3. Henry Mintzberg and J. Waters, "Of Strategies: Deliberate and Emergent," *Management Journal* 6, no. 3 (1985).
4. Rumelt, *Good Strategy, Bad Strategy: The Difference and Why It Matters*, p. 71, 169.
5. Ibid., p. 20, 64.
6. Stan Shih, *Me-Too Is Not My Style: Challenge Difficulties, Break through Bottlenecks, Create Values* (Taipei: The Acer Group, 1996).
7. Ram Mudambi, "Location, Control and Innovation in Knowledge-Intensive Industries," *Journal of Economic Geography* 8, no. 5 (2008).
8. McGrath, *Seeing around Corners: How to Spot Inflection Points in Business before They Happen*, p. 174.
9. James C. Collins and Jerry I. Porras, "Building Your Company's Vision," *Harvard Business Review* Sept–Oct (1996).
10. A. Thompson, A.J. Strickland III, and J.E. Gamble, *Crafting and Executing Strategy*, 16th ed. (New York: McGraw-Hill, 2010), p. 22.
11. Thomas J. Law, "17 Seriously Inspiring Mission and Vision Statement Examples," *Oberlo*, https://ie.oberlo.com/blog/inspiring-mission-vision-statement-examples#:~:text=Mission%20statement%3A%20We%20strive%20to,might%20want%20to%20buy%20online.
12. G.T. Doran, "There's a S.M.A.R.T. Way to Write Management Goals and Objectives," *Management Review* 70, no. 11 (1981).
13. Mudambi, "Location, Control and Innovation in Knowledge-Intensive Industries."

Chapter 8

Exerting Influence

For subsidiaries that are well established within their parent's network the routes to be followed in socialising and seeking support for a strategy may already appear clear. However, some caution is advised as relationships that have worked well on operational matters may not be sufficient sources of support for more ambitious agendas. While leveraging existing relationships to secure broader support will be a worthwhile tactic, it is important to think more deeply than this so that existing sources of support can be directed to where they can be of most help, and so that the need for additional allies can be analysed with a view to nurturing their support. Clearly, this will be even more important for a less established subsidiary, or especially one that is the result of an acquisition and does not have experience in navigating the complexities of the parent's decision-making processes.

There are several factors to consider when planning how to exert the required level of influence to secure support for the strategy (or at least for its first steps). All organisations will be subject to some degree of internal *politics*, so it is important to reflect on the more obvious political influences, but also those that may operate in the shadows. Good strategies harness *power* and apply it to where it will have the most effect,[1] so it is worthwhile to analyse the existing power of the subsidiary and other sources of power that can be channelled to desired ends, or which may present sources of resistance. It is also important not to under-estimate

DOI: 10.4324/9781003425502-11

the importance of building *trust* as a foundation on which the subsidiary can earn autonomy and give assurances that stakeholder expectations will be fulfilled. The *decision-making* processes and cultures that operate across the parent's network also merit some explicit analysis so that the sequences of decisions required and the influences that will apply to these decisions can be planned. There should also be some reflection on the *behaviours* that will be acceptable (e.g., Scout or Subversive), including those that may be necessary but will involve some risk. Lastly, but most importantly, a definitive approach to *stakeholder management* is required so that there is stewardship of most supportive stakeholders and management of those that may be less supportive or even hostile to the direction of the subsidiary strategy.

These factors are each explored in the following sections.

Politics

In their book detailing how companies can promote the incubation and development of entrepreneurial opportunities within their organisations, Block and MacMillan emphasise that the promoters of new ideas must carefully manage internal politics as "ignoring politics is tantamount to passively accepting its results."[2] Subsidiary managers should recognise that the internal market of a corporation does not follow normal market rules where the winners are usually those with superior resources and offerings. Rather, they operate as a hierarchy of power, or a network of decision-makers, where a subsidiary may be favoured even when it does not possess the strongest capabilities – other than its ability to influence internal politics.[3] This emphasises the criticality of developing clear political strategies, designed to encourage influencers to behave in ways that they may not otherwise choose.

Managing internal politics involves gathering information, lobbying, developing personal relationships and positioning to take advantage of emerging opportunities. This is made more challenging in a world where business travel is restricted, and online meetings are preferred. There is no substitute for walking the corridors of headquarters (HQ), having side-discussions at meetings and socialising with colleagues from sponsoring organisations or peer sites. Hosting visiting executives is also a very effective tactic in building relationships and gaining insights into how these executives think.

Where these visits include meetings with front-line employees, this can help to build affinity with the personality of the subsidiary, as well as giving value to the visitors in the form of front-line operational and customer insights.

Where possible, there is also great value to be gained from sending managers on extended assignments to HQ or other influential sites. Although this can be expensive, the developmental benefits to the manager in question, coupled with the relationships and sources of intelligence that this can develop, usually make it very worthwhile. Success will hinge on selecting a candidate who has the professional skills to represent the subsidiary in a favourable light, the social skills required to develop useful networks and the developmental potential to bring this value back to the subsidiary on return. Ensuring that the assignment is to a suitable role where the assignee can develop, and ideally exert influence, is also desirable.

All the above will help to build social capital that generates political intelligence and can be drawn upon when support is needed. But as well as developing sources of positive influence, the management of internal politics also requires the identification of potential sources of resistance and actions to pre-empt this resistance. Political blockers can be in the form of public opposition, reservations voiced through back-channels or just inertia that causes ideas to wither and die. Reasons for inertia or resistance can include distraction due to other business pressures, fear of competition with existing offerings, fear of cannibalisation of existing markets or threats to the existing power positions enjoyed by some.[4]

Developing a considered assessment of the political terrain within which influence must be exerted is therefore an important prerequisite to strategy execution. Figure 8.1 provides a template that can assist in doing this. The template can be used to consider the subsidiary strategy as a whole – assuming that it is a very cohesive one. If the strategy has several dimensions, it may be necessary to consider each of its major objectives separately. The initial question to be formulated is "*What* objective [embedded in the strategy] may invoke political positions?" This forces some reflection on areas where the subsidiary may be perceived as stepping outside the boundaries of its current remit, and where this might draw some overt or hidden reaction within the network. If the strategic objective in question is likely to instigate a reaction, it is important to assess "*Why* this position will be adopted?" and specifically why it may invoke

What objective may invoke the adoption of political positions?			

	RESAONS FOR SUPPORT	REASONS FOR AMBIVALENCE	REASONS FOR RESISTANCE
Why will positions be adopted?			

	SOURCES OF SUPPORT	AMBIVALENT or UNKNOWN	SOURCES OF RESISTANCE
Who will adopt these positions?			

	MEANS OF SUPPORT	AMBIVALENT or UNKNOWN	MEANS OF RESISTANCE
How will positions be expressed? — PUBLICLY			
PRIVATELY			

Figure 8.1   Mapping the political terrain

supportive, ambivalent or resistant reactions. This should force some contemplation on how the objective will be perceived outside the subsidiary – either consciously or subconsciously. The following question is *"Who will adopt these positions?"* whether they be driven by supportive, ambivalent or resistant reasoning. It may be unclear at this point what position a known stakeholder may take, in which case this should also be recorded for clarification or influencing later. Lastly, it is worth considering *"How will positions be expressed?"* and particularly whether this will happen publicly through a governance process or privately through back-channels (or both).

Subsidiary leaders who are new to strategy formulation may find it difficult to accurately complete a template such as this. Existing information on stakeholder positions may be limited, and many may still be open to influence. However, going through the thought process that is reflected in the template should reveal how much is known about the political terrain and where more intelligence must be gathered. Fundamentally, this is intended to provide input to stakeholder management as covered later in the chapter.

Continuing our fictitious example for HETSol Support Labs, Box 11 shows the initial mapping of the political terrain completed by that team.

BOX 11
HETSOL SUPPORT LABS
MAPPING THE POLITICAL TERRAIN

What objective may invoke the adoption of political positions?	To deliver the highest levels of value-add to HETSol and our customers through a culture of collaboration, teamwork, innovation and customer advocacy.		

	RESAONS FOR SUPPORT	REASONS FOR AMBIVALENCE	REASONS FOR RESISTANCE
Why will positions be adopted?	Ambitious and customer-focused.	Big deal – shouldn't you be doing that anyway?	SVP of Cust Support has responsibility for advocacy. Adding value is not a subject for internal competition.

	SOURCES OF SUPPORT	AMBIVALENT or UNKNOWN	SOURCES OF RESISTANCE
Who will adopt these positions?	SVP of Product Development.	SVP of Customer Support. SVP of Fee-earning Services. Corporate CFO. North American sister sites	SVP of Sales & Marketing. European sister sites.

		MEANS OF SUPPORT	AMBIVALENT or UNKNOWN	MEANS OF RESISTANCE
How will positions be expressed?	PUBLICLY	Corporate planning cycle concurrence.	Resist reassignment of skills.	Corporate planning cycle non-concurrence.
	PRIVATELY	Back-channels to CEO. Back-channels to CFO	Ambivalence to investment requests.	Back-channels to CEO. Back-channels to CFO

Notes:

This analysis of the political landscape highlighted that the strategy may face some sources of veiled or even outright resistance. The extent of any such reservations, and indeed the degree to which assumed sources of support may be relied upon, are not fully known at this point. Some preparing of the ground is needed to tease-out current feelings and to begin to influence opinions so that the political landscape is better understood.

A particular concern is that it is currently unknown what position that will be adopted by the senior vice president (SVP) of Customer Support in relation to the HETSol Support Labs strategic objective to be a leader in customer advocacy. There is a danger that this will be perceived as encroaching on that SVP's sphere of responsibility, or even a criticism of how this role has been carried out to date. A negative initial reaction from this individual could stall the initiative indefinitely. Assessing and influencing this position will require careful management, as will contacts with other executive stakeholders.

It also appears likely that the SVP of Sales and Marketing may adopt a negative position as this may threaten their traditional position as the focal point for current and future customer needs. There may be a specific concern that the focus on innovation in the mission statement implies the need for updates to existing offerings. This SVP may also be fearful that this emphasis by a subsidiary is a sign of it acting "above its station" and could lead to suggestions on new offerings that have the potential to erode current revenue streams.

A further key conclusion of this analysis is that the HETSol Support Labs management team has a limited understanding of the corporate annual planning process and any associated politics. A deeper understanding must be developed. More clarity is also required in the strategy on what level of investment will be sought through the planning process to enable its implementation.

Power

Fundamentally, power can be thought about as the ability to get another to do something that they would not otherwise do.[5] Even in the most authoritarian corporate cultures, there will be some level of free will and ability to resist instruction. To be effective, the exertion of power must be reciprocated by a willingness to comply with an instruction. Therefore, for our purposes, we can consider power and influence to be largely the same thing, albeit that they imply different methods of encouragement.

When we think of power in corporations, it is normal to think of it as a function of the position of an individual within the organisational hierarchy. That is, an individual can exert power based on the authority that the corporation has formally assigned to them, either through their position on an organisation chart or their role as an approver within decision-making or other governance processes. This is what is known as *legitimate* power which is formally allocated and recognised based on seniority within the hierarchy. However, there are several other ways in which individuals can earn and exert power:

■ *Expert* power can be earned by individuals who have a level of technical knowledge that is respected and relied upon when making critical decisions.

■ Individuals can also attract power through their *Personality*, particularly where this is charismatic, or a respected source of integrity.

■ Personal traits can also be manifest as *Coercive* power, where individuals use their intellect and force of personality to harass others to give a desired response.

■ Power based on the control of access to *Rewards* – such as promotions, salary increases or discretionary awards – can be exerted by HR or compensation committee members.

■ Some individuals will have *Informational* power if they control access to data or processes.

■ Others may use *Connection* power if they do not have formal positions of power themselves, but they are positioned to influence decision-makers, or if they are gatekeepers who control who is allowed time with these key individuals.

■ For completeness, we should not exclude *Physical* power. Even if companies should take strong action against instances where physical attributes are used to intimidate or attract a desired response, such practices still exist.

All the above are examples of individual power and the most proficient power practitioners use combinations of these skills when exerting influence up, down and across the organisation (hopefully, except for physical power).

For any subsidiary, it is useful to ponder on which individuals in the network have power and which sources of power they draw upon (i.e., Legitimate, Expert, Personality, Coercive, Rewards, Informational, Connection or Physical). It is also useful to make a mental inventory of the power of individuals within the subsidiary's own team, for example, based on their expertise, charisma and network connections. Some of these sources may be relatively immature, pointing to opportunities to develop them further as resources for exerting power and influence going forward.

When analysing sources of power and how to use them in corporations, it is also important to consider the power balances between different sub-unit entities and not just at an individual level. For example, what is the balance of power between HQ and a specific subsidiary, between a subsidiary and a supplier or between two peer subsidiaries? Each of these entities may be influencers or stakeholders, and encouragement may be needed at an inter-organisational level to secure their support. Therefore, the power dynamics between organisational entities also require attention.

Richard Emerson's early writings on *power–dependence relations* provide a useful structure for viewing these inter-organisational power relationships.[6] He pointed out that power is best viewed as a property of the relationship between two entities, and not as an attribute of either of them. That is, an organisational entity or an individual can be powerful in one setting (e.g., in the office) but not very powerful in another (e.g., at home). The difference in an individual's or an organisational entity's power is therefore a function of the nature of the relationship, and not an attribute of either of the entities engaged in that relationship.

Therefore, if we are assessing our own power or that of a third party, we cannot assume that this is a constant. It will vary by context and will be a function of the factors that govern the relationship and how these change over time. To understand power, we need to analyse the nature of this dynamic, recognising that relationships are founded on mutual dependency between the parties.

Emerson proposed that the power balance in a relationship is directly related to the level of mutual dependence that exists between the two parties. He also defined dependence as a function of two characteristics:

1. The strength of the *Need* that each party has for whatever the other provides through the relationship.
2. The availability of *Alternatives*. That is, are other sources of this support available from elsewhere or can they be substituted with an alternative form of support?

In simple terms, if one party has a high need for whatever the other provides and has few alternatives to satisfy this need, then they have a high dependency and are therefore in a low power position relative to the other. If the other party has low needs for whatever the first party provides and has access to other sources of support, then they are in a high relative power position. This is an unbalanced power–dependence relationship where the second party holds all the cards over the first.

Figure 8.2 presents a grid that can be used to map the power–dependence relationship between two parties. Two example relationships are included in the figure for illustration:

■ In the example relationship between A and B, A has moderate needs for what B provides but has a high number of alternatives. B has moderate needs for A but has few alternatives. This could be a case of a

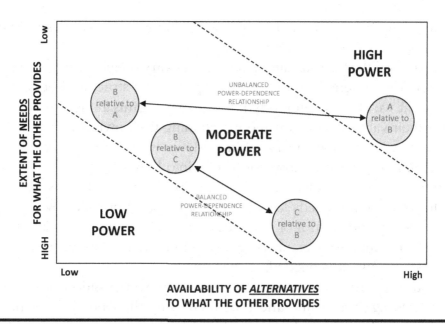

Figure 8.2   Mapping power–dependence relationships

parent organisation (i.e., A) using a range of subsidiaries to deliver a key service. The subsidiary (i.e., B) needs support from A and has limited other options for maintaining its critical mass. The arrow between the two circles shows this to be an unbalanced relationship in favour of A, who can exert more power over B. This arrow can be thought of as a vector – comprising a *force* indicating how stridently the power is exerted and a *direction* indicating how it is expected to change the balance of the relationship over time.

■ In the second example, B has moderate needs for C and a few alternatives. C has higher needs for B but also has more alternatives. This could be an example where one subsidiary (i.e., C) is providing secondary services to a peer subsidiary in the fulfilment of a critical offering. If the supports provided by C are no longer required in this relationship, then there is a market for them elsewhere. The primary subsidiary (i.e., B) has high need for these support services but can also source them from elsewhere. In this case, each party has moderate power–dependence over the other and this is a balanced relationship.

This is not to suggest that it is always desirable to have balanced power–dependence relationships. Clearly, most organisations would prefer to have relationships where the power is in their favour. Figure 8.2 merely provides a template to facilitate a critical assessment of where the power lies in important relationships, and why it is this way.

Like all good theoretical frameworks, Emerson's breakdown of the features of power–dependence relationships provides a structured perspective on what we already intuitively know – that organisations will jockey to increase their value to others while maintaining their own access to alternative sources of support in case of breakdown in current relationships. However, it also gives an important insight into how entities may seek to change the balance of power in a relationship. The most obvious way to do this is to decrease the needs for what the other party provides by gaining more autonomy and control of resources. This can be coupled with efforts to access alternative sources of sponsorship in case the current relationship does not deliver what is needed.

The other approach is to shift the relative power position of the other party by adding more value and thus increasing their needs for what the relationship provides. As we explored in the previous chapter, the value delivered is related to its uniqueness as a contributor to the differentiation of the company's offerings in the marketplace. However, in the context of power–dependence positions, research has also found that subsidiaries involved in activities that have the most immediate and severe impacts on end products are in more powerful positions.[7] For example, this research suggests that a subsidiary controlling critical finishing processes on products that require urgent delivery to customers (i.e., high immediacy and severe impact of failures) will have more power than upstream manufacturing activities, which will still be critical to the production process but will have less power as the process allows more time to rectify errors. This can be viewed as another manifestation of the Smiley Curve, where proximity to the customer gives additional value and power.

The other contributor to the power–dependence position of the other party is their access to alternatives. This can potentially be altered by negating the influence of competitors through political or other out-manoeuvring actions. Ultimately, alternatives can be reduced by making their offerings redundant or by bringing them under one's own control.

The grid provided in Figure 8.2 can be used as a tool to plot how the needs and alternatives of either party can be influenced to shift the dynamic of the power–dependence relationship. That is, additional arrows can be drawn to show actions designed to alter the needs and alternatives for either party.

For more complex corporate environments, the grid can also be used to gain a more in-depth understanding of the network of power relationships between the subsidiary's stakeholders and their sponsors. For example, in a HQ–subsidiary context, the HQ may appear to have a high level of power over the subsidiary. However, even HQ is dependent on customers, so if the subsidiary can increase the dependencies that customers have on its services, this can enable it to gain more power than could be expected based solely on needs and alternatives that apply directly between HQ and the subsidiary. In other words, becoming embedded in customer, or even supplier processes, can allow the leveraging of customer dependencies to the extent that this can alter the dynamics of the HQ–subsidiary relationship.[8]

Trust

Although politics and power are realities that require an evaluation and attentive management, it is also fair to say that they both have manipulative undertones – assumed to be aimed at orchestrating events in one's own favour. Our focus on these topics in the previous sections implies that large organisations will usually have a highly suspicious and controlling culture where collaborative behaviours are on the surface and not always supported by attitudes held in the background. Although there may be some truth to this impression, it is an unfair general representative of the mindset in most firms, where people are driven by their interpretation of what is best for the parent and for customers. In successful corporations, behaviours are largely motivated by the trust that people will fulfil commitments and do the right thing. Earning and maintaining trust is fundamental to achieving respect and exerting influence.

Trust can be defined as an indicator of the confidence that the other party will operate in good faith in endeavouring to fulfil expectations in a predictable manner.[9] In a trustful relationship, both parties allow themselves to become dependent on the other, and both assume that the other will not exploit their vulnerabilities.[10] At a more practical level, formal agreements such as Memoranda of Understanding cannot cater for all eventualities so there needs to be trust that there will be flexibility when faced with unforeseen events. This is particularly important for globally distributed operations, so there is trust that dispersed teams will be driven by a singularity of purpose, and that shared objectives will overcome differences between sub-units due to geography or cultural distances.[11]

Trust is developed through repeated contacts (*experience-based trust*), through calculations that it is also in the other's interest to demonstrate that they are reliable (*logic-based trust*) or through the norms that operate in a generally trustworthy system of contacts (*culture-based trust*). Trust can exist between individuals or between organisational entities. It is built through consistency of behaviour, adherence to contractual agreements and displays of competence, as well as through personal characteristics such as loyalty, concern, benevolence, goodwill, honesty, integrity and openness.[12]

Trust and power are linked, since personal sources of power such as expert, personality, connection and informational power will only have an effect if the other party trusts that these will deliver what is expected. Failures can significantly dent the belief that such sources of power are real. Also, in terms of Emerson's power–dependence theory, perceptions about the level of dependence of one organisation on another will only be maintained if the other can be trusted to deliver the expected benefits flowing from that dependence.

The level of trust between HQ and a subsidiary can also dictate the extent of delegated authority that will be granted and whether this is temporarily or permanently allocated. Various academic studies have found distinctions between responsibilities that are delegated to the subsidiary to act as an agent on behalf of a HQ function (referred to as *loaned* responsibilities), and those that are more clearly defined as part of the ongoing mandate of the subsidiary (*owned* responsibilities).[13] Trust between HQ and the subsidiary is fundamental to whether these functions will be loaned or owned. Several studies have also proved the intuitive hypothesis that higher levels of trust and embeddedness of the subsidiary in the HQ organisation will lead to increased levels of autonomy being afforded to the subsidiary as HQ managers gain confidence that their trust will be rewarded.[14] In other words, the investment of resources to get close to HQ and to build an open relationship results in a more hands-off management style later.

So, in corporations – like in life – a reputation for trustworthiness is very valuable and perceptions of untrustworthiness can be very damaging. The groundwork involved in nurturing trust is therefore a critical investment in building influence that can be drawn upon in times of need. Like a bucket of water that is filled drip-by-drip, trust can take a long time to grow, but if it is disrupted it can wash-away in an instant. Therefore, trust levels that are built-up should be protected and any perceptions that the subsidiary has breached its trust should be quickly addressed. This further emphasises why it is critical throughout the process of pursuing a strategy to continue to deliver operational results and to fulfil commitments so that the subsidiary maintains a reputation for trustworthiness.

Decision-Making

The ways in which decisions are made vary between organisations. Some are very clearly defined through governance processes, with matrices defining levels of concurrence required for different considerations that contribute to a final decision (e.g., financial, operational and legal). Levels of investment authority may also be set based on seniority. Some organisations have less well-defined decision processes, while most have a pragmatic hybrid of formality and flexibility, with some level of lobbying outside the formal decision governance processes. When seeking support within corporate structures, it is important to fully understand the decision-making processes that must be influenced. Researching these processes will be particularly important for early-stage subsidiaries and those that are the result of acquisitions into a corporation.

However, the first question is the more fundamental one of what decisions are required. It may be possible to fulfil some initial elements of the strategy using locally controlled resources, within the scope of existing mandates (even if the boundaries of these mandates must be loosely interpreted). There may be cases where it will be more expedient to ask for forgiveness later, rather than permission now. In other cases, the first steps may simply involve socialising ideas as a means of testing-the-water, and not looking for firm decisions in case these are not favourable and may be irreversible. However, ultimately at some point, a formal position of support will be needed, not only to secure investment but also to gain a seal of approval for the direction so that this becomes a recognised element of the subsidiary's charter. Being clear on what is being asked for is key, as well as ensuring that the groundwork has been done before the decision arises so that a favourable response can be expected. As a colleague of mine was fond of saying: "Never ask a question for which you don't know the answer."

Figure 8.3 provides a model of decision-making styles, adapted for a subsidiary context.[15] The model proposes that two main drivers of decision-making in corporations are (a) whether loyalty to corporate objectives is expected over the objectives of individual divisions of the company, or vice versa, and (b) whether decision-making power is a function of position within the organisational hierarchy, or alternatively whether a range of

	Power is Diffuse	Power is Concentrated
Corporate Loyalty trumps Divisional Loyalty	RULE-BASED DECISIONS	CORPORATE EXECUTIVE DECISIONS
Divisional Loyalty trumps Corporate Loyalty	COLLABORATIVE & NEGOTIATED DECISIONS	DIVISIONAL EXECUTIVE DECISIONS

Figure 8.3   Matrix of decision-making styles (adapted from Sibbet, 2010)

individuals are expected to contribute to decisions based on their expertise and functional areas of responsibility. Where corporate objectives are given priority over divisional agendas, and power is concentrated, corporate executives will be the decision-makers. When corporate objectives have priority and power is more diffuse, a rules-based approach to decision-making is more likely, incorporating indicators that must be achieved under various headings to earn concurrence from different stakeholders. In more diverse corporations where priority is given to divisional loyalty, if power is concentrated, then divisional managers will be in the driving seat. Where divisions require consideration of different agendas, some rules may apply, but the process is likely to be more collaborative and involve negotiation.

Recognising which of these styles, or which combination of them, applies to a decision being sought can help in the navigation of the decision-making process. Even where power is concentrated in executives for final decision-making, they are likely to seek the input of advisors, so key influencers should be identified and consulted. Rules-based decision-making processes may seem attractive as they provide clarity on the criteria that must be met. However, often rules will be risk-averse and will not lend themselves to speculative decisions, particularly when there are general resource constraints in force.

Collaborative and negotiated decision-making processes are more resource intensive. They can also be frustrating if representatives of many different functions have the authority to stall a decision by non-concurring (e.g., Finance, Business Controls, Operations and Customer Service). These functions can often have little to gain from an initiative, but they run the risk that this will come back to haunt them if they agree to something that creates problems later. In an increasingly networked and co-dependent environment, navigating this terrain requires some dexterity if everyone is to be brought on-board. In his book exploring how the increased connectivity and inter-dependencies resulting from globalisation have led to new global risks, Mark Leonard argues that managing the network has become a critical skill. Although he develops this for a geopolitical context, many of the sub-skills that he identifies can also apply in corporate networks where the emphasis is on collaborative decision-making. These include the active management of inter-dependencies, the identification of gatekeepers, gathering data, becoming embedded in related organisations, understanding rules and maximising autonomy.[16]

While plotting a way through the decision-making process may be tortuous in some cases, it is also important to recognise when the end point has been reached. In governance processes with formal approval mechanisms, this may be obvious. However, in other cases, a final push may be required to get a decision over the line and to make this stick. Sales experts sometimes refer to this as the *assumptive close*, where the customer is on the verge of a positive decision but has not explicitly confirmed this. A good salesperson will take the next step for the customer by using language that assumes their agreement and by moving the conversation on to implementation. Sometimes in corporate decision-making, the skill of using an assumptive close will also be required, although some emotional intelligence will be needed to avoid the approving party feeling that they are being manipulated. If the assumption holds, then it is best to stop making the case as to why this is the right decision, for fear that it will unravel – or to quote another hardened salesperson "when the sale is made, stop selling."

Behaviours

In Chapter 3, Scout and Subversive behaviours were introduced. These alternatives merit a reprise here as building and exerting influence to achieve a strategic end requires active behaviours. Choices can be made on the nature of the behaviours that will be most effective but still acceptable. Behaviours can be designed to build support within a network, to penetrate the network as a means of gaining more insights and influence or to seek approval for the next steps. The behaviours adopted in pursuing actions should take account of internal politics, should recognise the distribution of power, should be careful not to erode trust and should be targeted at encouraging favourable decisions.

When studying for my executive Master's degree I adopted an action-learning process to develop strategies appropriate to the business environment in which we found ourselves at that time. My interest was in how our small IBM subsidiary could improve its positioning within a very large software product division of the company. The identification of Scout versus Subversive behaviours was helpful to me and my IBM colleagues in showing that we had some alternatives in how we chose to act. However, I concluded that considering this as a binary choice was too simplistic. This did not reflect all factors that should dictate how to behave and these extreme ends of the spectrum did not cover all behavioural alternatives. I developed a more nuanced behavioural model based on the culture in that part of IBM at the time.[17] An adaptation of this, also taking account of what I have observed in the meantime, is shown in Figure 8.4.

The model is in two parts, based on the conclusion that there may be circumstances where the subsidiary is already strong enough not to require significant strategic action, or alternatively it may not be at a stage of maturity where such action will be credible. In the first instance, the model suggests that the factors to be considered are the subsidiary's maturity level, coupled with its ability to influence decision-making. If the subsidiary is already at a

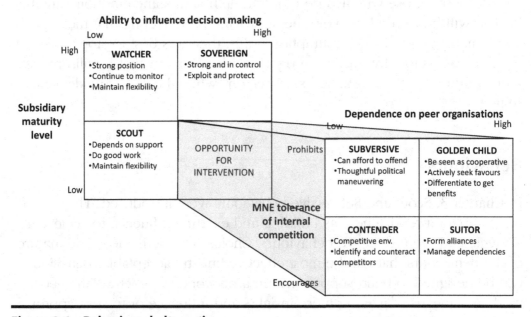

Figure 8.4   Behavioural alternatives

very mature level (as in Delany's model) and has high influence over decisions, it is in a very commanding position, where it can act like a *Sovereign*. If it is very mature but still only has limited control over decisions due to how authority is allocated by the multinational enterprise (MNE), then it is in a strong position but must carefully monitor the situation and continue to influence decisions that impact upon it (i.e., a *Watcher*). If the subsidiary is not sufficiently mature to credibly champion a strategic agenda, and if it is not yet in a position where it can actively influence decisions, then the only option may simply be to follow orders and wait for better opportunities to come its way (i.e., a *Scout*).

If the subsidiary is seeking a higher level of maturity and sees the opportunity to influence decisions, then the model identifies four further behavioural options. In the internal environment that existed when the original version of the model was developed, two factors were at play. Firstly, there was sensitivity at a corporate level to the circumstances in which visible competition between subsidiaries would be tolerated. During its most successful years, IBM faced limited competition in its markets so it often encouraged the internal development of competing products to cater for different needs in the market and to ensure that product teams would not become complacent. In more recent years, the political in-fighting that resulted from this was recognised as being dysfunctional so there was an increased expectation of cross-site collaboration. Therefore, it was important to take account of how any action deemed to be internally competitive would be judged. The second factor was the level of operational dependency that existed between peer subsidiaries. This is to reflect the observation that where sites require each other's support to fulfil their commitments there will be a greater sensitivity to upsetting another by being judged to be pursuing selfish political actions. Such perceptions could lead to a reticence by one subsidiary to providing support to another.

The combination of these two factors leads to the other behavioural options identified in this model. If competition is not tolerated and there is low dependence on other sites, then covert actions can be taken to pursue one's own agenda – as long as this does not raise objections from HQ (i.e., a *Subversive*). If the MNE tolerates internal competition, then the actions can be more visible and aggressive (i.e., a *Contender*). If dependence on other sites is higher and competition is prohibited, the subsidiary will have to work even harder to differentiate itself in a more active way than just being a passive Scout (i.e., a *Golden Child*). If competition is tolerated by HQ and there is high inter-dependence between subsidiaries, it may be necessary to form alliances, aimed at moving to a stronger competitive position while remaining close to other sites on which there are dependencies (i.e., a *Suitor*).

The factors that influenced this model were applicable in one corporate environment (i.e., IBM) at one point in time. They may not be relevant to your environment. However, the model is included here to make the point that there are other possible behaviours on the spectrum between Scout and Subversive. Some of the behavioural types shown in this model may be appropriate in your case – even if they are driven by different factors that exist in your environment.

It is also reasonable to assume that different behaviours can be adopted at different times, although this should be done consciously and with awareness of the potential consequences.

Stakeholder Management

The topics covered in each of the previous sections will ultimately inform how stakeholders should be managed. An assessment of the internal political terrain will help to identify stakeholders and encourage reflection on their likely priorities and positions relative to the intended direction. The power balance between the subsidiary and each stakeholder – and between stakeholders and their own immediate network – will influence the tactics that are advisable in managing stakeholders. Maintaining stakeholder trust will clearly be critical throughout. The behaviours that will be most effective and deemed acceptable by stakeholders should also be considered. Also, the decisions that are required of stakeholders, the optimum timing for requesting these decisions and the tactics needed to navigate decision-making processes all require thoughtful planning.

It is important not to focus only on stakeholders within the management hierarchy. It has long been acknowledged that organisational stakeholders include all "individuals, groups, and other organisations who have an interest in the actions of an organisation and who have the ability to influence."[18] Therefore, a broad view of stakeholders should be adopted, including employees and any representative groups they may have, internal and external customers, suppliers, peer organisations within the MNE network, government bodies and any other external alliances.

Stakeholders have the potential to provide active support to the organisation, but they can also have the potential to threaten its plans. This potential is a function of their power in the organisation coupled with their level of interest in taking a position either way. Some may have more potential to threaten than to support, some may be the opposite, some may have little real potential to influence plans and others may be able to threaten and support. These combinations lead to four categories of stakeholder, each of which requires a different management approach:[19]

- *Mixed Blessing* stakeholders have a high potential to threaten and a high potential to support. Efforts should be made to *collaborate* with them to secure their buy-in.
- *Supportive* stakeholders have the potential to support, but less potential to threaten. Actions should be taken to *involve* them where possible.
- *Non-supportive* stakeholders have the potential to threaten but without much ability or inclination to offer active support. Actions should be taken to *defend* against them.
- *Marginal* stakeholders have a low ability to threaten or support. The most appropriate management approach in this case is to continue to *monitor* them.

Mixed Blessing and Supportive stakeholders should be communicated with and nurtured to develop high levels of trust. In some cases, it may be enough just to ensure that they have no objections, without the need for their active support or championing of an initiative. However, in other cases specific interventions may be needed from them and inertia can become a problem. To counter this, it is important to be very clear on an initiative's critical short- and long-term objectives and to keep re-enforcing these messages. Predicting obstacles and being ready with answers on how these can be overcome will also reassure stakeholders that any potential pitfalls can be avoided.[20] It may also be useful to think about the decision-making styles of key stakeholders, and whether they are more inclined to respond to logic (based on data analysis, goals, consideration of alternatives), to process adherence (investment rules, existing processes, business controls) or to political considerations (how others will view it, what pushbacks there may be, consequences of failure).[21]

This focus on building coalitions of support is of course critical, but an equivalent level of attention should be given to the potential sources of resistance. Resistance can be in the form of active lobbying against a proposal, the withholding of necessary resources or non-concurrence in collective decision-making processes. When objections are publicly voiced, a logical reason will have to be given to justify this position. It is important to anticipate these arguments and to try to placate the objector in advance, or to be ready with counterarguments that can be made directly or fed to supporters.

For subsidiaries operating in very complex internal networks, it may be helpful to complete a structured mapping of stakeholders to reach a consensus on who they are, the extent to which they are positioned to support or threaten the subsidiary's desired direction, how they should be categorised and managed and their current level of support or resistance (if known). Figure 8.5 provides a template that can be used for this purpose. For each stakeholder listed, it is also suggested in the template that a primary contact point within the management team be identified to own that relationship. This does not mean that this individual is the only contact point with the stakeholder, but it ensures that someone is thinking about the range of contacts with that individual so that messaging is consistent and regular. This also ensures that one person on the management team feels responsible for understanding the overall disposition of the stakeholder and the reasons why they are adopting this position. Actions to further develop the stakeholder relationship can also be recorded on the template.

Box 12 shows how stakeholder mapping was completed by the HETSol Support Labs management team, while taking into consideration all their previous analysis.

STAKEHOLDER	POTENTIAL TO SUPPORT 1=Low; 5=High; 0=Unknown	POTENTIAL TO THREATEN 1=Low; 5=High; 0=Unknown)	STAKEHOLDER TYPE / APPROACH	CURRENT POSITION 1=Resistant; 5=Supportive; 0=Unknown	RELATIONSHIP OWNER	PLANNED ACTIONS

Figure 8.5   Stakeholder management planning

BOX 12
HETSOL SUPPORT LABS
STAKEHOLDER MAPPING

STAKEHOLDER	POTENTIAL TO SUPPORT 1=Low; 5=High; 0=Unknown	POTENTIAL TO THREATEN 1=Low; 5=High; 0=Unknown)	STAKEHOLDER TYPE / APPROACH	CURRENT POSITION 1=Resistant; 5=Supportive; 0=Unknown	RELATIONSHIP OWNER	PLANNED ACTIONS
SVP Product Development	4	4	Mixed blessing: Collaborate	4	DM	Visit HQ to socialize the direction, confirm support
SVP Cust Support	4	4	Mixed blessing: Collaborate	0	MM	Develop positive rationale from Cust Service perspective.
SVP Fee earning Services	0	0	Unknown	0	FK	Suggest visit to HETSol Support Labs to develop relationship
Corporate CFO	2	5	Non-supportive: Defend	0	PE	Develop financial case. Research the annual planning process.
SVP of Sales & Marketing	4	4	Mixed blessing: Collaborate	0	FH	Develop Sales benefits of proposition. Solicit input from SVP of Prod Dev't on how to engage.
North American sister sites	2	2	Marginal: Monitor	0	BJ	Schedule tour of NA sites as a learning process
European sister sites	2	4	Non-supportive: Defend	2	PB	Schedule tour of sites to
Employees	5	5	Mixed blessing: Collaborate	5	MB	Convene employee discussion forums
Local university	4	2	Supportive: Involve	0	JK	Begin discussions on opportunities to collaborate
Government agency	4	2	Supportive: Involve	4	JG	Plan workshop to investigate opportunities for support

Notes:

In the first phase of the strategy, the emphasis is on socialising ideas, seeking input and developing relationships with key stakeholders. The stakeholder mapping exercise recognises that the position that a number of the stakeholders may take is not fully known. A delicate process must be undertaken to gather information while not yet being ready to present firm plans – except to some stakeholders where there is strong likelihood of support.

Through this stakeholder mapping exercise ownership has been assigned for each relationship and initial actions are identified. Many of the internally focused actions recommend travel to HQ and other sites, as well as invitations to executives to visit the HETSol Support Labs site. These are intended to build relationships. The visits can be positioned as learning exercises, with the added intention of beginning the conversation on where more value can be added in collaboration with other sites.

The exercise also recommends interaction with employees through the establishment of new discussion forums between senior management and front-line staff. The intention is to encourage involvement in the innovation and customer advocacy dimensions of the strategy.

Outreach contacts are also recommended to the government agency responsible for encouraging foreign direct investment (FDI) so that opportunities for grant aid or other supports can be investigated. It is also recommended that the opportunity for a more established relationship with the local university should be explored. This may provide a valuable research capability to allow the development of some of the ideas that have emerged on the use of digital libraries, blockchain and other new technologies to complement existing offerings for assisted learning and to allow more robust online student assessment.

Summary

The landscape to be considered when seeking to exert influence is multidimensional, involving issues of politics, power, trust, behaviours and decision-making processes – all of which ultimately guide how stakeholders should be managed. None of these factors are constants, as political forces change, power shifts, trust builds or declines etc. Therefore, this is more a process of maintaining environmental awareness than one of making immutable assessments that hold true over extended periods.

That said, for subsidiaries that have not previously spread their wings within their internal markets, it is worthwhile to invest time in purposefully thinking about each of these dimensions to build an initial base of awareness. The templates and examples that are provided in this chapter are designed to help subsidiary managers to unpick these issues and to encourage them to ask questions that will help to reveal how they apply in their case.

As always, the relevance of the templates will vary between environments. Some will resonate; some may not. However, often the value of this kind of reflection is in realising what you don't know as much as what you think you know. Affording time to consider each dimension is worthwhile before starting a journey that requires the exertion of influence. The old maxim attributed to Benjamin Franklin is very relevant in this case: "Failing to prepare is preparing to fail."

Notes

1. Rumelt, *Good Strategy, Bad Strategy: The Difference and Why It Matters*, p. 95.
2. Block and MacMillan, *Corporate Venturing: Creating New Businesses within the Firm*, p. 283.

3. C. Dörrenbächer and J. Gammelgaard, "Subsidiary Role Development: The Effect of Micro-Political Headquarters–Subsidiary Negotiations on the Product, Market and Value-Added Scope of Foreign-Owned Subsidiaries," *Journal of International Management* 12, no. 3 (2006).

4. Block and MacMillan, *Corporate Venturing: Creating New Businesses within the Firm*, p. 288.

5. R.A. Dahl, "The Concept of Power," *Behavioral Science* 2 (1957).

6. Richard M. Emerson, "Power-Dependence Relations," *American Sociological Review* 27, no. 1 (1962).

7. David J. Hickson et al., "A Strategic Contingencies' Theory of Interorganizational Power," *Administrative Science Quarterly* 16, no. 2 (1971).

8. C.A. Bartlett and S. Ghoshal, *Transnational Management: Text, Cases, and Readings in Cross-Border Management* (Irwin, 1992).

9. Peter Smith Ring and Andrew H. Van De Ven, "Structuring Cooperative Relationships between Organizations," *Strategic Management Journal* 13, no. 7 (1992).

10. Jurian Edelenbos and Jasper Eshuis, "The Interplay between Trust and Control in Governance Processes: A Conceptual and Empirical Investigation," *Administration & Society* 44, no. 6 (2012).

11. Alaka N. Rao, "Understanding the Role of Power Distance in Global Outsourcing Relationships," *International Management Review* 9, no. 1 (2013).

12. Paul S. Adler, "Market, Hierarchy and Trust: The Knowledge Economy and the Future of Capitalism," *Organization Science* 12, no. 2 (2001).

13. Alvaro Cuervo-Cazurra, Ram Mudambi, and Torben Pedersen, "Subsidiary Power: Loaned or Owned? The Lenses of Agency Theory and Resource Dependence Theory," *Global Strategy Journal* (2019).

14. Ambos, Asakawa, and Ambos, "A Dynamic Perspective on Subsidiary Autonomy."

15. David Sibbet, *Visual Meetings*, ed. Grove Consultants International (Hoboken, NJ: John Wiley & Sons, 2010), p. 205.

16. Mark Leonard, *The Age of Unpeace: How Connectivity Causes Conflict* (London: Bantam Press, 2021), p. 139–41.

17. Paul Lyons, "Unpublished Thesis Submission for Masters Degree in Management Practice," (Trinity College Dublin and Irish Management Institute, 1995).

18. Grant T. Savage et al., "Strategies for Assessing and Managing Organizational Stakeholders," *Academy of Management Executive* 5, no. 2 (1991): 61.

19. Ibid., p. 65.

20. Block and MacMillan, *Corporate Venturing: Creating New Businesses within the Firm*, pp. 295–305.

21. G. Allison, *Essence of Decision* (Boston: Little, Brown, 1971).

Chapter 9

Managing the Change Within

The topics covered in the previous chapter are largely concerned with exerting influence outside the organisational boundaries of the subsidiary. This is obviously crucial, but there is a risk of seeing the problem only as one where the capabilities of the subsidiary are underappreciated and where the focus is solely on encouraging others to see where it can add more value. This would miss the point that as well as reaching outwards to build support for the subsidiary's ambitions, the organisation must also look inwards to realise where it must change if it is to fulfil the promise that it can add more value.

This chapter focuses on the change management that is required within the subsidiary to deliver on the strategy. This requires reflection on where we need to get to, where we are today, what needs to change and how this change should be managed.

An internet search using the term "change management" will result in a high volume of books, articles, podcasts and offers of consultancy support on the subject. It is not possible to do full justice to the topic here, especially as so much will depend on the environment within which the subsidiary operates and the nature of the change that is required. Therefore, the intent of this short chapter is merely to raise awareness of the need for

DOI: 10.4324/9781003425502-12

active change management and to suggest some ways in which this can be approached.

Readers who want to delve deeper into the subject can refer to books such as those in the endnotes that have stood the test of time to earn their place as definitive guides to managing organisational change.[1,2] Much of this body of work approaches the topic from the point of view of large corporations requiring major transformational change programmes to reshape and reposition their offerings and their organisations. The insights provided can also be useful to smaller organisations that require transformational change. Other contributions approach change management more from a line-manageable perspective and recommend practical steps to drive business unit change and to secure buy-in as you do so.[3,4] Some notable contributions to the literature specifically focus on change that is driven from outside the organisation and how to cope with this.[5] These provide important learnings on how to deal with enforced change (such as those imposed by the COVID-19 pandemic), especially where this involves a *burning platform* that puts a time pressure on the need for change and focuses minds on the need to transition to a new world.

Whatever the scale, nature and drivers of change that are in force, leadership is required to avoid the reality that 70% of change management programmes fail to achieve all that they set out to achieve.[6] To encourage subsidiary leaders to think about the change required in their organisations and how this may be managed, three subsections make up the remainder of this chapter. First, we consider the question of what needs to change. A deep reflection on the real requirements for change will avoid us addressing the symptoms, but not the causes of why change is needed. Second, a summary of change management processes is provided, with reference to some of the most well-regarded contributions from the literature. We then discuss the governance processes required to monitor progress and keep the programme on track while remaining flexible to changes in the surrounding environment.

Change What?

In Chapter 7, we considered ways of analysing what success might look like, including the development of vision and mission statements. The ambitions represented in these statements can be considered the *desired future state* of the organisation. This can be fleshed out under a number of headings to provide a clearer articulation of what this future might look like. A classic approach to identifying what needs to change is to define the *current state* of the organisation under the same headings, and then to list the gaps between current and future states that need to be addressed.

Changes can be classified as those that are economic (e.g., costs per unit, employee retention levels and budgets) or those that are organisational (e.g., culture, skill levels and employee morale).[7] Most change programmes will involve a balance of economic and organisational elements but with a primary emphasis on one or the other.

Whatever category that is associated with a particular change, there can be a tendency to express it in operational terms so that it can be benchmarked and quantified. For example, the need to improve business performance can be expressed in key performance indicators (KPIs), or the need to improve capability can be expressed in quantifications of skill levels and employee survey results. This comes naturally to managers who are driven by the mindset that you can't change what you can't measure. It reflects a propensity to regard all changes as *technical* changes, which can be approached by applying existing constructs for viewing problems and existing management know-how to fix them.

However, these are measurements of outputs, and they may mask where real change can only be achieved by winning the hearts and minds of individuals throughout the organisation – encouraging them to get involved or to alter their ways. This is *adaptive* change, which is more difficult to orchestrate, usually requires more time, but is also more lasting. Framing a change as one that is technical is the natural inclination for executives who are used to taking ownership of issues and solving them through the existing management system. Realising that an adaptive change is needed presents more challenges, as it involves transferring the ownership of problems to others who must change their behaviours. Approaching a change only from a technical perspective – by focusing solely on KPIs, process improvements, etc. – can be attractive and can show some promising short-term results. However, this will ultimately be unsuccessful if the real need is for adaptive change, including the groundwork needed to address the fundamental causes of problems.[8]

BOX 13
HETSOL SUPPORT LABS
CHANGE MANAGEMENT GAP ANALYSIS

Vision: HETSol Support Labs will be recognized as the European hub for the highest value-adding functions in the company.
Mission: To deliver the highest value-add to HETSol and to our customers through a culture of collaboration, teamwork, innovation, and customer advocacy.

INDICATORS	CURRENT STATE	DESIRED FUTURE STATE
PEOPLE:		
- New employee attraction	Competitive but undifferentiated	"Employer of choice" in sector
- Existing employee retention	10% staff turnover p.a.	<5% turnover p.a.
- Skill development	Training plans set by managers	Employee ownership
- Employee involvement	Managers drive improvements	Employees drive improvements
PROCESS:		
- Operational results	KPI averages consistent with other sites	All KPI results in 4th quartile
- Cost vs value equation	Seen as increasingly expensive	Seen as excellent value
- Customer insight	Limited analysis of customer feedback	Experts on customer feedback & needs
- Innovation	Patchy across the organisation	Embedded throughout the organisation
TECHNOLOGY:		
- Toolkits	Outdated / Delivered by HQ functions	State of the art / driven by needs
- Staff training systems	Adequate, but stretched	Exemplar across HETSol Corp.

Notes:

The changes required are grouped under the headings of People, Process and Technology. The indictors that dictate the shape of the current state and the desired future state are listed in each case.

Under a number of these headings, it is clear that technical changes are needed to improve the results that are currently being achieved. In some cases, this will require a more diligent focus on KPIs and improvement plans monitored through the operational management system. These include all performance indicators that are reported externally. More robust tracking of other indicators, such as attrition levels, reasons for attrition and labour market reputation, is also required. New indicators should also be developed to cover trends in customer feedback and skill development.

Other dimensions of the desired future state are more difficult to quantify and will require adaptive change. Specifically, change efforts are needed to encourage higher levels of employee involvement, including personal ownership for skill development, innovation and the proactive identification of customers' issues. These changes will require the organisation to do a better job of winning employee trust by demonstrating a commitment to these objectives. New employee forums should be established to encourage a culture of innovation and customer advocacy. More robust budgets for employee training are needed, while resisting the tendency to cut these when faced with budget challenges. Management must also grow more responsive to feedback on the inadequacy of toolkits used by employees in the course of their work. Senior management should monitor progress in all of these areas, with the assistance of external reviews where required to ensure that messages are not diluted.

To illustrate how gap analysis between current and future states may be completed, including the identification of technical and adaptive changes, Box 13 shows how this was done by the HETSol Support Labs leadership team.

The Change Process

In his book *Leading Change* and in his subsequent consultancy work, John Kotter provides one of the most often-quoted theories on what is required to deliver enduring change.[9] He identifies eight steps:

1. **Create a sense of urgency**: The vision should be bold, clear and aspirational, to the extent that it will inspire passion, purpose and urgency.
2. **Build a guiding coalition**: There should be a shared purpose by people who want to be involved in designing the vision and guiding the organisation towards its achievement. Members of the guiding coalition should feel like champions for the aspiration, and they should be capable of motivating others by communicating its benefits.
3. **Form a strategic vision**: As we have seen, the vision should show how the future will be different and it should signpost the areas that need to change.
4. **Enlist a volunteer army**: Large-scale change requires the involvement of many people who are committed to the cause and prepared to contribute their efforts to its achievement.
5. **Enable action by removing barriers**: Anything that will slow progress should be identified and roadblocks should be removed so that

people feel empowered to act more flexibly, to innovate and to drive impacts more quickly.

6. **Generate short-term wins**: Early wins increase momentum, give confidence and create an increased sense of involvement in something that feels worthwhile.

7. **Sustain acceleration**: Don't let up. Change programmes require that you stay-the-course, do not skip steps and continually learn from progress and setbacks.

8. **Institutionalise change**: Constantly remind people how new behaviours have resulted in organisational successes, until these behaviours are institutionalised and replace old habits. Make changes stick by ensuring that management practices and monitoring systems reinforce these new ways of working.

The first three of these steps (i.e., create a sense of urgency; build a guiding coalition; form a strategic vision) have been addressed in our strategy formulation discussions so far. As the focus of Kotter's work is on large-scale pan-organisational change, it is understandable that the subsequent steps have an emphasis on maintaining widespread buy-in from within the organisation to sustain lasting behavioural change. However, these steps merit some further consideration in a subsidiary context.

In the world of corporate-wide change management, the leadership team controls all the initiatives and can dictate the pace. The need to move on from the vision and involve the wider organisation in its implementation is self-evident in this case. But, for subsidiaries that are dependent on others for support (or acquiescence) and allocation of resources, a more measured approach may be needed. For example, it will be unwise to march on to the fourth step (i.e., enlist a volunteer army) until the support of key stakeholders is assured. This suggests that in the world of subsidiaries, there is a need for an interim step between steps 3 and 4 to solicit stakeholder support. Even when the time is right to extend the change programme beyond this initial group, it is important to remember in the subsequent steps that continuing support is needed from a broad church. When removing barriers, celebrating wins, maintaining momentum and institutionalising new behaviours, it is equally important to involve the organisation and its stakeholders.

Even if the main players and the subsidiary organisation generally appear to be on-board with the change process, there can still be resistance.[10] Change leaders need to engage with sources of resistance, but they also need to be able to step away from the fray so they can see the bigger

picture without allowing emotion to cloud their judgment. Objectively understanding the reasons for resistance, and addressing these causes, is more
effective than responding to the symptoms.

Resistance often comes from the side-lines, with naysayers questioning
the motivation or pointing out how similar initiatives have been tried and
failed before. It can be helpful to identify influential opinion-formers within
staff groups and to ensure that they are on-board. Ultimately, involving those
with reservations rather than marginalising them is often most successful. If
the change programme is built on a well-thought-out foundation that is good
for the corporation, its customers, the subsidiary and its employees, there
should be no fear of flushing-out objections and dealing with these head-
on. Therefore, change leaders should actively court sources of resistance, so
they understand criticisms and deal with them. Sharing the burden, promoting empowerment and expecting ownership are usually more effective than
ignoring objectors and hoping they will go away.

The pressures of driving change while continuing to deliver on day-to-
day operational requirements can also lead to tension and disagreement
within the leadership team. The subsidiary leader will need to deal with this
by finding compromises and potentially creating spaces where it is acceptable to have disagreements without these being seen as a sign of breakdown
in teamwork.

Governance

It should not be underestimated that as well as leading the change process
necessary to support the subsidiary strategy, managers will still be expected
to give their primary focus to the "day job" of delivering their charters. In
some cases, the drive for strategic improvement can be integrated seamlessly into daily operations, but this can be especially difficult for longer
term adaptive changes. Where subsidiaries are comprised of a collection of
disparate charters reporting into different parts of a corporation and without
much local operational synergy, relying mostly on existing management systems to drive strategic change usually fails. There is also the challenge that
delivering the strategy generally requires a blend of internal change management and external influencing, both of which risk being overwhelmed by
day-to-day operational challenges unless they receive special attention.

For these reasons, it is advisable to create a separate governance process to oversee the strategy implementation. As well as monitoring internal

change, this process can cover the initiatives taken to promote the strategy in the broader corporate environment. For more complex strategy programmes, it may be necessary to appoint a dedicated programme manager. This individual should manage the overall change plan by identifying dependencies, tracking progress on actions and bringing issues to the attention of management. This should not allow managers to abdicate their own responsibility to drive the programme or to avoid their responsibility to deliver actions assigned to them. But it is important to be realistic when there is a need for dedicated resources to maintain momentum with the strategy process. The programme manager should have sufficient heft to hold managers to account for the completion of their actions, and to call out when they are remiss or are shirking their responsibility. This individual should also have a direct line to the subsidiary leader, who must be prepared to support them and to protect them from peer pressure. It may even be advisable to bring someone in from outside the organisation to fulfil this task. As well as ensuring that the role is properly resourced and not assigned to someone who already has a busy job, using an outside programme manager can help to ensure that internal politics or career concerns do not get in the way.

It is best to schedule dedicated meetings to ensure regular tracking of progress. If this is not feasible, then a separate agenda item at an existing meeting can work, but this creates a big danger that the strategic initiatives will become an afterthought that struggles to get airtime in the face of the "crisis du-jour." A separate governance process to oversee the strategic change process is highly preferable.

A proper governance process for change management should include:

- Terms of reference indicating the objectives of the forum, any linkages to other forums and its decision-making authority.
- A schedule of meetings with stipulations on the requirement for a quorum and the level of delegated representation allowed if the primary invitee is not available.
- Rolling documentation on key agreements, actions, owners of actions and deadlines.
- Progress indicators expressed where possible as KPIs with long-term and interim targets. In the most developed instances, these can include current indicators (status as currently measured), lagging indicators (previous trends that have led to current performance) and leading indicators (factors that may be important in the future, or signals indicating how current indicators may develop).[11]

Importantly, any such governance forum should allow space for general discussion and sharing of information. Particularly in disparate subsidiaries, it is critical to maintain openness and understanding of the pressures that each sub-unit is facing. Contacts with stakeholders, customers and employees should be maintained and inputs from these sources should continue to be fed into the discussion. This also helps to keep the process vibrant, while remembering that strategy-making is an iterative and evolving process where it is important to remain open to adjustment when needed.

Summary

The creativity that was invested in developing a subsidiary strategy and planning how to secure stakeholder support will all be in vain if energy levels are not maintained through the implementation phase. There will be very few cases where the strategy will only require lobbying to win charter extensions, without commensurate improvements to capabilities. Especially where there are dependencies on stakeholders, it will be easier to get support if the emphasis is on capability and value-add improvements. This requires internal change, supported by the potentially energy-sapping task of driving this change through the organisation. Therefore, the emphasis of this chapter has been on the change within – to stress the point that expecting others to see the potential of the subsidiary in a new light should be coupled with a recognition that local improvement is also needed.

Change management is the process of translating the strategy from a paper exercise to one that is embedded in the subsidiary's ways of working. Hopefully, the vision of a desired future state will be sufficient to sustain this transition. This vision can be translated into a more granular analysis of the features that will manifest that desired future state, and a realistic assessment of the current state under these headings. The gaps between these states will spotlight where actions to drive change are needed.

The change process involves motivating stakeholders and the local team around the ambition, overcoming barriers, celebrating wins, demonstrating persistence and learning from experience. The drumbeat of the change management governance system should keep the organisation in-step and marching towards its objectives. It will be necessary to constantly repeat core messages until they become part of the core fabric of the organisation.

It is often helpful to give an identity to the change strategy by coming up with a tagline that captures its essence and by investing a little in branding, communications materials and even merchandise. However, it is important to be realistic that such branding will have a limited lifespan before it looks tired and something else will then be needed to support the next phase of the strategy. There is also a danger here that management may think that a promotional campaign is doing the job for them and that they do not need to reinforce messages and demonstrate commitment through their actions. If, like me, you have seen examples of this, you will know that it does not fool employees who will recognise it as all form and little substance. This will just re-enforce cynical views that run totally counter to the trust and buy-in that are the foundations of a successful change programme.

Notes

1. John P. Kotter, *Leading Change* (Boston, MA: Harvard Business Review Press, 2012).
2. John Hayes, *The Theory and Practice of Change Management*, 6th ed. (London: MacMillan International and Red Globe Press, 2022).
3. Richard Smith et al., *The Effective Change Manager's Handbook: Essential Guide to the Change Management Body of Knowledge* (London, New York, New Delhi: Kogan Page Ltd, 2015).
4. William Bridges and Susan Bridges, *Managing Transitions: Making the Most of Change*, 4th ed. (London and Boston: Nicholas Brealey Publishing, 2017).
5. John Kotter and Holger Rathgeber, *Our Iceberg Is Melting: Changing and Succeeding under Any Conditions* (New York: Portfolio/Penguin, 2017).
6. Michael Beer and Nohria Nitin, "Cracking the Code of Change," *Harvard Business Review*, no. May–June 2000 (2000).
7. Ibid.
8. Ronald A. Heifetz and Marty Linsky, "A Survival Guide for Leaders," June 2002 (2002).
9. J. Kotter, "The 8 Steps for Leading Change," https://www.kotterinc.com/methodology/8-steps/.
10. Heifetz and Linsky, "A Survival Guide for Leaders."
11. McGrath, *Seeing around Corners: How to Spot Inflection Points in Business before They Happen*, pp. 44–47.

Chapter 10

Parental Responsibilities

The focus throughout this book is on how subsidiary leaders should analyse their environment and plot a course to develop their strategy. While this
assumes that the subsidiary is acting on its own initiative, it is also important
to give some attention to what support and encouragement can be expected
from the parent organisation. That is, what role (if any) should headquarters
(HQ) play in fuelling and lubricating the internal network to empower subsidiaries to fulfil their potential as value contributors to the corporation?

Some early writings on multinational enterprise (MNE) strategy recommended that HQ should seek to add value to individual businesses by
making vital strategic decisions, by offering a range of high-quality services
to support remote operations, by establishing useful connections between
business units where these did not already exist and by executing merg-
ers, acquisitions and divestments to continually fine-tune the network.[1] This
perspective remains valid, even if it views the MNE as a conglomerate with
tentacles into a diverse set of industry sectors that operate under different conditions. Under more contemporary MNE operational models – with
high levels of intra-organisational integration, fine-slicing and hybrid sourcing strategies – more should be expected of HQ to facilitate the controlled
operation of the network.

In the remainder of this chapter, five responsibilities for HQ managers are
recommended to create a terrain on which subsidiaries can maximise their
contributions:

1. Ensure clear definitions of the boundaries of responsibility between
   sub-units;

2. Find a balance between delegating responsibility to counter the "head-quarters knows best" syndrome, and avoiding the abdication of oversight responsibility;

3. Develop sourcing strategies that clearly differentiate between activities suitable for execution by internal business units or third parties;

4. Encourage and facilitate business units, but take strong corrective action when any are seen to prioritise their selfish objectives over the wider needs of the corporation; and

5. Ensure that clear governance processes are in place to maintain lines of communication while ensuring proactive support and control across the network.

In the final part of this chapter, we step back to consider what the future might hold in relation to the nature of work and how this might influence the further development of subsidiaries. Parent organisations also have a responsibility to all stakeholders, including their subsidiaries, to consider emerging trends and the consequences of these for investment decisions.

Define Boundaries

Clear boundaries should be established so that subsidiaries and third parties understand any limitations imposed on how they should fulfil their mandates and contribute to corporate strategy. This involves defining the scope of activities that should be executed centrally and those that may be regionally oriented. For example, the organisational guidelines that have proved most effective in companies adopting a primarily *Global* (as distinct from *Multidomestic*) strategy include the following:[2]

■ Primary activities of the company, such as manufacturing, distribution and sales, can be dispersed geographically across a selected number of sites. Where these primary activities are executed to a superior level by a regional subsidiary, these units may earn responsibility for a global or cross-regional mandate for the activity.

■ Support functions such as R&D, Finance and HR should be assigned to single locations and delivered as shared services.

■ There should be an emphasis on efficiency-seeking, by standardising processes and products and keeping local variations to a minimum. This requires clear communication on standards and governance mechanisms to ensure that these are enforced. This should not stifle debate on where truly unique local variations are needed, although implementation of any such variations should be supported by their own business cases.

■ Mandates should be clearly articulated and commonly understood, creating less reliance on managing duplication. However, there remains an emphasis on the need for flexibility by managers in response to unforeseen events.

At the other end of the spectrum, where the organisational emphasis is on catering for the particular needs of each individual market (i.e., a *Multidomestic* approach), the boundaries will more likely include stipulations such as:

■ HQ retains responsibility for defining general strategy in relation to offerings and market participation.

■ Subsidiaries are authorised to identify changes to offerings that respond to specific local needs. This should include the development of business cases to justify investments in any changes to offerings.

■ Subsidiaries have sign-off on the launch, marketing and promotional activities for offerings in their local market.

■ Subsidiaries also act as approvers for policy matters in areas such as Human Resources, to verify compliance with local laws and cultures.

■ HQ monitors subsidiary performance and retains the right to request audits and mediation plans if results for a particular region are at variance with those in comparable regions.

The above are just examples of boundaries that may be set for the extremes of global and multidomestic strategies. Most MNEs will aim for a hybrid of these, but this does not remove the need to ensure clarity of boundaries across all internal and external elements in the supply chain.

Delegation, Not Abdication

Any sensible organisational strategy should allow for the delegation of functional responsibility from HQ to dispersed units acting on behalf of the company. This is one approach to countering the "headquarters knows best" syndrome. This may also include the creation of a hierarchical structure across operating units, whereby units that are more established are given management oversight of less experienced units, or those with less operational scope. Even if reporting lines are not changed, a more competent subsidiary can earn the right to contribute to, or even approve, policy or product decisions. In this way, subsidiaries can be given licence to push for more responsibility and fulfil their potential, where they demonstrate the required abilities.

For example, sales subsidiaries of MNEs operating in Ireland are frequently organised under the UK subsidiary, where it is perceived that broader levels of competence may exist. It can also be logical for factories that manufacture sub-components to be structured under the factory that assembles final products. Such factories can be given sign-off on R&D decisions so that manufacturing and supply chain considerations are factored in.

An openness by HQ to the delegation of responsibility in this way can be effective in streamlining internal supply chains and promoting cross-organisational learning. It also signals that subsidiaries can have ambitions to increase their levels of contribution, as long as this remains consistent with the overall boundaries of the internationalisation strategy (e.g., a sales unit can seek to extend its influence over other sales units, but it cannot develop support services that compete with shared services units).

One potential downside of this delegation from HQ to a hierarchy of operational subsidiaries is that it can stoke dysfunctional political tensions between units as they jockey for power within this structure. A subsidiary that has manoeuvred itself into a more influential position can protect its position by limiting the potential contributions of less powerful subsidiaries or third parties for which it has oversight. HQ still needs to keep a watching brief on this and not abdicate its responsibility to oversee the network.

Develop Clear Sourcing Strategies

Particularly with the emergence of advanced globalisation concepts such as fine-slicing and the advent of multiprovider networks, corporations need some generally agreed principles on activities that must be performed within the company versus those that can be performed by third parties. It is a risky strategy to allow for a free-for-all, where internal units compete on equal terms with external providers. Although in-house units may have some advantages, such as the fact that their existence is usually not contingent on them making a profit, they do not operate on a level playing field.

They cannot make a loss, which puts them at a disadvantage relative to third parties who may be prepared to suffer financial pain temporarily to win the business and entrench their position by shutting-out competition.

A more robust approach is to develop more thoughtful policies on the sourcing of work. This ensures clarity of thought on where greater levels of control are needed, as well as giving subsidiaries more direction on where they can develop their potential.

The growth of outsourcing providers – whether for components, products or services – confirms that these companies continue to provide real value in the marketplace. This can be in the form of additional capacity, additional flexibility or lower costs. Outsourcers such as original equipment manufacturers (OEMs) and original design manufacturers (ODMs) can provide invaluable sources of innovation to complement a company's existing offerings.[3] For example, Apple could not produce iPhones at the speed and reliability required by the market, were it not for their manufacturing partner Foxconn and their network of third-party logistics providers.

Despite the benefits, it has traditionally been recommended in the literature that outsourcing should be avoided where the function (a) has strategic importance, (b) provides an identifiable competitive advantage, (c) is unique to the company, (d) is already delivered efficiently internally, (e) risks leakage of competency to outside firms, or (f) presents little opportunity for creating additional value with an external partner.[4] When making an outsourcing decision, the hidden costs should be realistically assessed (procurement costs, travel costs, training, etc.)[5] and governance costs should be factored in (estimated at 5–8% of contract value).[6]

These considerations remain valid, but as companies have grown more adept at managing outsourced functions, decisions on what to outsource and what to retain in-house have become less binary. It is now quite common to spread single functions across multiple outsource providers or to use a mix of in-house subsidiaries and outsourcers for the same process. Virgin Media UK, for example, has in the past used a range of onshore and offshore outsourcing partners for contact centre services while also maintaining an in-house function. Using a primary outsourcer supplemented by some smaller providers promotes healthy competition (sometimes referred to as a *champion/challenger model*). Maintaining an in-house competence keeps options open should a decision be made to return to insourcing the entire function in the future. The competence of the in-house teams can also be used as a benchmark for the performance of outsourcers and as a test-bed for new service features or production practices.

A more fluid insource/outsource model such as this is an example of the network organisation in action. Enabling it has required higher levels of investment in managing the network. For example, increased sector knowledge by procurement specialists ensures that a blend of outsource partners with different strengths can be commissioned, achieving an effective mix of costs, skills and flexibility. Legal teams have learned from experience in designing contracts that balance protections against underperformance, with flexibilities to allow providers to work together in responding to changing needs. Contract management offices have grown more specialised in managing multiple providers to deliver on common key performance indicators (KPIs).

This is achievable where outputs and linkages are reasonably well-defined. It becomes more problematic when there are high levels of interdependency between sub-processes, making it difficult to agree on root causes of problems and remedies in the event of underperformance. In a more integrated environment like this, much energy can be wasted on arguing about blame when something goes wrong.

Velvet Glove and Iron Fist

In an open market system, there are buyers, sellers and regulators who oversee the smooth running of the system. In capitalist market systems, the regulators see themselves as facilitators for smooth trading, but also as legislators for the rules of engagement and the remedies that must be made when rules are broken. The same should apply in a complex organisational network that seeks to deliver some of the benefits of a market system. HQ may wear a *velvet glove* to encourage and facilitate contributions from different sources, but where players misbehave, it must reserve the right to use an *iron fist*.

Consider, for example, the case of shared services, where HQ directs that functions such as HR, Finance or IT services must be delivered centrally – either by an in-house subsidiary or a third party. Front-line units act as customers of the service. The triumvirate of customers, providers and HQ overseers are all stakeholders in the service and this presents a new dynamic in the network that subsidiary and HQ managers must manage. Centralisation of service delivery to remote locations is seldom popular, particularly in cases where the service was previously delivered by familiar faces locally. Shared services cannot deliver the anticipated benefits unless service design is standardised as much as possible. This can cause further resistance by service users who see this as a way in which the corporation exerts soft-control over them. Sub-units receiving shared services are often subsidiaries themselves and will argue that their unique service requirements should be handled locally if they are to remain differentiated and to deliver on their own potential. Some units served may get a cost saving from centralisation, but others may not, adding to the cacophony of interests that must be managed. Unlike in other markets, customers in the internal market are usually not permitted to "vote with their feet."

This puts the onus on HQ to ensure the development of shared service designs that find compromises between all needs. It also needs to establish funding models that encourage the adoption of these services (e.g., in IBM EMEA, country units are charged for shared services based on their country revenue, irrespective of the extent to which they used the service). When valid issues are raised, HQ may have to get involved to put pressure on the service delivery unit or to negotiate a solution. However, where customer units make unreasonable demands or (worse) commission duplicate services, HQ must reserve the right to act strongly to bring things back into line. Without this air-cover, service providers cannot fulfil the objectives that they are expected to deliver.

Governance

Implied in each of the above recommendations is the need for robust governance processes between HQ and its subsidiaries. These should include tiered meeting structures at different levels of management. Regular meetings should focus on different dimensions of how the network operates, with appropriate frequencies and stakeholder participation depending on the focus of the meeting. KPIs and reports should also be institutionalised and performance should be regularly assessed. Planning processes should be formalised and matrices of responsibilities should be defined to clarify who is accountable for what and how decisions are made.

This level of formality can be an anathema to some companies who may see it as stifling and inflexible. While the comprehensiveness of governance processes can be adjusted so that it is in tune with corporate culture, some minimum level of governance should be installed if the system is to be directed, rather than being chaotic.

Even under the most formal governance structures, it is important that some level of informal connections should still be encouraged. Social contacts and informal networking provide channels for more open discussion on problems and opportunities to enhance the contributions made by business units.

What Might the Future Hold?

Dani Rodrik's – the insightful economist and commentator on globalisation – proposes the *inescapable trilemma of the world economy*, whereby "democracy, national sovereignty and global economy integration are mutually incompatible; we can combine any two, but never have all three simultaneously and in full."[7] His inference is that in recent decades, we have enjoyed the fruits of global economic integration under democratic systems, but we have had to sacrifice national sovereignty in the process. With increases in nationalism and the push-back on multilateralism that has been seen across many countries, something else has to give. Rodrik argues that the retraction is most likely to be in the level of economic integration that has fuelled the current system of globalisation.

Others are less pessimistic about the demise of globalisation, but they still accept that disruptions such as the rise in populism, nationalism and shifts in geopolitical power are causing subtle changes to the version of globalisation that we have lived through in recent times. Martin Wolf of the *Financial Times* acknowledges the accusations that globalisation has amplified contagious economic impacts across the world, particularly through its facilitation of fluid capital markets. Rising inequality and risks to national supply chain security have also encouraged anti-globalisers to point the finger of blame at the openness of current global trading systems. However, Wolf argues that this overlooks the positive contribution that global trade has made to combat global poverty, and the need to continue open trade as the lifeblood for smaller economies. The alternative of national self-centredness and unilateralism also threatens the global cooperation that is required to tackle climate change.[8,9]

While analysts' predictions may differ on the nature of any change to the globalisation system, it would require a major decline and disinvestments to reverse the impact of the growth in MNE investments abroad that has occurred over the past three decades. The number of MNEs across the world grew from 30,000 in 1990[10] to, by some estimates, 60,000 in 2018, controlling more than 500,000 subsidiaries.[11] Data from the US Bureau of Economic Analysis indicates that one in three of every employee of US MNEs is now based abroad, compared to one in five in the 1980s.[12] Despite recent economic setbacks, there has been no sign of slow-down to this growth in the global sprawl of companies. In April 2022, the OECD reported that global FDI flows surged by 88% since the previous year, rising 37% above pre-pandemic levels.[13] Completed cross-border M&A transactions exceeded pre-COVID levels by 50% in advanced economies and by 25% in developing economies. This level of cross-border investment was made possible because lower percentages of earnings were distributed to shareholders and unprecedented levels were re-invested. The USA remained by far the highest source of FDI outflows, followed by Germany, Japan, China and the UK.

Therefore, to paraphrase Mark Twain, reports of the death of globalisation are an exaggeration, although there is likely to be some degree of retrenchment. A survey by McKinsey in May 2020 found that 93% of global supply chain leaders were planning steps to make their supply chains more resilient by building in more redundancy and implementing nearshoring to move more elements in the production process nearer to the regions that they service.[14] The pandemic, the war in Ukraine, government-driven concerns about supply security and geopolitical tensions between the USA, the EU and China are all likely to be contributing causes.

We can conclude some sensible rationalisation is currently underway, although corporations will continue to find it difficult to resist the allure of new markets and new sources of efficiency as they fight to remain competitive and grow their business. Despite pressures to level the playing field for FDI – as seen from the recent intense negotiations on corporate tax harmonisation across countries – governments will continue to closely guard their sovereignty in deciding the benefits they offer to investing companies in return for the jobs they attract.

Assuming that the FDI climate remains healthy, it will be interesting to monitor the extent to which fine-slicing in supply chains continues. This may be one area of shake-out as companies increase their focus on the risks that such fragmentation across multiple specialised partners may cause.

Particularly for manufacturing MNEs, an additional consideration will be the sustainability of their chains. Concerns about the environmental impacts of globally dispersed supply and distribution networks will bring increased pressure on companies to demonstrate that the carbon emissions resulting from long geographic links are costed and offset in some other way.

Companies can also no longer hide from the societal and human rights impacts that globally dispersed operations may cause. The deaths of at least 1,132 people as a result of the 2013 collapse of the Rana Plaza building in Bangladesh[15] brought the realisation that MNEs should be held responsible for the conditions that underpinned their global supply chains. If they are to enjoy the rewards of low-cost foreign investments and third-party relationships, they must also accept responsibility for the conditions that enable these costs to be achieved. MNEs will therefore be expected to become increasingly proactive in auditing the sustainability, integrity and fairness of their global supply chains, not just for tier-1 or tier-2 suppliers, but as deep into the supply network as they can reasonably be expected to burrow.[16]

One other important factor that will contribute to the subsidiary and MNE organisations is the nature of work and employment. The global pandemic showed how employees can work remotely and still collaborate without the need for expensive office space. At the time of writing, there is much debate about the viability from a control and productivity perspective of continuing extensive working from home. Yet many companies are struggling in their efforts to encourage employees back to the office. In a job market where skilled employees are scarce to find and difficult to retain, companies are tentative in how they approach this sensitive issue.

Dispersed teams working remotely from each other are not a new phenomenon for many large organisations. For a long time it has been possible for team members in different regions to collaborate by phone, email and a wide array of groupware applications. The pandemic normalised this and brought it to the next level with the wider adoption of technologies such as videoconferencing, screen sharing and new collaboration tools available across multiple device types. Particularly in services operations, where the asset is the skill of an individual rather than facilities or machinery, remote working through the COVID crisis instigated a more fundamental debate about why employees need to be aligned with physical work locations. This could lead to questions within corporations on the very nature of its subsidiaries and whether these still need to be constructed as cohesive location-based units. How work is dispersed across subsidiaries and whether subsidiary mandates need to be as rigidly defined as in the past could also come into question.

For answers to these questions, forgive me while I briefly digress into what management theory says about why organisations exist. We can even go as far back as 1937 when Ronald Coase, the influential English economist, theorised on *The Nature of the Firm*.[17] Embedded in this discussion was a fundamental exploration of why firms exist and why all work is not carried out by ad hoc groupings of independent workers collaborating on a task (who Coase refers to as the 'plain man'). Later, this led to Transaction Cost Economics theory,[18] which (among other things) says that firms will enter into longer-term contracts for work when the cost of agreeing a contract is less than the cumulative cost of transacting for each individual task separately. Therefore, firms hire employees to ensure continuity of production, to control labour as a factor of that production and to avoid the cost of recruiting every time a new project is commenced. Firms exist because they are an effective mechanism for integrating and coordinating individual activities so that the whole is greater than the sum of the parts. Through collaboration between employees, firms and their sub-units can also develop organisational-level capabilities that remain an asset as individual employees come and go.

This may all sound self-evident – which a management theory should be if it is to be accepted as an aid to our understanding of why things are the way they are. When we apply this to the current *nature of work* discussion, it tells us that it is unlikely that future MNEs will be made up of groups of employees who basically act as freelancers within the organisation. This would imply that the company has no requirement for oversight, organisational learning and resource planning. The cost of managing a stable of individual professionals would be prohibitive and inefficient, unless they are structured under some organisational groupings. Norms for the levels of autonomy that are allowed to individual employees will continue to vary from sector to sector, just like they do today. Consider, for example, how professional services firms such as business consultants, legal practices and medical surgeries tend to have flat structures with high levels of autonomy delegated to the individual skilled practitioners. This shows that where skills are highly specialised, there is a greater opportunity for employees to work independently and unsupervised, albeit that they will still be expected to contribute to the wider development of the organisation. However, in the majority of cases, the need for supervision and co-working will remain, even if some of that work is done remotely.

In summary, while working remotely is here to stay, it really won't change very much in terms of how the organisation needs to be structured into logical functional groups, each with a purpose and identity. Subsidiaries will still exist with defined mandates, even if their employees are dispersed. They may even be distributed across different regions, except where government agencies that are providing grant aid to employment in a specific region object. The alternative is that HQ manages teams of individuals on tasks, which is simply not scalable. It will, however, be important for the cohesion of any given subsidiary to maintain control over its resources and also to ensure that it can adequately influence all other resources contributing to the execution of its mandates (e.g., third parties, sub-contractors, satellite individuals and groups in other subsidiaries). Where physical assets such as buildings and other infrastructure no longer act as the anchor point for the cohesion of the subsidiary, it is all the more important to have a strategy to optimise the contribution of all of its other resources and processes.

Just as it has done in the past, technological advances will continue to influence the activities of companies and the nature of their investments. For example, robotics, artificial intelligence, additive manufacturing and 3D printing will all play a part in continuing to oscillate the priorities that corporate strategists set between capital and labour-oriented investments. These technologies will also create new needs and opportunities – for example in research and development and in data analytics. While HQ organisations will want to keep close control over the development of such technologies in their early stages, most will not have the concentration of skills needed to adequately develop them into sources of advantage. Making full use of the network of partners, suppliers and subsidiaries will remain critical in an environment where, if the company does not develop new opportunities, existing or new competitors will.

Summary

A headquarters organisation has a responsibility to its stakeholders to maximise the potential returns from all investments. This includes creating the conditions that will enable subsidiaries to increase their capacity to contribute to corporate growth. Without some level of encouragement and nurturing, subsidiaries will either need to stifle the ambitions of their workforce or pursue their development using exclusively subversive strategies. While this may ultimately prove effective, it is likely to be more resource intensive. It will also only serve to encourage an "Us versus Them" relationship between HQ and business units. Therefore, concerted action is required from HQ leaders to take advantage of investments already made in the supply chain network, by ensuring controlled delegation, by carefully considering sourcing strategies and by implementing a thoughtful governance model that encourages innovative development while discouraging dysfunctional behaviour.

The frailties that were exposed by the COVID-19 pandemic, coupled with a confluence of geopolitical pressures that were already brewing, has triggered much speculation on the future of global supply chains. While there may be some sensible rationalisation of supply chains, this will not reverse the results of the globalisation of the business environment that we have seen in recent decades. The pervasiveness of organisational structures that have enabled a global expansion of firms will continue and ambitious companies will still be attracted by the lure of new markets and the possibility of achieving competitive advantage by accessing capabilities that are only available in other parts of the world.

It is reasonable that recent issues should trigger some reflection, but it is better to view these events as transient setbacks for international business development. Companies that respond by taking impulsive retrenchment actions risk "throwing the baby out with the bath water." They are also in danger of being blinded by issues that cause them to miss out on the opportunities that currently exist. Technological advances will continue to offer new possibilities for how processes can be distributed across supply chains. Changes to how work is aligned (or not) with locations are a further factor that will be part of the next evolutionary stage. The most successful MNEs will recognise the potential for their subsidiaries to contribute to any rationalisation of their supply chains to shape this future. Not to do so would represent a derogation of parental responsibility, by not taking advantage of insights and capabilities that should be expected from investments already made in subsidiary organisations.

Notes

1. Michael Goold, Andrew Campbell, and Marcus Alexander, *Corporate-Level Strategy: Creating Value in the Multibusiness Company* (New York: John Wiley & Sons Ltd, 1994).
2. Kendall Roth and Allen J. Morrison, "Implementing Global Strategy: Characteristics of Global Subsidiary Mandates," *Journal of International Business Studies* 23, no. 4 (1992).
3. Dan Breznitz, *Innovation in Real Places: Strategies for Prosperity in an Unforgiving World* (New York: Oxford University Press, 2021), p. 82.
4. Paul Lyons and Louis Brennan, "A Typology and Meta-Analysis of Outsourcing Relationship Frameworks," *Strategic Outsourcing: An International Journal* 7, no. 2 (2014).

5. P. Davies, "Offshoring: Hidden Benefits and Hidden Costs," in *Technology and Offshore Outsourcing Strategies*, ed. P Brudenall (New York: Palgrave Macmillan, 2005).

6. M. Lacity and L. Willcocks, *Advanced Outsourcing Practice: Rethinking Ito, Bpo and Cloud Services*, ed. L.P. Willcocks and M.C. Lacity, Technology, Work and Globalization (Basingstoke: Palgrave Macmillan, 2012).

7. Dani Rodrik to Unconventional thoughts on economic development and globalization, 25 October, 2007, https://rodrik.typepad.com/dani_rodriks_weblog/2007/06/the-inescapable.html.

8. Martin Wolf, "The Big Mistakes of the Anti-Globalisers," *Financial Times*, June 21 2022.

9. "In an Era of Disorder, Open Trade Is at Risk," *Financial Times*, June 28 2022.

10. Daniels, Radebaugh, and Sullivan, "Chapter 12: Country Evaluation and Selection." citing Gabel & Bruner (2003)

11. Mondial, "Multinational Corporations: World Atlas of Global Issues."

12. Goddard, "Activities of U.S. Multinational Enterprises, 2020."

13. OECD, "Fdi in Figures: April 2022."

14. McKinsey, "Risk, Resilience, and Rebalancing in Global Value Chains," ed. Lisa Renaud (2020).

15. International Labour Organisation, "The Rana Plaza Accident and Its Aftermath," https://www.ilo.org/global/topics/geip/WCMS_614394/lang--en/index.htm.

16. Jodi L. Short, Michael W. Toffel, and Andrew R. Hugill, "Monitoring Global Supply Chains," *Strategic Management Journal* 37, no. 9 (2016). Summarised on YouTube: Harvard Business School, "Monitoring Global Supply Chains" (2016). https://www.youtube.com/watch?v=wl2CoRiosPw.

17. R.H. Coase, "The Nature of the Firm," *Economica* 4, no. 16 (1937).

18. Oliver E. Williamson, "Transaction-Cost Economics: The Governance of Contractual Relations," *Journal of Law and Economics* 22, no. 2 (1979).

Chapter 11

Conclusion

My hope is that the chapters of this book have helped to shape your think-ing on the need for subsidiaries to have a strategy, and how to structure, develop and execute one. It was never anticipated that every idea that is contained here will resonate with every reader. The roles of subsidiaries, the environments in which they operate and the cultures of their parents are far too disparate for that.

I also recognise the likelihood that the approaches outlined here may be seen as being overly prescriptive and restrictive for some. This is to be expected, but readers are encouraged to push through this so that the foun-dations of a strategy are sound. My experience in using similar approaches with a broad range of subsidiary leadership teams is that, even when they are not a perfect match, they still provide useful reference points that help to unravel complex thinking. I come back to the point made in the introduc-tory chapter that subsidiaries can reasonably argue that they are different – but not in as many ways as they think. Where there are valid differences, significant insights can still be stimulated by contrasting one's own environ-ment to a more standardised case.

The templates provided are intended to be used as tools to encourage reflection, debate and consensus. They will be particularly useful in group situations where it is often good to have a focus for debate and sharing of perspectives, rather than unstructured discussion which are often dominated by the more vocal players. Using these templates encourages a more foren-sic approach to analysis, with less inclination to overlook issues or rely on preconceptions. Having said this, it may be necessary to modify some of the templates to fit your environment. When completed, none of these templates

DOI: 10.4324/9781003425502-14

should ever be regarded as final. Good strategy should adapt to new insights and changing circumstances.

Throughout this book, there is the implication that subsidiary leaders have a responsibility to push their organisations and their parents towards new strategic ambitions. This differs from the traditional view of corporations, where subsidiaries are expected to operate within set boundaries and at the direction of headquarters (HQ). However, that view is long outdated and subsidiary leaders who do not foster ambitions for their organisations can justifiably be accused of not leveraging the potential for increased returns from the investment made by the parent. Of course, the time is not always right for action and, as we have seen, often the focus needs to be on stabilising operational performance before setting sights elsewhere. However, this does not negate the responsibility that is on subsidiary leaders to constantly consider when might be the right time to begin the process of developing more value-adding capabilities.

Taking on the leadership responsibility for a more strategic drive requires thoughtfulness, persistence and the interpersonal skills needed to influence fellow managers and stakeholders. The concepts, process and toolkit of templates that are detailed throughout this book provide guidance on how to do this. But on their own, these cannot substitute for a further management attribute that is required to sustain this journey. That is, the courage to start. One objective of this book is to emphasise that subsidiary managers should see that building this courage is an intrinsic part of their leadership responsibility – to their local units, their employees and their parent organisation.

In the current business and geopolitical climate, the imperative for subsidiary leaders to develop their organisations is even more pronounced. There is currently much speculation that tectonic shifts are changing the nature of globalisation that has formed the backdrop for subsidiary growth in recent decades. In her book *Homecoming: The Path to Prosperity in a Post-Global World*,[1] Rana Faroohar makes a compelling case that globalisation is not dead – as has been asserted by some commentators – but it is changing. There are tussles for geopolitical power and influence over the global economy between West and East. There are definite trends to move more production activities closer to consumption in efforts to avert supply chain risks that have bitten in recent years. These moves are encouraged by governments, but also driven by more cautious corporate mindsets. Countries and firms are increasingly motivated towards vertical integration so that they own their supply networks, rather than be at the mercy of open markets. New technologies such as additive manufacturing and 3D printing will create new opportunities to move certain production systems closer to the customer, thus challenging current organisational models.

It is possible that any major changes to the global trading environment will be slow to crystallise, giving companies and their subsidiaries time to adjust. However, recent events and current economic circumstances appear to have accelerated the pace of change – creating dangers for those who are not thinking ahead. Over the short- to medium-term, this will present opportunities and threats that should be considered by subsidiaries, so they are ready for them. The quotation attributed to Charles Darwin is relevant in this case: "It is not the strongest of the species that survives, nor the most intelligent, but the one that is most responsive to change." In business, like in nature, evolution is as much about the survival of fitting as it is about the survival of the fittest.[2]

Against this backdrop there are also important considerations for government policy makers tasked with encouraging more investment in their regions. The traditional gauge of success in this world has been the number of jobs created by a new investment. Although this is good for newspaper headlines, it is a crude measurement that puts the emphasis on the volume rather than the economic and broader social impact of investments. In developed economies, there should be at least equal emphasis on the quality and sustainability of these jobs, in terms of their salary levels and their potential to contribute to clusters of specialised skills that will be self-sustaining and differentiating for the local economy.

Similarly, government supports aimed at developing the footprint of existing corporate investments should not only consider the potential for additional jobs. To be more forward-thinking, these should also encourage strategies to evolve the maturity of a subsidiary and its added value to the parent. In some cases, this may even result in fewer total jobs, but this accepts the reality that as economies develop their potential as sources of low-cost labour reduces, and different objectives should be encouraged if hosted subsidiaries are to remain vibrant and sustainable.

Corporations should also not be fearful of subsidiary ambitions. Of course, any political behaviours that are damaging or which encourage dysfunctional internal competition should be discouraged. However, just like among ambitious employees, subsidiaries that are driven by a desire to add more value so they earn more benefits should be encouraged within self-confident multinational enterprise (MNE) organisations. If subversive behaviour emerges, this should be taken as a sign that there is something wrong with the openness of the parent's management system. It should not immediately be seen as a bad reflection on the subsidiary. Subversive behaviour is usually driven by good intentions but also a fear that this will be misinterpreted and ambition will be thwarted.

Fundamentally, subsidiary leaders, government policy makers and HQ organisations alike should all remember that subsidiary strategy will only be successful if it is pursued for the sake of the parent.

Notes

1. Rana Faroohar, *Homecoming: The Path to Prosperity in a Post-Global World* (New York: Crown, 2022).
2. Gareth Morgan, *Images of Organization* (London: Sage Publications Inc, 2006).

Bibliography

Adler, Paul S. "Market, Hierarchy and Trust: The Knowledge Economy and the Future of Capitalism." [In English]. *Organization Science* 12, no. 2 (Mar/Apr 2001): 215–34.

Aguilar, Francis. *Scanning the Business Environment*. New York: Macmillan, 1967.

Allison, G. *Essence of Decision*. Boston: Little, Brown, 1971.

Ambos, Bjorn, Kazuhiro Asakawa, and Tina C. Ambos. "A Dynamic Perspective on Subsidiary Autonomy." *Global Strategy Journal* 1 (2011): 301–16.

Andersson, Ulf, Mats Forsgren, and Ulf Holm. "Balancing Subsidiary Influence in the Federative Mnc: A Business Network View." *Journal of International Business Studies* 38 (2007): 802–18.

Ansoff, H.I. "Conceptual Underpinnings of Systematic Strategic Management." *European Journal of Operational Research* 19, no. 1 (1985): 2–19.

———. *Strategic Management*. London: Macmillan, 1979.

Barney, Jay. "Firm Resources and Sustained Competitive Advantage." [In English]. *Journal of Management* 17, no. 1 (Mar 1991): 99.

Barney, Jay, and Delwyn N. Clark. *Resource-Based Theory: Creating and Sustaining Competitive Advantage*. Bloomington, IN: Oxford University Press, 2007.

Bartlett, C.A., and S. Ghoshal. *Transnational Management: Text, Cases, and Readings in Cross-Border Management*. Homewood, IL: Irwin, 1992.

Bartlett, Christopher A., and Sumantra Ghoshal. "Tap Your Subsidiaries for Global Reach." *Harvard Business Review* 64, no. 6 (1986): 87–94.

Beatie, Alan. "Brussels Sharpens a Weapon That Might End up Spearing Its Friends." *Financial Times*, July 18 2022.

Beer, Michael, and Nohria Nitin. "Cracking the Code of Change." *Harvard Business Review*, no. May–June 2000 (2000): 133–41.

Beugelsdijk, Sjoerd, Tatiana Kostova, Vincent E. Kunst, Ettore Spadafora, and Marc van Essen. "Cultural Distance and Firm Internationalization: A Meta-Analytical Review and Theoretical Implications." *Journal of Management* 44, no. 1 (2018): 89–130.

Birkinshaw, J. "Foreign-Owned Subsidiaries and Regional Development: The Case of Sweden." In *Multinational Corporate Evolution and Subsidiary Development*, edited by J. Birkinshaw and N. Hood. Basingstoke: Macmillan Press, 1998.

Birkinshaw, J., and N. Hood. "Multinational Subsidiary Evolution: Capability and Charter Change in Foreign-Owned Subsidiary Companies." *Academy of Management Review* 23, no. 4 (1998): 773–95.

Birkinshaw, J., and T. Pedersen. "Strategy and Management in Mne Subsidiaries." In *The Oxford Handbook of International Business Studies*, edited by A. Rugman. Oxford: Oxford University Press, 2009.

Block, Zenas, and Ian C. MacMillan. *Corporate Venturing: Creating New Businesses within the Firm*. Boston: Harvard Business School Press, 1993.

Boffey, Daniel. "Eu Starts Legal Action against Astrazeneca over Vaccine Shortfalls." *The Guardian International Edition*, April 26 2021.

Bouquet, C., J. Birkinshaw, and J.-L. Barsouz. "Fighting the 'Headquarters Knows Best' Syndrome." *MIT Sloan Management Review* 2016, no. Winter (2016):59–66.

Bradshaw, T. "'Tech Debt': Why Badly Written Code Can Haunt Companies for Decades." *Financial Times Magazine*, 27 November 2019.

Brennan, L. "How Netflix Expanded to 190 Countries in 7 Years." *Harvard Business Review Digital Articles* (October 12 2018): 16–20. https://search-ebscohost-com.elib.tcd.ie/login.aspx?direct=true&db=bth&AN=132377634 (Accessed: 8 May 2023).

Breznitz, Dan. *Innovation in Real Places: Strategies for Prosperity in an Unforgiving World*. New York: Oxford University Press, 2021.

Bridges, William, and Susan Bridges. *Managing Transitions: Making the Most of Change*. 4th ed. London and Boston: Nicholas Brealey Publishing, 2017.

Buckley, Peter J. "International Integration and Coordination in the Global Factory." *Management International Review* 51 (2011): 269–83.

Carney, Mark. *Value(s): Building a Better World for All*. London: HarperCollins Publishers, 2021.

Cerrato, Daniele. "The Multinational Enterprise as an Internal Market System." *International Business Review* 15, no. 3 (2006): 253–77.

Christensen, Clayton M., Scott D. Anthony, and Erik A. Roth. *Seeing What's Next: Using the Theories of Innovation to Predict Industry Change*. Boston: Harvard Business School Press, 2004.

Christopher, Martin. "The Agile Supply Chain: Competing in Volatile Markets." *Industrial Marketing Management* 29, no. 1 (2000): 37–44.

Coase, R.H. "The Nature of the Firm." *Economica* 4, no. 16 (1937): 386–405.

Collins, James C., and Jerry I. Porras. "Building Your Company's Vision." *Harvard Business Review* Sept–Oct 74, no. 5 (1996): 65–77.

Cuervo-Cazurra, Alvaro, Ram Mudambi, and Torben Pedersen. "Subsidiary Power: Loaned or Owned? The Lenses of Agency Theory and Resource Dependence Theory." *Global Strategy Journal* 9, no. 4 (2019): 491–501.

Dahl, R.A. "The Concept of Power." *Behavioral Science* 2 (1957): 201–18.

Daniels, J.D., L.H. Radebaugh, and D.P. Sullivan. "Chapter 12: Country Evaluation and Selection." In *International Business: Environment and Operations*, edited by J.D. Daniels, L.H. Radebaugh, and D.P. Sullivan. Essex: Pearson Education Ltd, 2015.

Davenport, Thomas H. "The Coming Commoditization of Processes." *Harvard Business Review* 83, no. 6 (2005): 100–8.

Davies, P. "Offshoring: Hidden Benefits and Hidden Costs." Chap. 4 In *Technology and Offshore Outsourcing Strategies*, edited by P. Brudenall, 80–93. New York: Palgrave Macmillan, 2005.

Davies, Rob. "Ex-Bt Bosses Named in Investigation into Alleged Fraud in Italy Unit." *The Guardian International Edition*, February 13 2019.

Delany, Ed. "Strategic Development of the Multinational Subsidiary through Subsidiary Initiative-Taking." *Long Range Planning* 33 (2000): 220–44.

Doran, G.T. "There's a S.M.A.R.T. Way to Write Management Goals and Objectives." *Management Review* 70, no. 11 (1981): 35–36.

Dörrenbächer, C., and J. Gammelgaard. "Subsidiary Role Development: The Effect of Micro-Political Headquarters–Subsidiary Negotiations on the Product, Market and Value-Added Scope of Foreign-Owned Subsidiaries." *Journal of International Management* 12, no. 3 (2006): 266–83.

Edelenbos, Jurian, and Jasper Eshuis. "The Interplay between Trust and Control in Governance Processes: A Conceptual and Empirical Investigation." *Administration & Society* 44, no. 6 (September 1, 2012): 647–74.

Emerson, Richard M. "Power-Dependence Relations." *American Sociological Review* 27, no. 1 (1962): 31–41.

Evans, Vaughan. *25 Need to Know Strategy Tools*. Harlow: Pearson Education Limited, 2014.

EY. "How Will Europe Compete for Investment Amid Ongoing Turbulence: Ey Attractiveness Survey Europe. May 2022." Edited by Marc Lhermitte, 2022.

Faroohar, Rana. *Homecoming: The Path to Prosperity in a Post-Global World*. New York: Crown, 2022.

Fildes, Nic. "Bt Breaks up Italian Business with Sale to Telecom Italia." *Financial Times*, December 10 2020.

Forrester. "Shattering the Offshore Captive Center Myth." 2007.

Gabel, M., and H. Bruner. *Globalinc.: An Atlas of the Multinational Corporation*. The New York Press, 2003.

Giles, Chris. "Oecd Drafts Principles for $100bn Global Tax Revolution." *Financial Times*, October 12 2020.

Goddard, Mark. "Activities of U.S. Multinational Enterprises, 2020." USA Bureau of Economic Analysis, 2022.

Goold, Michael, Andrew Campbell, and Marcus Alexander. *Corporate-Level Strategy: Creating Value in the Multibusiness Company*. New York: John Wiley & Sons Ltd, 1994.

Grant, Robert M. *Contemporary Strategy Analysis*. 8th ed. Oxford: Blackwell, 2013.

Grove, Andrew S. *Only the Paranoid Survive: How to Exploit the Crisis Points That Challenge Every Company and Career*. New York: Doubleday, 1996.

Hay, Jon. "Esg, Trump and Covid Hasten Gathering Trend to Re-Shore." *Global Capital*, July 9 2020.

Hayes, John. *The Theory and Practice of Change Management*. 6th ed. London: MacMillan International and Red Globe Press, 2022.

Heifetz, Ronald A., and Marty Linsky. "A Survival Guide for Leaders." *Harvard Business Review* 80, no. 6 (2002): 65–74.

Henderson, Rebecca. *Reimagining Capitalism: How Business Can Save the World*. UK: Penguin Random House, 2020.

Hickson, David J., Christopher R. Hinnings, Charles A. Lee, Rodney E. Schneck, and Johannes M. Pennings. "A Strategic Contingencies' Theory of Interorganizational Power." *Administrative Science Quarterly* 16, no. 2 (1971): 216–29.

IMI. "Leading with Strategic Intent (Fdi)." https://www.imi.ie/leading-with-strategic -intent/.

Ireland, IDA. "Annual Report and Accounts 2020." IDA Ireland, 2020.

Kahneman, Daniel. *Thinking, Fast and Slow*. UK: Penguin Random House, 2011.

King, William R. "Creating a Strategic Capabilities Architecture." *Strategic Planning* Winter 1995 (1995): 67–69.

Kotter, J. "The 8 Steps for Leading Change." https://www.kotterinc.com/methodol-ogy/8-steps/.

Kotter, John P. *Leading Change*. Boston: Harvard Business Review Press, 2012 [1996].

Kotter, John, and Holger Rathgeber. *Our Iceberg Is Melting: Changing and Succeeding under Any Conditions*. New York: Portfolio/Penguin, 2017.

Lacity, M., and L. Willcocks. *Advanced Outsourcing Practice: Rethinking Ito, Bpo and Cloud Services*. Technology, Work and Globalization. Edited by L.P. Willcocks and M.C. Lacity. Basingstoke: Palgrave Macmillan, 2012.

Law, Thomas J. "17 Seriously Inspiring Mission and Vision Statement Examples." *Oberlo*. https://ie.oberlo.com/blog/inspiring-mission-vision-statement-exam-ples#:~:text=Mission%20statement%3A%20We%20strive%20to,might%20want %20to%20buy%20online.

Leonard, Mark. *The Age of Unpeace: How Connectivity Causes Conflict*. London: Bantam Press, 2021.

Lonergan, J. "Address to Social Care Conference." Institute of Technology, Tralee, 2006.

Lyons, Paul. "Unpublished Thesis Submission for Masters Degree in Management Practice." Trinity College Dublin and Irish Management Institute, 1995.

Lyons, Paul, and Louis Brennan. "Assessing Value from Business-to-Business Services Relationships: Temporality, Tangibility, Temperament, and Trade-Offs." *Journal of Service Research* 24, no. 1 (2019): 27–43.

———. "A Typology and Meta-Analysis of Outsourcing Relationship Frameworks." *Strategic Outsourcing: an International Journal* 7, no. 2 (2014): 135–71.

McGrath, Rita. *Seeing around Corners: How to Spot Inflection Points in Business before They Happen*. New York: Mariner Books, 2021.

McGrath, Rita Gunther, and Ian C. MacMillan. *The Entrepreneurial Mindset: Strategies for Continuously Creating Opportunities in an Age of Uncertainty.* Boston: Harvard Business School Press, 2000.

McKinsey. "Risk, Resilience, and Rebalancing in Global Value Chains." Edited by Lisa Renaud, 2020.

Mele, Cristina, and Valentina Della Corte. "Resource-Based View and Service-Dominant Logic: Similarities, Differences and Further Research." *Journal of Business Market Management* 6, no. 4 (2013): 192–213.

Mintzberg, Henry. *The Rise and Fall of Strategic Planning.* New York: Free Press, 1994.

———. "That's Not 'Turbulence,' Chicken Little, It's Really Opportunity." *Planning Review* 22, no. 6 (1994): 7–9.

Mintzberg, Henry, and J. Waters. "Of Strategies: Deliberate and Emergent." *Management Journal* 6, no. 3 (1985): 257–72.

Molloy, Edmond, and Edward Delany. "Strategic Leadership of Multi-National Subsidiaries: An Overview for Senior Executives." Edited by M.D.L. Management Consultants Ltd. Quantum International, 1998.

Mondial, Espace. "Multinational Corporations: World Atlas of Global Issues." https://espace-mondial-atlas.sciencespo.fr/en/topic-strategies-of-transnational-actors/article-3A11-EN-multinational-corporations.html#:~:text=At%20the%20present%20time%2C%20there,controlling%20more%20than%20500%2C000%20subsidiaries.

Monroe, K.B. *Pricing—Making Profitable Decisions.* New York, NY: McGraw Hill, 1991.

Moose, Sandy. "The Growth Share Matrix Revisited—A Ted Animation." Boston Consulting Group. https://www.bcg.com/publications/2014/corporate-strategy-growth-share-matrix-revisited-ted-animation.

Morgan, G., and P.H. Kristensen. "The Contested Space of Multinationals: Varieties of Institutionalism, Varieties of Capitalism." *Human Relations* 59, no. 11 (2006): 1467–90.

Morgan, Gareth. *Images of Organization.* London: Sage Publications Inc, 2006.

Mudambi, Ram. "Location, Control and Innovation in Knowledge-Intensive Industries." *Journal of Economic Geography* 8, no. 5 (2008): 699–725.

OECD. "Fdi in Figures: April 2022." OECD, 2022.

Organisation, International Labour. "The Rana Plaza Accident and Its Aftermath." https://www.ilo.org/global/topics/geip/WCMS_614394/lang--en/index.htm.

Pan, Y., and D.K. Tse. "The Hierarchical Model of Market Entry Modes." *Journal of International Business Studies*, no. 4 (2000): 535.

Patterson, S.L., and D.B. Brock. "The Development of Subsidiary Management Research: Review and Theoretical Analysis." *International Business Review* 11 (2002): 139–63.

Perlmutter, Howard. "The Tortuous Evolution of Multinational Enterprises." *Columbia Journal of World Business* 1 (1969): 9–18.

Porter, Michael E. *Competitive Strategy: Techniques for Analyzing Industries and Competitors.* New York: Free Press, 2008.

Quinn, James Brian, and Frederick G. Hilmer. "Strategic Outsourcing." *Sloan Management Review* 35, no. 4 (1994): 43.

Rao, Alaka N. "Understanding the Role of Power Distance in Global Outsourcing Relationships." [In English]. *International Management Review* 9, no. 1 (2013): 5–18, 87.

Reichert, Julia, and Steven Bognar. "American Factory." Netflix, 2019.

Ridley, Matt. *How Innovation Works*. London: 4th Estate, 2020.

Ring, Peter Smith, and Andrew H. Van De Ven. "Structuring Cooperative Relationships between Organizations." [In English]. *Strategic Management Journal* 13, no. 7 (Oct 1992): 483.

Rodrik, Dani. "The Inescapable Trilemma of the World Economy." In *Unconventional Thoughts on Economic Development and Globalization*, edited by Dani Rodrik. Palgrave Macmillan, 2007.

Roth, Kendall, and Allen J. Morrison. "Implementing Global Strategy: Characteristics of Global Subsidiary Mandates." *Journal of International Business Studies* 23, no. 4 (1992): 715–35.

Rumelt, R.P. *Good Strategy, Bad Strategy: The Difference and Why It Matters*. New York: Crown Business, 2011.

Sandbu, Martin. "The Death of Globalisation Has Been Greatly Exagerated." *Financial Times*, May 26 2022.

Sargeant, L.W. "Strategic Planning in a Subsidiary." *Long Range Planning* 23, no. 2 (1990): 43–54.

Savage, Grant T., Timothy W. Nix, Carlton J. Whitehead, and John D. Blair. "Strategies for Assessing and Managing Organizational Stakeholders." *Academy of Management Executive* 5, no. 2 (1991): 61–75.

Schein, Ed. "Ed Schein - Let's Focus on (National, Organizational, and Occupational) Culture." https://www.youtube.com/watch?v=UUBPsO1jCcU. Youtube 2015.

School, Harvard Business. "Monitoring Global Supply Chains." https://www.youtube .com/watch?v=wl2CoRiosPw. 2016.

Shaw, Hollie. "Target Corp's Spectacular Canada Flop: A Gold Standard Case Study for What Retailers Shouldn't Do." https://financialpost.com/news/retail-market-ing/target-corps-spectacular-canada-flop-a-gold-standard-case-study-for-what -retailers-shouldnt-do. 2015.

Shih, Stan. *Me-Too Is Not My Style: Challenge Difficulties, Break through Bottlenecks, Create Values*. Taipei: The Acer Group, 1996.

Short, Jodi L., Michael W. Toffel, and Andrew R. Hugill. "Monitoring Global Supply Chains." *Strategic Management Journal* 37, no. 9 (2016): 1898–987.

Sibbet, David. *Visual Meetings*. Edited by Grove Consultants International. Hoboken, NJ: John Wiley & Sons, 2010.

Smith, Brian. "How Europe, India and Africa Are Incentivizing Foreign Investment." *EY*, 2021.

Smith, Richard, David King, Ranjit Sidhu, and Dan Skelsey. *The Effective Change Manager's Handbook: Essential Guide to the Change Management Body of Knowledge*. London, New York, New Delhi: Kogan Page Ltd, 2015.

Tam, Donna. "Remember Bebo? Yeah. That's Why the Founder Is Killing the Site." *CNET*. https://www.cnet.com/tech/services-and-software/remember-bebo-yeah-thats-why-the-founder-is-killing-the-site/.

Thomas, Daniel. "Uk Manufactuers Reshore Supply Chains after Pandemic and Brexit." *Financial Times*, May 16 2022.

Thompson, A., A.J. Strickland III, and J.E. Gamble. *Crafting and Executing Strategy*. 16th ed. New York: McGraw-Hill, 2010.

Tooher, Patrick. "The Future's Not So Bright as Orange Gets the Red Light in Ulster." *Independent*, July 12 1996.

van den Berghe, Douglas. "A Guide to Fdi: What Is the Point of Incentives?" *Investment Monitor*. https://www.investmentmonitor.ai/investment-promotion/guide-to-fdi-what-is-the-point-of-incentives.

Vlaskovits, Patrick. "Henry Ford, Innovation, and That 'Faster Horse' Quote." *Harvard Business Review Online* (29 August 2011). https://hbr.org/2011/08/henry-ford-never-said-the-fast#:~:text=%E2%80%9CIf%20I%20had%20asked%20people,and%20air%20of%20self%2Devidence.

Wild, J.J., K.L. Wild, and K.C.Y Han (Eds). "Chapter 13: Selecting and Managing Entry Modes." In *International Business: An Integrated Approach*. Upper Saddle River, NJ: Prentice Hall, 2000.

Williamson, Oliver E. "Transaction-Cost Economics: The Governance of Contractual Relations." *Journal of Law and Economics* 22, no. 2 (1979): 233–61.

Wolf, Martin. "The Big Mistakes of the Anti-Globalisers." *Financial Times*, June 21 2022.

———. "In an Era of Disorder, Open Trade Is at Risk." *Financial Times*, June 28 2022.

Toolkit

The templates used throughout the book are reproduced on a larger scale in this appendix for ease of reproduction when they are to be used in group discussions.

The following templates are included:

1. Charter evolution analysis (adapted from Delany).
2. Charter portfolio analysis (influenced by the BCG Growth Matrix).
3. Capability assessment and identification of sustained competitive advantage.
4. Analysing capabilities using the SWOT framework.
5. Assessment template for environmental changes.
6. Macro environmental impact analysis.
7. Bringing it all together – charters, capabilities and macro environmental influences.
8. Mapping the political terrain.
9. Mapping power–dependence relationships.
10. Stakeholder management planning.

CURRENT TIMEFRAME: _____   FUTURE TIMEFRAME: _____

CURRENT CHARTERS:	STAGE 1: Establishing start-up	STAGE 2: Carrying out mandate satisfactorily	STAGE 3: Fulfilling basic mandate in a 'superior way'	STAGE 4: Extending basic mandate – low risk moves	STAGE 5: Extending basic mandate – strategic development	STAGE 6: Becoming strategic centre for the MNE	STAGE 7: Becoming strategic pivot for the MNE	STAGE 8: Becoming strategic apex for the MNE

Charter evolution analysis (adapted from Delany)

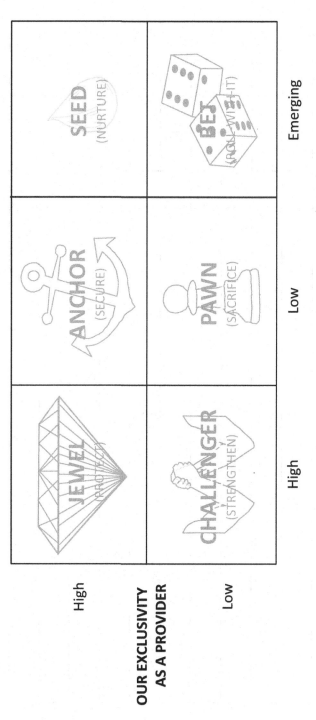

STRATEGIC IMPORTANCE TO PARENT

Charter portfolio analysis (influenced by the BCG Growth Matrix)

CREST CATEGORY	VALUED	RARE	DIFFICULT TO COPY	DIFFICULT TO SUB.
CAPABILITY				

Capability identification and assessment of sustained competitive advantage

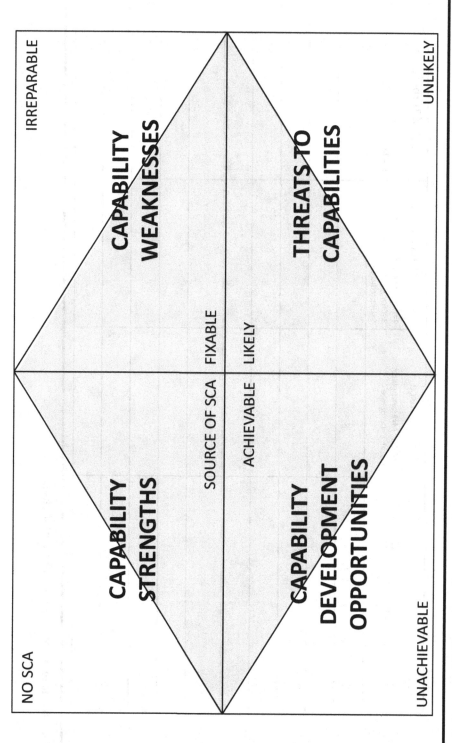

Analysing capabilities using the SWOT framework

Environmental Factor	Source G=Global; M=Marketplace; L=Local; C=Corporate.	Level of Turbulence 1=Repetitive; 2=Expanding; 3=Changing; 4=Discontinuous; 5=Unpredictable	Effect of Turbulence ← = Headwind; → = Tailwind

Assessment template for environmental changes

Macro environmental impact analysis

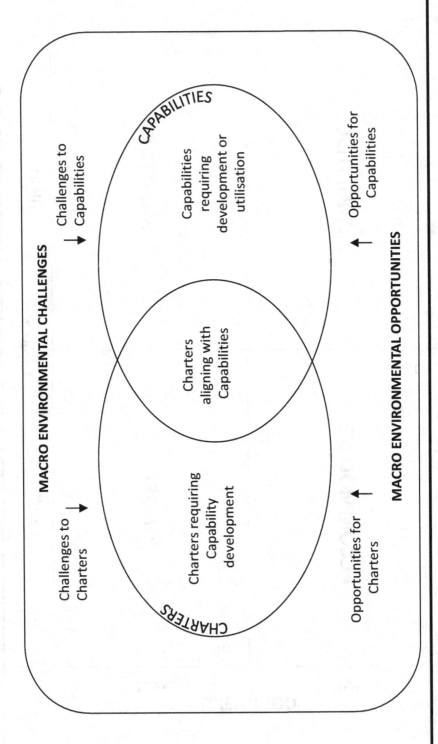

Bringing it all together – charters, capabilities and macro environmental influences

What objective may invoke the adoption of political positions?

RESAONS FOR SUPPORT	REASONS FOR AMBIVALENCE	REASONS FOR RESISTANCE

Why will positions be adopted?

SOURCES OF SUPPORT	AMBIVALENT or UNKNOWN	SOURCES OF RESISTANCE

Who will adopt these positions?

	MEANS OF SUPPORT	AMBIVALENT or UNKNOWN	MEANS OF RESISTANCE
PUBLICLY			
PRIVATELY			

How will positions be expressed?

Mapping the political terrain

HIGH
POWER

MODERATE
POWER

LOW
POWER

Low　　　　　　　　　　High

AVAILABILITY OF *ALVERNATIVES*
TO WHAT THE OTHER PROVIDES

EXTENT OF <u>NEEDS</u>
FOR WHAT THE OTHER PROVIDES

Low

HIGH

Mapping power–dependence relationships

STAKEHOLDER	POTENTIAL TO SUPPORT 1=Low; 5=High; 0=Unknown	POTENTIAL TO THREATEN 1=Low; 5=High; 0=Unknown)	STAKEHOLDER TYPE / APPROACH	CURRENT POSITION 1=Resistant; 5=Supportive; 0=Unknown	RELATIONSHIP OWNER	PLANNED ACTIONS

Stakeholder management planning

Index

Printed in the United States
by Baker & Taylor Publisher Services